THE POETICS OF FRAGMENTATION IN CONTEMPORARY BRITISH AND AMERICAN FICTION

Edited by
Vanessa Guignery, *École Normale Supérieure in Lyon*
and
Wojciech Drąg, *University of Wrocław*

Series in Literary Studies

VERNON PRESS

www.vernonpress.com

In the Americas:
Vernon Press
1000 N West Street,
Suite 1200, Wilmington,
Delaware 19801
United States

In the rest of the world:
Vernon Press
C/Sancti Espiritu 17,
Malaga, 29006
Spain

Series in Literary Studies

Library of Congress Control Number: 2019932594

ISBN: 978-1-62273-729-1

Also available:
Hardback: 978-1-62273-616-4
E-book: 978-1-62273-646-1

Table of Contents

Acknowledgements

This volume is the outcome of an international conference entitled "Fragmentary Writing in Contemporary British and American Fiction," which was held in Wrocław, Poland, on 22-23 September 2017. Organized by Prof. Vanessa Guignery and Dr. Wojciech Drąg, the conference gathered forty scholars from eleven countries. It was made possible thanks to the financial support by the Institute of English Studies at the University of Wrocław and the IHRIM research laboratory at the École Normale Supérieure in Lyon.

Our volume contains a selection of fifteen articles based on the papers presented at the conference, including two texts written by the plenary speakers – Prof. Merritt Moseley and Prof. Grzegorz Maziarczyk. The third keynote speaker, Prof. Alison Gibbons, has written the afterword. The editors wish to express their gratitude for their great contribution to the project since its inception in 2015. They also extend their thanks to Dr Marcin Tereszewski, Ewa Błasiak, Krzysztof Jański, Agata Słowik and Angelika Szopa for helping in various ways in organizing the Wrocław conference.

This publication has received the support of UMR 5317 – IHRIM (Institut d'histoire des représentations et des idées dans les modernités), under the authority of the CNRS, the ENS de Lyon, and the Universities Lumière-Lyon 2, Jean-Moulin-Lyon 3, Jean-Monnet-Saint-Etienne and Clermont Auvergne.

List of figures

Introduction: the art of the fragment

Vanessa Guignery,
École Normale Supérieure in Lyon

Wojciech Drąg,
University of Wrocław

In 1966, Donald Barthelme had the narrator of his short story "See the Moon?" declare, "Fragments are the only forms I trust" (157). A number of contemporary British and American novelists could also make this statement theirs as the last few decades have seen a renewed popularity of fragmentation in works of fiction that deny completeness, linearity and coherence in favor of incompletion, disruption and gaps. According to Hans-Jost Frey, the fragment "is not a popular subject for literary scholarship" because it "does not fulfil the presupposition of wholeness" and "cannot be controlled" (32). However, the resurgence of fragmentation at the turn of the twentieth and twenty-first centuries deserves to be examined in order to ascertain whether contemporary forms of fragmentary writing constitute a return to the modernist episteme or the fragmented literature of exhaustion of the 1960s, whether they mark a continuity with some aspects of the postmodernist aesthetics or signal a major deviation from previous structures. Additionally, the relation between the fragment and the whole needs to be reconsidered so as to determine if the two notions are mutually exclusive in contemporary fiction and if the loss of the ideal of totality and unity is viewed with nostalgia or accepted and even welcome. This volume also purports to examine whether thinking up new modes and practices of fragmentation in literature, which can accommodate multimodal and transmedial forms, might be a way for contemporary writers to reflect today's accelerated culture of social media and over-communication within which long-form fiction seems increasingly anachronistic. If the novel is not quite dead despite Will Self's dogged insistence that "this time it's for real" and that, in the digital age, "the novel is absolutely doomed to become a marginal cultural form" (qtd. in Clark), the genre is undergoing significant transformations which seem necessary if one is to overcome the "novel-nausea" that writers like Zadie Smith have expressed (Smith, "An Essay"). While the most innovative fiction sometimes veers towards the anti-novel in its extreme discontinuity (Drąg) or creates hybrid genres, less experimental works rely on fragmentation to shake the novel "out of its present complacency" (Smith, *Changing My Mind* 94), mimic the fissures of the self (Gibbons, *Multimodality* 201–02) or echo the shattering effects of trauma.

Defining the fragment

Before examining the ways in which contemporary forms of fragmentariness differ from, refurbish or repeat past models, one should start with the near-impossible task of trying to define the fragment. In *The Fragment: Towards a History and Poetics of a Performative Genre* (2004), Camelia Elias argues that "much of the appeal to the fragment relies on the fact that one can never be sure of what exactly constitutes a fragment" (2). For Frey, the fragment is "hostile to meaning and resists understanding" (25) because it cannot be accommodated into a whole: defining the fragment would amount to giving it well-delineated contours and considering it as a self-contained object, thereby disavowing its fragmentariness. Despite this proviso, critics have attempted to pinpoint some characteristics of this elusive object and have insisted in particular on its incompleteness: "a fragment appears incomplete, be it a sliver cut off from a larger whole, an unfinished work, or a work that seems insubstantial" (Metzer 106). David Metzer adds that the central relationship for a fragment is "that between part and whole" (106), a relationship that is predicated on loss. The etymology of the word certainly highlights these aspects. As noted by Alain Montandon, in Latin, the words *fragmen* and *fragmentum* derive from *frango*, which means "to break, to shatter, to crash." A fragment is a piece of a whole which has been ruptured and fragmentation therefore implies "an endured violence, an intolerable disintegration" (Montandon 77).[1] André Guyaux also draws attention to the etymology which emphasizes the cut, the separation and even "the wound" (7) while Sébastien Rongier refers to "a fracture" and "a tear." Fragmentariness is therefore commonly associated with loss, lack and vulnerability – a word whose etymology is significantly *vulnus*, i.e., the wound. It might thereby come as no surprise that in our "era of the vulnerable" (Ganteau, *The Ethics* 5), works of fiction which relate personal and collective traumas, with a focus on bodily frailty and a dramatization of loss, should opt for the trope of vulnerability and for modes of fragmentation and dislocation.

---

[1] All quotations from French sources are provided in our own translation.

A historical overview of the fragment

In earlier centuries, however, the fragment was not necessarily considered as the sign of a fracture to be deplored. Critics usually locate the origins of theoretical interest in the fragment in two European traditions. Firstly, French moralists and essayists from the sixteenth to the eighteenth century including Montaigne, Pascal, La Rochefoucauld and Chamfort favored the form of the *pensée*, the sentence, the maxim, the aphorism – a form taken up again by David Markson and David Shields in the contemporary period, as analyzed by Wojciech Drąg in this volume. According to Françoise Susini-Anastopoulos, unlike the fragment, the aphorism of the French moralists is marked by its "excessive closure" and "perfect completeness" (31), and for Elias, it "does not possess the same potential as the fragment to be performative" (9). The second European tradition of the fragment privileges a more open form: the late eighteenth-century Jena group of the first period of German Romanticism (including Schlegel and Novalis) set out their theory of the fragment in the journal *The Athenaeum* – a tradition Marcin Tereszewski recalls in this volume to differentiate it from the relationship of the fragment to totality in J. G. Ballard's fiction. According to D. F. Rauber, the classical literary stance centered on the finite and developed forms that enhanced "effects such as balance, harmony, perfection" (214). On the other hand, the Romantic artist was looking for a finite and discreet form that would "reflect the infinite and the indeterminate" (Rauber 214). For Schlegel and Novalis, but also for Goethe, Schiller or Nietzsche, the fragment seemed to offer the best solution to fulfil this ideal, which has led Rauber to call it "the ultimate romantic form" (215) and Philippe Lacoue-Labarthe and Jean-Luc Nancy to name it "the romantic genre *par excellence*" (40). The two French critics insist that the German Romantics, contrary to the etymological definition proposed earlier, never confuse the fragment with "the residue of a broken ensemble," nor do they emphasize the fracture that produces the fragment (42).

This marks a contrast with the perception of fragmentation in the twentieth and twenty-first century, as noted by Elizabeth Wanning Harries in *The Unfinished Manner: Essays on the Fragment in the Later Eighteenth Century* (1994): "We tend to think of fragmentary forms as radically discontinuous, reflecting a discontinuous, unstable, uncentered universe. The world is in chaos, and we represent that chaos in fragments. In the eighteenth century, however, and even into the nineteenth, fragments were not necessarily signs of a broken reality" (34). Instead, the Romantics gesture towards an impossible totality which remains an ideal. They acknowledge that the fragment "involves an essential incompletion" (42) because it is a project, engaged in the process of becoming – a "fragment of the future" as noted in *Athenaeum* fragment 22 (qtd. in Lacoue-Labarthe and Nancy 43). Simultaneously, however, they insist that the fragment relies on a form of unity, integrity and individuation, as suggested by Schlegel's famous description in *Athenaeum* fragment 206: "[a] fragment, like a small work of art, has to be entirely isolated from the surrounding world and be complete in itself like a hedgehog" (qtd. in Lacoue-Labarthe and Nancy 43). The Romantic fragment, therefore, reaches out towards an impossible whole and does not bring "the dispersion or the shattering of the work into play" (Lacoue-Labarthe and Nancy 48).

A century later, the modernists repudiated Romanticism, and yet several critics traced the lineage of modernism, commonly labeled as an art of rupture, to Romantic modes of writing. For Anne Janowitz, the Romantic fragment poem was "the precursor form to the modernist fragment poem" (442), and for Rebecca Varley-Winter, "modernist fragments respond to Romantic fragments" (15). At the beginning of the twentieth century, chaos, confusion and a sense of crisis prevailed in the context of technological, social and economic modernization, scientific breakthroughs such as Einstein's theory of relativity, the decline of philosophical, religious and moral certainties and the catastrophe of the First World War. Susini-Anastopoulos attributes the development of fragmentary writing in that period to what she calls modernity's triple crisis of completeness, totality and genre (2) – notions which are deemed obsolete. Ricard Ripoll adds to that list the modern crisis of the subject (*L'écriture* 17–18), whereas Isabelle Chol proposes the crisis of meaning – prompted by the experience and awareness of lack, emptiness and discontinuity – as yet another philosophical context for the emergence of fragmentary literature (Chol 18–22). Moving further into the twentieth century, Rongier indicates a historical crisis as the motivation for the adoption of fragmentary style by thinkers such as Theodor Adorno. Rongier regards the choice to write in fragments as a "testimony of rupture" precipitated by the Holocaust and calls it "a thought of the radical mutilation of thought." In the aftermath of Auschwitz, fragmentary writing signifies, according to Rongier, the "loss of every form of innocence," the impossible "suture of the historical wound" and the exhaustion of "the affirmative conciliatory or reconciliatory thought." Rongier associates formal disintegration with the "sense of an ending," interprets the rise of fragmentation as literature's admission of its own impotence and cites Adorno's remark that art's "turn to the friable and the fragmentary is in truth an effort to save art by dismantling the claim that artworks are what they cannot be" (Adorno 190).

In the first decades of the twentieth century, disillusioned poets were intent on devising new strategies that could capture the complexity of the contemporary world. In *The Waste Land* (1922), T. S. Eliot juxtaposed the refuse, shards and debris of Western culture, "confronting the reader with a collage of seemingly unrelated fragments and abandoning the narrative that might hold them together" (Gasiorek 11). Eliot's poem concludes with snippets from other works (a children's song, the Upanishads, an ancient Latin poem and works by Dante, Thomas Kyd, Gérard de Nerval, Alfred Lord Tennyson and Algernon Swinburne, each of them in its original language), presented by the Fisher King as "these fragments I have shored against my ruins" (Eliot 75). Characteristically, Eliot does not provide any bridges or transitions which would account for the coexistence of so many distinct fragments.

While poetry is conducive to fragmentary writing and fragmentariness is integral to the short story (as examined by David Malcolm and Teresa Bruś in this volume), the novel has been considered as the genre that is the most distant from fragmentation (Ripoll, *L'écriture* 15). And yet, modernist novelists – wary of unifying plots, autonomous characters, reassuring sequentiality and closure – turned their backs on "realism as an unwarrantedly stable and epistemologically confident narrative mode" and "developed novelistic forms that were fragmented, deployed multiple viewpoints, emphasized the subjective nature of experience, disrupted narrative chronology" (Gasiorek 6). William Faulkner deprived the reader of any organizing narratorial figure and unified representation of the world, favoring instead the juxtaposition of a multitude of points of view in *The Sound and the Fury* (1929) and *As I Lay Dying* (1930) while Virginia Woolf linked herself "to dispersion, to intermittency, to the fragmented brilliance of images, to the simmering fascination of the instant" (Blanchot 101), famously asking readers to "tolerate the spasmodic, the obscure, the fragmentary, the failure" (Woolf 111). Significantly, most theorists of modernist literature highlight the primacy of fragmentation and put forward related concepts or notions which Stephen Kern has enumerated in *Modernism after the Death of God: Christianity, Fragmentation, and Unification* (2017):

> *rupture* (Marjorie Perloff), *disintegration* (Erich Kahler), *discontinuity* (William Everdell), *nihilism* (Shane Weller), *crisis* (Jacques Le Rider), *meltdown* (Marshall Berman), *trauma* (Ariela Freedman), *shock* (Robert Hughes), *exploded form* (James Mellard), *break-up* (Katharine Kuh), *broken images* (Robert Schwartz), *fragmentation* (Sarah Haslam), and *self-fragmentation* (Dennis Brown). (6)

Kern adds however that this emphasis on fragmentation, disintegration and dislocation is often balanced by a process of reconstruction and a desire for unification. Thus, James McFarlane reinterpreted William Butler Yeats's famous line from "Second Coming" (1919) – "Things fall apart; the

Introduction: the art of the fragment

centre cannot hold" (Yeats 158) – by arguing that "the defining thing in the Modernist mode is not so much that things fall *apart* but that they fall *together*" (McFarlane 92). According to Joshua Kavaloski, Yeats was not only mourning "the perceived collapse of the order that had previously provided structure and meaning to human life" but he was also "longing for a new center" and articulating "the desire to reestablish order out of the shocks, crises, and violations of modernism's early phase" (1). In the same way, Eliot in *The Waste Land* aimed to "piece together or reconcile the jigsaw of the myriad references, half-lines, non-sequiturs and quotations," thereby trying to "hold in the chaos" (Childs 182). In "Spatial Form in Modern Literature," Joseph Frank argued for a spatial and non-sequential reading of modernist works, following the model of imagist poetry. Taking the example of James Joyce's *Ulysses* (1922), he wrote, "the reader is forced to read *Ulysses* in exactly the same manner as he reads modern poetry, that is, by continually fitting fragments together and keeping allusions in mind until, by reflexive reference, he can link them to their complements" (20). These examples suggest that fragmentation in modernist literature needs to be set up against the wish to synthesize what has been taken apart in order to recover some form of unity. Thereby, as suggested by Varley-Winter in *Reading Fragments and Fragmentation in Modernist Literature* (2018), crises within modernist literature "are more than purely negative" (21).

While in France in the 1950s and 60s, the *nouveau roman* as practiced by Alain Robbe-Grillet, Nathalie Sarraute, Michel Butor and Claude Simon was bringing radical changes to the novel, and in the United States in 1967, John Barth published his famous essay "The Literature of Exhaustion" about "the used-upness of certain forms or exhaustion of certain possibilities" (71), in Britain, mainstream social realism was the dominating trend and traditional novels were flourishing. Writers such as Eva Figes, B. S. Johnson, Ann Quin, Alan Burns or Brigid Brophy showed their frustration with this "reaction against experiment" – the title of Rubin Rabinovitz's study of the English novel of the period. Figes recalls, "We were concerned with language, with breaking up conventional narrative, with 'making it new' in our different ways. We all used fragmentation as a starting point, and then took off in different directions" (70). Just as William S. Burroughs devised his cut-up technique to reflect the randomness of consciousness and the fragmented nature of the real, Johnson kept looking for forms that would reflect the chaos and fragmentation of reality, or, quoting Samuel Beckett, "a form that accommodates the mess" (Johnson, *Aren't You Rather Young* 17). In *Albert Angelo* (1964), the author-narrator describes his own book as being "about the fragmentariness of life, too, attempts to reproduce the moment-to-moment fragmentariness of life, my life, and to echo it in technique, the fragmentariness" (169). In *The Unfortunates* (1969), Johnson's famous novel-in-a-box composed of twenty-seven unbound sections, the novelist used the dislocated form of the book as a metaphor for the random workings of the narrator's mind, the arbitrary progression of a football match and the proliferation of cancer cells.

Critics have considered Johnson either as "a Modernist stranded on the inimical shores of the late twentieth century" (Ganteau, "Anatomy" 113) or as a paradoxical precursor of postmodernism, "a postmodernist who wasn't postmodern" (White and Tew 6). This hesitation points to the continuities and points of contact between modernism and postmodernism despite the addition of the polysemic prefix "post–," and one of them is specifically "the shattered fragment" (Metzer 104). For Jean-François Lyotard, the postmodern condition is characterized by an "incredulity towards metanarratives" (xxiv): master narratives that would grant meaning and rationality to events no longer exist and are replaced by a multitude of stories, a polyphony of voices, a plurality of versions. Therefore, as noted by Paul Virilio in 1983, "[w]e're in the age of micro-narrative, the art of the fragment" (35): the unity of continuity has been displaced "onto the notion of fragment, of disorder" (36). While Romantic and modernist artists were still longing for unity, the postmodernist writer "only disconnects.... His ultimate opprobrium is 'totalization,' any synthesis whatever, social, epistemic, even poetic. Hence his preference for montage, collage, the found or cut-up literary object, for paratactical over hypotactical forms" (Hassan 19). Several theorists have highlighted that major difference with modernism, for instance, Alan Wilde, who wrote that "Postmodernism has given up Modernist attempts to restore wholeness to a fragmented world and has accepted the contingency of experience" (42). For such American writers as Barthelme, Richard Brautigan or Thomas Pynchon, the fragments "never come together under the aegis of an explanatory rationale, be it that of history, myth, or psychology" because all such metanarratives are distrusted (D'haen 220). This also explains why the narrator of Salman Rushdie's *Shame* (1983), in his attempt to tell the history of Pakistan, is "forced to reflect that world in fragments of broken mirrors" and has to reconcile himself to "the inevitability of the missing bits" (69). Whereas modernist fiction "endorsed the reader's will to read the fragment into a totality," in postmodernist fiction, "this move to reconstruction breaks down, for both the reader and the fictional characters" (Mepham 146). Postmodernist texts made of unconnected fragments destroy the idea of connectivity and "challenge the literary code that predisposes the reader to look for coherence" (Fokkema 44).

Now that postmodernism is "over" (Hutcheon 165), "dead and gone," "buried" (Federman 245), and has "run out of steam" (Mullins 1), one needs new theoretical tools to analyze the types of fragmentation practiced by British and American contemporary writers, which is what the present volume seeks to provide. On the one hand, contributors examine to what extent contemporary literature draws inspiration or moves away from earlier models, such as, for example, Mariano D'Ambrosio, who sees Laurence Sterne's *Tristram Shandy* as a precursor of fragmentary writing or Jarosław Hetman, who shows how David Foster Wallace has moved beyond postmodernist fragmentation to counter this brokenness with a sense of transcendence. On the other hand, contributors offer new taxonomies and categories to define the specificity of the modes of fragmentation implemented by contemporary writers in the digital age. A brief review of existing taxonomies and of the main features of fragmentary writing will be proposed below before we turn to the characteristics of fragmentary writing in British and American fiction of the last few decades.

Attempts at taxonomy

A number of critics agree on the basic distinction between works whose fragmentation is the result of the author's conception and those which are incomplete for other reasons, such as the writer's inability to finish them or the loss of some of its parts over time. In *The Romantic Fragment Poem* (1986), Marjorie Levinson uses the terms "authorized" and "accidental" to differentiate between those two categories (19). The element of chance signaled by the latter notion is also conspicuous in Merritt Moseley's choice of the word "fortuitous" to account for this group of texts in the present volume. Harries, in turn, prefers the terms "planned" and "unplanned" (3), whereas Metzer chooses to distinguish between "invented" and "remnant" fragments (105). The invented, or "new," fragments are, in Metzer's words, "fragments of nothing," as their origin is not a complete existing work but rather the concept of the fragment, informed by "the notions of incompletion, loss, and vagueness." Metzer concludes that despite their differences in genesis both types employ a very similar rhetoric (105–06).

Beyond the general agreement about the existence of the two outlined groups of fragmentary writing, there is little or no critical consensus on any further subdivisions and classifications. Elias proposes a classification of ten kinds of literary fragments, which she divides into two categories: those that historically *are* fragments and those that *become* fragments "by being theorized in critical discourse." The former group, composed of coercive, consensual, redundant, repetitive and resolute fragments, manifests "agency," while the latter, comprising ekphrastic, epigrammatic, epigraphic, emblematic and epitaphic fragments, performs "representational functions" (20). By the coercive fragment Elias understands texts (like the writings of Heraclitus) which forcefully aim to elicit a reception emphasizing their incompletion (25). The consensual kind, exemplified by the works of Schlegel, is also defined with reference to the way the text is interpreted; in this case, the text agrees to being "stretched to infinity and engages on a path of 'forever becoming'" (26). Redundant, repetitive and resolute fragments, in turn, are distinguished on the basis of what they mean rather than how they are perceived. The three kinds represent different "stages in modernist writing" as epitomized by the works of Louis Aragon, Gertrude Stein and Emil Cioran, respectively (27). Elias embeds her discussion of the second group of fragments in the context of the poetics of postmodernism. The first subtype, the ekphrastic fragment, is one which comments verbally on its visual properties. The next three – epigrammatic, epigraphic and emblematic – "represent three stages in deconstructive thinking" which are informed, respectively, by writing as performance, writing as paratext and writing as metadiscourse (29–30). The final type, the epitaphic fragment, illustrated by the works of David Markson (discussed in this volume in the articles by Moseley and Drąg), is defined as an "event that puts performativity to rest" (30).

In the present volume, the most comprehensive attempt at classifying deliberately fragmentary works is undertaken by Moseley, who proposes three categories: the braid, the bricolage and the mosaic, each of which is exemplified by a variety of contemporary works including the novels shortlisted for the 2016 Man Booker Prize. The braid is conceived of by Moseley as a series of distinct narrative projects which are interspersed with one another rather than offered in sequence. The bricolage is a category referring to works which are composed out of radically heterogeneous materials, whereas the mosaic comprises texts consisting of many narratives that are complete in themselves. Moseley concedes that his taxonomy is not exhaustive, as there exist numerous *sui generis* works that elude his classification.

The polyphonic novel, explored in this volume by D'Ambrosio, is another possible category of fragmentary writing. It relies on a juxtaposition of multiple voices and the employment of numerous narrators. Rather than amounting to a "messy cacophony," works like Colum McCann's *Let The Great World Spin* (2009) and Jennifer Egan's *A Visit from the Goon Squad* (2010) combine the various voices "with a virtuosity akin to that demon-

strated by the great contrapuntal composers" (Gioia 4).[2] David Mitchell's
Cloud Atlas (2004) is a work which could be classified as a polyphonic
novel as well as what A. E. van Vogt has dubbed the "fix-up" (qtd. in Liptak). Also referred to as the short-story novel, the "fix-up" is a notion applied to texts whose degree of coherence between consecutive chapters,
regarding subject matter and genre, is greater than in the case of a collection of short stories and lesser than in a traditional novel. Further examples, including other works by Mitchell and, to a certain extent, Ali Smith's
Hotel World (2001), are examined in this volume by Gerd Bayer and Alicia
Rouverol. The two other categories connected with fragmentary writing
which are discussed in other chapters are collage (Drąg) and the shuffle
narrative (Côme Martin). Among other relevant critical labels are lexico-
graphic fictions – texts imitating the form of encyclopedias, lexicons or
dictionaries, such as Xiaolu Guo's *A Concise Chinese-English Dictionary for
Lovers* (2007) and David Levithan's *The Lover's Dictionary* (2010) – and
question-and-answer texts, as exemplified by Jeanette Winterson's "The
Poetics of Sex" (1993) and Lydia Davis's "Jury Duty" (2001).

The poetics of fragmentary writing

Since fragmentary writing is not a widely established category, the list of
its distinctive features has not been authoritatively codified. As Moseley
notes in the opening chapter of this volume, in order for a text to be regarded as fragmentary, it certainly needs to *appear* that way to the reader.
That subjective impression is often evoked by the division of the text into
single paragraphs or sentences which are separated by space. In such
works, exemplified by the writings of Roland Barthes, Maurice Blanchot,
David Markson and Maggie Nelson, fragmentariness is evident at first
glance – from the moment the reader sets eyes on the page. One alternative are works composed of blocks of continuous text – like Smith's *Hotel
World* and Mitchell's *Cloud Atlas* – where fragmentation is only apparent at
the level of the narrative, which frequently intersperses various elements
and stories in a non-linear manner. The third common strategy of fragmentary writing is asserting its hybridity by employing multimodality.
Composed of "a multitude of semiotic modes," multimodal texts "cognize
and integrate meaning from the creative synthesis of word, image, and
tactility" (Gibbons, *Multimodality* 4; Gibbons, "Multimodal Literature"
433). Multimodal fragments have become particularly prominent over the
last decades, therefore a separate section of the volume has been devoted

---

[2] Ted Gioia's article "The Rise of the Fragmented Novel" is an electronic publication
divided into sections, whose numbers are provided in parenthetical references.

to the analysis of their poetics: Grzegorz Maziarczyk provides an overview of various multimodal and transmedial strategies in contemporary fiction, while Zofia Kolbuszewska and Deborah Bridle examine the formal characteristics of specific examples of works combining text, visuals and sound.

As suggested earlier, among the most common characteristics of fragmentary literature, regardless of which of the above categories they may fit into, are incompleteness, discontinuity and heterogeneity. The defiance of completeness, cohesion and continuity in the syntactic structure and the arrangement of text on the page appears suited to convey content that challenges the status quo. Susini-Anastopoulos sees fragmentary literature as "a space of conflict and tension" and as a "writing of intersection" on many levels, including the "aesthetic, generic [and] logical" (258). Its anarchic and irreverent mixture of incommensurate elements may evoke a strong reaction in the reader, including shock (Rongier), as is the case in sexually explicit literary collages by Burroughs and Kathy Acker. Related to fragmentary writing's propensity for critique and contestation is its frequently adopted position of skepticism and resistance to ideology. The mistrust of systematic truth and of any received hierarchies is, according to Werner Helmich, the intrinsic property of this kind of literature and has made it a useful tool for feminist literature. Authors such as Joan Didion and Annie Leclerc have, according to Ripoll, employed the fragment as a gesture of opposition towards "masculine writing, which would rest on the will to impose a unicity against a specifically feminine *multiplicity*" ("Vers une pataphysique" 18, emphasis original). The programmatic egalitarianism of fragmentary writing invites polysemy (28), as a result of which individual works make no pretense to unity and lay bare their contradictions.

The rejection of the principle of coherence makes fragmentary writing particularly suited to represent the chaos and contingency of reality, as noted by Chol (12) and Marc Botha (213). It can thus be regarded as endowed with a capacity to be a "truer" form of realism than ostensibly realist art. This paradox has been asserted memorably in Burroughs's manifesto for the cut-up technique: "Take a walk down a city street and put down what you have just seen on canvas. You have seen a person cut in two by a car, bits and pieces of street signs and advertisements, reflections from shop windows – a montage of fragments" ("Fall" 76). In fragmentary writing, the seams between the numerous scraps out of which the text is interwoven are deliberately exposed rather than concealed. Hence the stylistic preference for all kinds of lists and inventories as well as for citation and other forms of appropriation, especially those that do not smoothly integrate the borrowed content with the rest of the text. Although some works considered in this volume, especially those by David Foster Wallace and David Mitchell, amount to several hundred or even over a thousand pages, fragmentary writing is generally associated with brevity and stylistic economy (Helmich 29), as exemplified by Johnson's *The Unfortunates* and Will Eaves's *The Absent Therapist* (2014).

The earlier noted heterogeneity of fragmentary writing is usually the result of combining a number of distinct components, such as genres, discourses, registers, external sources and even passages in different languages. The rhetorical strategy adopted in many texts discussed in this volume, including those by Winterson (in Maria Antonietta Struzziero's paper), Markson, Shields and Eaves, is parataxis – a seemingly arbitrary and non-hierarchical juxtaposition of elements which do not bear any obvious logical relation to one another. A similar mechanism can be observed on a larger scale – when considering the structure of the entire work being composed of sections that vary significantly as regards genre, style or content. Some of the most critically acclaimed examples of generic hybridity, also referred to as generic eclecticism, have been Julian Barnes's *Flaubert's Parrot* (1984) and *A History of the World in 10 ½ Chapters* (1989), Mitchell's *Ghostwritten* (1999) and *Cloud Atlas*, and Egan's *A Visit from the Goon Squad*.

The lack of explicit connections between consecutive passages or parts results in the appearance of what Ripoll calls "a space of the not-said which permits ambiguity" ("Vers une pataphysique" 17). Wolfgang Iser's notion of the gap could be invoked here to elucidate the mechanism of the reading process of fragmentary texts. Iser argues that whenever the reader is confronted with such a space of ambiguity, they are offered an opportunity to "bring into play [their] own faculty for establishing connections" and "fill in the gaps left by the text itself" (284–85). Chol's analogical term to Iser's gap is "lacunary interval," which she defines as the text's refusal to provide the "syntactic links of causality," as a result of which the plot of a fragmentary novel may veer towards the antiplot (19). For the same reason, the fragmentary novel often comes close to what is called the antinovel – a work that challenges novelistic expectations, such as the employment of a linear narrative, a single protagonist and a consistent setting. Ballard's *The Atrocity Exhibition* (1970) and Markson's *This Is Not a Novel* (2001) could be cited as cases in point.

Because of its use of ambiguity, discontinuity and other strategies of disorientation, fragmentary writing may be liable to the charges of obscurity and inaccessibility (Veikat; Metzer 106). In order for the reader to succeed in drawing all the necessary connections, they need to pay scrupulous attention to the text, which may involve having to reread some of its parts. Iser notes that while reading a radically fragmented work, "one's attention is almost exclusively occupied with the search for connections between the fragments" (285). When commenting on certain strategies adopted by "modern experimental works," Gerald Graff notes that their frequent renunciation of a straightforward plot makes them "depend much more heavily on the reader's ability to locate thematic propositions capable of giving their disjunctive, fragmentary, and refractory details some exemplary meaning and coherence" (qtd. in McHale 221). Although the rejection of plot is by no means obligatory for fragmented fictions, Graff's insistence on the strengthened role of the reader applies to all of its varieties. Fragmentary writing could thus be said to belong to the category of "writerly" (*scriptible*) rather than "readerly" (*lisible*) works, as prescribed by Barthes in *S/Z* (4). Their multiple gaps and lacunae compel the reader to increase their engagement with the text and to become an active co-author of its meanings.

Fragmentation today

This volume originates from two convictions: first, that over the last years one can observe a revival of interest in fragmentary literature and, secondly, that its contemporary examples do not restrict themselves to cultivating the poetics of their modernist and postmodernist antecedents but often propose alternative formal solutions. The validity of the former claim can be illustrated by the fact that the year 2014 alone saw the publication of three critically acclaimed and radically fragmentary works: Richard McGuire's *Here* – a graphic novel created out of over 150 images (non-chronologically arranged) of the same location throughout several million years, Jenny Offill's *Dept. of Speculation* (shortlisted for the Folio Prize) – an account of a marriage crisis narrated with the use of several hundred loosely connected paragraphs, and Eaves's *The Absent Therapist* (shortlisted for the Goldsmiths Prize) – an amalgam of the voices of 150 speakers. The mere list of authors considered in this volume – including Barnes, Mitchell, Ali Smith, Winterson, Wallace and Jonathan Safran Foer (whose mechanics of fragmentation are analyzed by Caroline Magnin) – testifies to the significance of this literary phenomenon.

In "The Rise of the Fragmented Novel" (2013), Ted Gioia locates the resurgence of contemporary fragmentary literature at the time of publication of Don DeLillo's *Underworld* (1997). The critic singles out this work as a harbinger of a new kind of fragmented novel, which despite offering a "sprawling and multivalent" narrative remains "meticulously controlled and orchestrated" (21). Novels such as the earlier mentioned *Cloud Atlas* and *A Visit from the Goon Squad*, as well as Ian McEwan's *Atonement* (2001) and Zadie Smith's *NW* (2012), are cited by Gioia as paradigms of the twenty-first century reinvention of the tradition of postmodernist experiments with fragmented narratives as practiced by Burroughs, Ballard and Gilbert Sorrentino. "Instead of relying on fragmentation as a means of disjunction and dissolution," as the postmodernists did, writers like Mitchell and Egan weave fictions out of scraps in such a way as to make them "holistic and coalescent" (Gioia 3). Their overall coherence, combined with greater attention to plot and pacing, makes them a lot more accessible to the general reader. While remaining experimental in their commitment to mixing multiple voices, genres and narrative scraps, Gioia argues, they become palatable to a mainstream audience, thus enabling the fragmented novel to emerge from the niche it occupied in the 1960s and 70s (8). Works like Burroughs's *The Naked Lunch* (1959) and Ballard's *The Atrocity Exhibition* may have developed a cult following some years after their publication, but they did not manage to attract a mass readership. On the contrary, *Atonement* and *Cloud Atlas* not only achieved bestseller status (the former – with close to 1.4 million copies sold in the UK alone by 2010 – was ranked 21 in *The Guardian*'s list of "Top-selling 100 Books of All Time") but were made into high-profile and high-budget films starring Keira Knightley, Tom Hanks and Halle Berry. Other works mentioned in Gioia's essay that testify to the high marketing potential of fragmentary fictions are Audrey Niffenegger's *The Time Traveler's Wife* (2003), Roberto Bolaño's *2666* (2004) and Hari Kunzru's *Gods Without Men* (2011). Another evidence of the domestication of fragmented fictions is the awarding of major literary prizes to such works as McCann's *Let The Great World Spin* (National Book Award), Egan's *A Visit from the Goon Squad* (Pulitzer Prize), George Saunders's *Lincoln in the Bardo* (2017, Man Booker Prize) and Olga Tokarczuk's *Flights* (2007/2017, International Man Booker Prize).

What may seem problematic about Gioia's argument is his use of the "mainstream" label to refer to works by authors like Egan, Wallace and Zadie Smith. Although it is true that they have attracted a vast readership and that some of them do make concessions to accessibility in their use of fragmentation, their works remain more ambitious and demanding of the reader than most works of literary fiction. Furthermore, when Gioia states that in twenty-first century literature "the techniques of disjunction and fragmentation, once pursued as part of an *avant-garde* movement, have been tamed and subdued," he omits to notice the continued and thriving tradition of the more experimental (and certainly far removed from the mainstream) fragmentary writing (25). Its representatives include older writers, such as Gabriel Josipovici, David Markson (who died in 2010) and Mary Robinson; younger and established authors like Maggie Nelson, Jenny Offill, Lance Olsen, David Shields and Steve Tomasula, as well as young and aspiring writers such as Zinzi Clemmons, Sheila Heti and Harry

Parker. Much of what many of their works share – besides the usual prop-erties of fragmentary writing outlined in the previous section – and what appears to distinguish them from their postmodernist counterparts can be subsumed under David Shields's notion of "reality hunger" – the desire to "break larger and larger chunks of 'reality'" into the text (1) and, conse-quently, a greater commitment to representation. In place of irony and playfulness, those works offer seriousness and engagement, which mani-fests itself in their choice of subject matter: working through traumatic loss (Nelson's *Bluets*, 2009, and Clemmons's *What We Lose*, 2017), the crisis of a marriage (Offill's *Dept. of Speculation*), the experience of losing both legs during the war in Afghanistan (Parker's *Anatomy of a Soldier*, 2016) and the assassination of Theo van Gogh by a Muslim fundamentalist (Ol-sen's *Head in Flames*, 2009), to name but a few.

In *Reality Hunger: A Manifesto* (2010), Shields diagnoses the arrival of lit-erary works which, among other characteristics, incorporate "'raw' mate-rial, seemingly unprocessed, unfiltered, uncensored" and obliterate the distinction between fiction and non-fiction by frequently absorbing auto-biography and criticism (3). Both strategies can be observed in the works of many of the authors mentioned above. The inclusion of "authentic" material occurs in them on a scale much greater than in earlier fragmen-tary works, which relied on appropriating quotations from other texts. At the extreme, *Reality Hunger* alone, Jonathan Lethem's "The Ecstasy of Influence" (2007) and Jeremy Gavron's *Felix Culpa* (2018) are avowed pla-giarisms (or collages) which are almost exclusively composed of fragments from other works. One of many other strategies of "breaking reality" into one's text is Sheila Heti's practice of incorporating large portions of record-ed and transcribed conversations with friends in her debut novel *How Should a Person Be?* (2010).

While remaining committed to the label of the novel, many examples of contemporary fragmentary literature, including works by Heti, Offill and Ben Lerner, transcend its boundaries. Shields sees it as a consequence of their embracing of "reality": "Our lives aren't prepackaged along narrative lines and, therefore, by its very nature, reality-based art – underprocessed, underproduced – splinters and explodes" (70). According to Shields, there also exists a vital link between fragmentary form and sincere content: "As a work gets more autobiographical, more intimate, more confessional, more embarrassing, it breaks into fragments" (70). This insight may account for the frequent use of fragmentation in life writing, as exemplified by Joe Brainard's *I Remember* (1970), Rick Moody's "Primary Sources" (1995) and Shields's own *How Literature Saved My Life* (2013).

Whereas Shields appears to attribute the resurgence of fragmentary writing to "reality hunger," critics such as Gioia, Tiina Veikat, Dominique Rabaté and Pierre Schoentjes point to the influence of the recent developments of technology. Veikat regards literature's "increasing tendency towards brevity and fragmentation" as a reaction to the massive influx of information available on the Internet and the sense that one is incapable of processing all that data. Rabaté and Schoentjes indicate the quickening pace of the Internet, video games and TV programs as evidence of "our epoch's inability to take things slowly" and as the genesis of "fictions of extreme brevity" (3). Gioia, in turn, draws a parallel between the radical increase in the number of editing cuts in TV commercials and the fragmentation of the mainstream novel. He also adds that in this respect literature is merely following a general and global tendency rather than setting a new trend (9). Jonathan Bastian, likewise, sees the fragmentation of contemporary narratives – particularly in the context of the polyphonic novel – as a symptom of literature "keeping pace with these shifting times." The arrival of digital culture, with its emphasis on visuality, has also influenced twenty-first-century literature and contributed to the earlier noted rise of richly multimodal works. The present volume aims to illustrate the great variety and originality of fragmentary writing in contemporary British and American fiction by examining how electronic literature and print books, experimental works and more traditional ones, develop their own strategies to practice and perfect the art of the fragment.

Works Cited

Adorno, Theodor W. *Aesthetic Theory.* Eds. Gretel Adorno and Rolf Tiedemann. Trans. Robert Hullot-Kentor. London: Continuum, 1997.

Barth, John. "The Literature of Exhaustion." 1967. *The Novel Today.* Ed. Malcolm Bradbury. 1977. London: Fontana, 1990. 71–85.

Barthelme, Donald. "See the Moon?" 1966. *Unspeakable Practices, Unnatural Acts.* New York: Farrar, Straus and Giroux, 1973. 153–70.

Barthes, Roland. *S/Z.* 1970. Trans. Richard Miller. New York: Hill and Wang, 1974.

Bastian, Jonathan. "'Goon Squad' Ushers in an Era of New Perspectives." *National Public Radio,* 19 Apr. 2011, http://www.npr.org/2011/04/19/135546674/goon-squad-ushers-in-an-era-of-new-perspectives. Accessed 20 Aug. 2018.

Blanchot, Maurice. *The Book to Come.* 1959. Trans. Charlotte Mandell. Stanford: Stanford UP, 2003.

Botha, Marc. "Microfiction." *The Cambridge Companion to the English Short Story.* Ed. Ann-Marie Einhaus. New York: Cambridge UP, 2016. 201–20.

Burroughs, William S. "The Fall of Art." *The Adding Machine: Selected Essays.* By William S. Burroughs. New York: Arcade, 201–80.

Childs, Peter. *Modernism*. 2000. New York: Routledge, 2008.

Chol, Isabelle. "Avant-propos." *Poétiques de la discontinuité: De 1870 à nos jours*. Ed. Isabelle Chol. Clermont-Ferrand: PU Blaise Pascal, 2004. 7–22.

Clark, Alex. "Will Self: 'The Novel is Absolutely Doomed.'" *The Guardian*, 17 Mar. 2018, https://www.theguardian.com/books/2018/mar/17/will-self-the-books-interview-alex-clark-phone-memoir. Accessed 20 Aug. 2018.

D'haen, Theo. "Postmodernism in American Fiction and Art." *Approaching Postmodernism*. Eds. Douve W. Fokkema and Hans Bertens. Amsterdam: John Benjamins, 1986. 211–31.

Drąg, Wojciech. "'A Novel Against the Novel': David Markson's Antinovelistic Tetralogy." *Polish Journal of English Studies* 1 (2015): 11–25.

Elias, Camelia. *The Fragment: Towards a History and Poetics of a Performative Genre*. Bern: Peter Lang, 2004.

Eliot, T. S. *The Complete Poems and Plays of T. S. Eliot*. London: Faber, 1982.

Federman, Raymond. *Aunt Rachel's Fur*. Normal: Fiction Collective Two, 2001.

Figes, Eva. "B.S. Johnson." *The Review of Contemporary Fiction* 5.2 (1985): 70–71.

Fokkema, Douve W. *Literary History, Modernism and Postmodernism*. Amsterdam: John Benjamins, 1984.

Frank, Joseph. *The Idea of Spatial Form*. New Brunswick: Rutgers UP, 1991.

Frey, Hans-Jost. *Interruptions*. Trans. Georgia Albert. Albany: State U of New York P, 1996.

Ganteau, Jean-Michel. "Anatomy of an Obsession: B. S. Johnson's *Aren't You Rather Young to be Writing Your Memoirs?*" *Études britanniques contemporaines* 33 (2007): 103–13.

---. *The Ethics and Aesthetics of Vulnerability in Contemporary British Fiction*. London: Routledge, 2015.

Gasiorek, Andrzej. *A History of Modernist Literature*. Chichester: Wiley Blackwell, 2015.

Gibbons, Alison. "Multimodal Literature and Experimentation." *The Routledge Companion to Experimental Literature*. Eds. Joe Bray, Alison Gibbons and Brian McHale. Abingdon: Routledge, 2012. 420–34.

---. *Multimodality, Cognition, and Experimental Literature*. New York: Routledge, 2012.

Gioia, Ted. "The Rise of the Fragmented Novel." *Fractious Fiction*, 17 July 2013, http://fractiousfiction.com/rise_of_the_fragmented_novel.html. Accessed 20 Aug. 2018.

Guyaux, André. *Poétique du fragment: Essai sur les Illuminations de Rimbaud*. Neufchâtel: À la Baconnière, 1985.

Harries, Elizabeth Wanning. *The Unfinished Manner: Essays on the Fragment in the Later Eighteenth Century*. Charlottesville: U of Virginia P, 1994.

Hassan, Ihab. *Rumors of Change: Essays of Five Decades*. Tuscaloosa: U of Alabama P, 1995.

Helmich, Werner. "Discontinuité donnée et discontinuité recherchée: Plaidoyer pour une désambiguïsation de certains termes littéraires." *Poétiques de la discontinuité: De 1870* à *nos jours*. Ed. Isabelle Chol. Clermont-Ferrand: Presses Universitaires Blaise Pascal, 2004. 25–34.

Hutcheon, Linda. *The Politics of Postmodernism*. 1989. 2nd ed. New York: Routledge, 2002.

Iser, Wolfgang. *The Implied Reader: Patterns of Communication in Prose Fiction from Bunyan to Beckett*. 1972. Baltimore: John Hopkins UP, 1978.

Janowitz, Anne. "The Romantic Fragment." *A Companion to Romanticism*. Ed. Duncan Wu. Oxford, Blackwell, 1998. 442–51.

Johnson, B. S. *Albert Angelo*. 1964. *Omnibus*. London: Picador, 2004.

---. *Aren't You Rather Young to be Writing Your Memoirs?* London: Hutchinson, 1973.

Kavaloski, Joshua. *High Modernism: Aestheticism and Performativity in Literature of the 1920s*. Rochester: Camden House, 2014.

Kern, Stephen. *Modernism after the Death of God: Christianity, Fragmentation, and Unification*. New York: Routledge, 2017.

Lacoue-Labarthe, Philippe, and Jean-Luc Nancy. *The Literary Absolute: The Theory of Literature in German Romanticism*. Trans. Philip Barnard and Cheryl Lester. Albany: State University of New York P, 1988.

Levinson, Marjorie. *The Romantic Fragment Poem: A Critique of a Form*. Chapel Hill: U of North Carolina P, 1986.

Liptak, Andrew. "A. E. van Vogt and the Fix-Up Novel." *Kirkus Reviews*, 5 Aug. 2013, https://www.kirkusreviews.com/features/e-van-vogt-and-fix-novel/. Accessed 20 Aug. 2018.

Lyotard, Jean-François. *The Postmodern Condition: A Report on Knowledge*. 1979. Trans. Geoff Bennington and Brian Massumi. Minneapolis: U of Minnesota P, 1984.

McFarlane, James. "The Mind of Modernism." 1976. *Modernism: A Guide to European Literature. 1890–1930*. Eds. Malcolm Bradbury and James McFarlane. London: Penguin, 1991. 71–93.

McHale, Brian. *Postmodernist Fiction*. London: Routledge, 2007.

Mepham, John. "Narratives of Postmodernism." *Postmodernism and Contemporary Fiction*. Ed. Edmund J. Smyth. London: Batsford, 1991. 138–55.

Metzer, David. *Musical Modernism at the Turn of the Twenty-First Century*. Cambridge: Cambridge UP, 2009.

Montandon, Alain. *Les formes brèves*. Paris: Hachette, 1992.

Mullins, Matthew. *Postmodernism in Pieces: Materializing the Social in U.S. Fiction*. Oxford: Oxford UP, 2016.

Rabaté, Dominique, and Pierre Schoentjes. "Micro-scopies." *Revue critique de fixxion française contemporaine 1* (2010), http://www.revue-critique-de-fixxion-francaise-contemporaine.org/rcffc/article/view/fx01.01/480. Accessed 20 Aug. 2018.

Rabinovitz, Rubin. *The Reaction Against Experiment in the English Novel, 1950–1960*. New York: Columbia UP, 1967.

Rauber, D. F. "The Fragment as Romantic Form." *Modern Language Quarterly* 30 (1969): 212–21.

Ripoll, Ricard, ed. *L'écriture fragmentaire: théories et pratiques.* Perpignan: Presses Universitaires de Perpignan, 2002.

---. "Vers une pataphysique de l'écriture fragmentaire." *Capa* 4 (2006): 11–22.

Rongier, Sébastien. "La modernité, esthétique et pensée du fragmentaire." *Recherches en esthétique* 14 (2008), http://sebastienrongier.net/article55.html.

Rushdie, Salman. *Shame.* 1983. London: Picador, 1984.

Self, Will. "The Novel is Dead (this time, it's for real)." *The Guardian*, 2 May 2014, http://www.theguardian.com/books/2014/may/02/will-self-novel-dead-literary-fiction. Accessed 20 Aug. 2018.

Shields, David. *Reality Hunger: A Manifesto.* New York: Knopf, 2010.

Smith, Zadie. *Changing My Mind: Occasional Essays.* New York: Penguin, 2009.

---. "An Essay is an Act of Imagination." *The Guardian*, 21 Nov. 2009, http://youmightfindyourself.com/post/252362834/zadie-smith-on-the-rise-of-the-essay. Accessed 20 Aug. 2018.

Susini-Anastopoulos, Françoise. *L'écriture fragmentaire: définitions et enjeux.* Paris: Presses Universitaires de France, 1997.

"This Week's Bestsellers: September 15, 2014." *Publishers Weekly*, 12 Sept. 2014, https://www.publishersweekly.com/pw/by-topic/industry-news/bookselling/article/63997-this-week-s-bestsellers-september-15-2014.html. Accessed 20 Aug. 2018.

"Top-selling 100 Books of All Time." *The Guardian*, 1 Jan. 2011, https://www.theguardian.com/news/datablog/2011/jan/01/top-100-books-of-all-time. Accessed 20 Aug. 2018.

Varley-Winter, Rebecca. *Reading Fragments and Fragmentation in Modernist Literature.* Eastbourne: Sussex UP, 2018.

Veikat, Tiina "Collage et inventaire poético-méditatif: écrire de la littérature fragmentaire au XXIe siècle: analyse comparative de *Vanishing Point* de David Markson et *Ombres errantes* de Pascal Quignard." *Academia.edu*, 2014, https://www.academia.edu/8133499/Inventaire_po%C3%A9tico-m%C3%A9ditatif_-_%C3%A9crire_de_la_litt%C3%A9rature_fragmentaire_cas_de_Vanishing_Point_par_David_Markson_et_des_Ombres_errantes_par_P._Quignard. Accessed 20 Aug. 2018.

Virilio, Paul, and Sylvère Lotringer. *Pure War.* Trans. Mark Polizzotti. New York: Semiotext(e), 1983.

White, Glyn, and Philip Tew. "Introduction: Re-reading B. S. Johnson." *Re-reading B. S. Johnson.* Eds. Philip Tew and Glyn White. Houndmills: Palgrave Macmillan, 2007.

Wilde, Alan. *Horizons of Assent: Modernism, Postmodernism, and the Ironic Imagination.* Baltimore: John Hopkins UP, 1981.

Woolf, Virginia. "Mr. Bennett and Mrs. Brown." 1924. *The Captain's Death Bed, and Other Essays.* London: Hogarth Press, 1950. 90–111.

Yeats, William Butler. *The Collected Poems of W. B. Yeats.* Hertfordshire: Wordsworth Editions, 2000.

Part One

Forms of fragmentation: past and present

Chapter 1

What is fragmentary fiction?

Merritt Moseley,
University of North Carolina at Asheville

Fragmentary fiction is not a simple term or a simple category; its meaning is contestable, its reach comprehensive, the understanding of its techniques dependent on prior definitions. Before attempting an analysis of types of fragmentary fiction, or an explanation of how fiction may be fragmented, it is necessary to begin at the beginning. What, then, *is* fragmentary fiction? I will first offer a tentative definition of a term wielded with looseness and often aligned with some particular period or *Zeitgeist*. I will then focus on examples of fortuitous fragmented works before moving on to specific cases of intentionally fragmented novels that are *sui generis* and could not adequately fit into a taxonomy. I will finally suggest that part of fragmentary fiction could fall into three categories – the braid, the bricolage and the mosaic – which I will illustrate by pointing to early examples in literature and then focusing on three novels on the 2016 shortlist for the Man Booker Prize: Madeleine Thien's *Do Not Say We Have Nothing*, Graeme Macrae Burnet's *His Bloody Project* and David Szalay's *All That Man Is*.

To define fragmentary fiction, it might be helpful to start by asking what fiction is like if it is *not* fragmentary. Is it a seamless whole, complete and entire, leaving no margins around the edges, with nothing left out in the middle? Does it neither consist of fragments, nor constitute in itself a fragment of something larger? If we try to imagine such an achieved work, we will find there is none. Henry James, who was writing from a commitment to verisimilitude and the obligation of fiction to produce the sensation of reality, wrote: "Really, universally, relations stop nowhere, and the exquisite problem of the artist is eternally but to draw, by a geometry of his own, the circle within which they shall happily *appear* to do so" (vii). Relations stop nowhere; but novels *have* to stop somewhere, and they will, necessarily, require some sort of fragmentation. The work itself is, and must be, a fragment of something larger, even if that something larger is a fictive whole.

However, to say that fragmentary fiction is nothing less than all fiction is of little help. Perhaps we can move toward more useful discrimination by suggesting that the fragmentary fiction we are interested in is fiction that *feels* fragmented, broken, unfinished, incomplete, incoherent. It might also be useful to think of works that are themselves fragments, alongside works that are made up of fragments, and some texts can have both characteristics.

Any overview of fragmentation in fiction will include many possibilities for the subgenre including forking-path narratives, polyphonic voices, novels built of self-contained parts and collages. Many of these are not new – as Borges's forking paths narrative from 1941 will show – but others constitute forms of radically fragmented fiction based on modern technology. The first mobile phone novel, delivered in text messages, called *Deep Love*, appeared in Japan in 2003. Each of its chapters is less than 200 words long. This kind of fragmentation has been quickly eclipsed in Twitter novels, in which each installment is limited to 140 characters.

Despite the richness of the term, "fragmentary fiction" is not commonly used in Anglophone literary criticism. When it does appear, it is wielded with some looseness. Sometimes "fragmentary novel" is the term assigned to a collection of short stories. It has been applied to Sherwood Anderson's *Winesburg, Ohio* (1919), and to James Joyce's *Dubliners* (1914), usually thought of as short-story collections. In another example of the term's looseness, a reviewer writing about Michael Chabon's 2016 novel, *Moonglow*, calls it "Chabon's least linear, most fragmentary novel, achieving its considerable effects by means of an accumulation of layers of feeling rather than from any sense of one incident leading to another and another" (Nance D5). This sounds like what used to be called "episodic" narrative, and the principle of construction something like emotional rather than logical sequence. In a comment on A. S. Byatt's *Babel Tower* (1996), Thuan Chye Kee wrote that "this fragmentary novel of the fragmented '60s contains an argument with D. H. Lawrence and E. M. Forster, a throwback to The Hobbit, and the idea of towers from the Tower of Babel to the Tower of the 120 Days of Sodom" and that "it is held together by its metaphors" (Kee 11). The suggestion here is of a gallimaufry of different types of content, combined with a looseness of the logical structure that seems to be what Nance means by a novel not being "linear."

The review of *Babel Tower* is characteristic in aligning fragmentary fiction with some particular *period* in which supposedly the culture or the *Zeitgeist* or the human consciousness or experience itself is notably fragmented – "the fragmented '60s." It is not quite clear what it means to say that the 1960s were "fragmented" or, if they were, what unfragmented time we might appeal to for contrast; and other periods have also been cited as explanations for the fragmentation of literature. J. G. Ballard, for instance, commenting on his 1970 novel *The Atrocity Exhibition*, explains, "Its landscape is compounded of an enormous number of fictions, the fragments of the dream machine that produces our lifestyle right now" – "right now" being either 1970, when the novel first appeared, or 1990, when he wrote his introduction (Ballard 6). Tom McCarthy recently defended *avant-garde* writing by saying that it does justice to the fragmentary and discontinuous consciousness of human beings and is, therefore, more realistic than texts that pursue realism through more conventional forms (McCarthy 21–22). Something similar may underlie the statement by Clarice Lispector: "Coherence ... I don't want it any more. Coherence is mutilation. I want disorder. I can only guess at it through a vehement incoherence" (Daniels). Another recent comment by Guy Patrick Cunningham linked fragmentary writing to the digital age. Our reading, he insists, is fragmentary because of digital texts, hyperlinks, and other features of The Way We Read Now:

> And because of that, works that deal with fragmentation, that eschew not only a traditional narrative structure but the very idea of a work comprising a single, linear whole – take on a special kind of relevance. Fragmentary writing is (or at least feels) like the one avant-garde literary approach that best fits our particular moment. (Cunningham)

Surprisingly, Cunningham then goes on to look back to Beckett and Kafka as precursors though their particular moment did not have the digital universe to provoke their fragmentariness. Since T. S. Eliot's celebrated discussion of the dissociation of sensibility was really in an important sense a diagnosis of fragmentation, which he traced to the seventeenth century, the move of explaining fragmentary fiction by the time in which it appears becomes problematic.

Fortuitous fragments: unfinished and incomplete works

The first group of texts that may be regarded as fragmentary fictions are those which are *fortuitously* fragmented. Among them are unfinished works – fictions which are truncated by the death of the author and published posthumously. Examples include Nikolai Gogol's *Dead Souls* (1842), Charles Dickens's *The Mystery of Edwin Drood* (1870), Franz Kafka's *Amerika* (1927), Albert Camus's *The First Man* (1994), Vladimir Nabokov's *The Original of Laura* (2009) and David Foster Wallace's *The Pale King* (2011). All of these works are fragments of a whole of which their authors' deaths prevented the completion. Some marginal cases would include Truman Capote's *Answered Prayers* (1986), the incompleteness of which was *revealed* by his death, though it was probably uncompletable, and the heartbreaking case of Ralph Ellison's *Juneteenth*. Ellison worked on this, his second novel, from 1952, when he published *Invisible Man*, to his death in 1994. Part of the manuscript was apparently destroyed by fire in 1967, and during the remaining 27 years of Ellison's life he did not finish it. Some books lack ending for other reasons. Novalis left two unfinished novels, but this may reflect not incapacity or death, but rather the Romantic admiration for the idea of the unfinished, much as Herman Melville wrote in *Moby-Dick* (1851): "God keep me from ever completing anything" (159). On the other hand, Paul Valéry's famous comment reverses the idea that death prevents completion: "A work is never completed except by some accident such as weariness, dissatisfaction, the need to deliver, or death" (qtd. in Baum 147).

Another kind of fragmentary text is the one not missing its ending or truncated, but incomplete through missing some of the intermediate parts that it formerly contained. The *Satyricon* of Petronius exists in a highly fragmented form such that what remains amounts to a short novel less than 300 pages long. Estimates of the length of the whole work vary widely; it may have been 400,000 words when complete (Rimell 2, fn. 12). Another ancient text, the *Epic of Gilgamesh*, not only lacks many lines of its poetry – to be expected since it exists on fragile clay tablets over 3000 years old – but its order is also debatable, for the same reason. The discovery of the tablets in a scattered and partial state gave no clue of the order in which they were to be arranged. A more recent example, Franz Kafka's *The Trial* (1925) has also aroused critical disagreement over whether Kafka's friend Max Brod has properly ordered the chapters. Misordered chapters would constitute the kind of fragmentation people mean by "non-linear."

All these are unavoidably fragmented fictions – either unfinished, or missing some of their parts – either fragments themselves, or made up of fragments. In the late twentieth century, there are many works whose fragmentation is intentional, and these are our subject here. Novelists have acknowledged, in a way that would have horrified Henry James, that literature is – *must be* – fragmentary and have made a feature of it. Universally, the more contemporary novelist seems to say that relations stop nowhere; so why should the novelist go to so much trouble to practice an exquisite geometry designed to disguise this fact? Why not acknowledge the finitude and necessary incompleteness of fiction? In fact – some go on to say – why not flaunt it, celebrate it, have some fun with it? Though the foregrounding of such fragmentation is a literary device most often found in the modernist and postmodernist novel, it is worth remembering that it has a long pedigree. Henry Mackenzie's *The Man of Feeling* (1771) is made up of loosely connected (non-linear) parts and the "editor" explains the condition of the text by blaming a curate who possessed the manuscript but regularly tore pieces of it off to use for wadding in his rifle: "The Reader will remember," the editor explains, "that the Editor is accountable only for scattered chapters, and fragments of chapters; the curate must answer for the rest" (7). Mackenzie, like his master Sterne, reminds us that post-modernism, at least in its foregrounding of fragmentation and self-reference, is also pre-modernism.

Intentionally fragmented fictions

Before offering a tentative and partial taxonomy of fragmentary fictions, I would like to draw attention to specific cases of fragmentation in novels that are *sui generis* and therefore could not fit into my taxonomy. These books are fragmentary in part because they present themselves, so strenuously, as something so different from a novel. For instance, Nabokov's *Pale Fire* (1962) comprises a 999-line poem, with its introduction and commentary provided in an apparatus of footnotes. Milorad Pavić's *Dictionary of the Khazars* (1984) is aptly identified in its subtitle as a lexicon novel. Georges Perec's *Life: A User's Manual* (1978) is based on the structure of a Parisian apartment house, with fragments devoted to each of the flats and its inhabitants, with some other constraints – some of them derived from jigsaw puzzles – that remind us that a fertile source of fragmentary literature is the OULIPO group of which Perec was a founding member. Finally, a recent novel, Paul Ewen's *London Pub Reviews* (2007), appears in the form of forty-four quirky two- to three-page reviews of real London pubs.

Among less unique examples of the fragmentary, one which is by now so familiar that it probably does not register with most readers as being fragmented, is the fiction operating under many of the conventions of film. Such works are not presented in the form of a film script, but with the kind of loose connectivity, lack of explicit transitions, unsignposted slippages in time sequence, and quick "cuts" that are so recognizably a part of the cinematic technique. The rise of cinema in the early twentieth century affected fiction; an early exemplar is Evelyn Waugh's *Vile Bodies* (1930), influenced both by the cinema and by T. S. Eliot's *The Waste Land* (1922), and characterized by fragmentary dialog (presentation mostly in the form of dialog is also a feature of film) and rapid scene changes. Over the past thirty years or so, the convention of using present tense narration, often but not exclusively in a filmic fiction, loosens the chronological linearity that in traditional novels militates against fragmentation. The use of present, past and past perfect tenses, signaling different degrees of pastness, gives an apparent coherence to the narrative, which is impossible to achieve with the exclusive use of the present tense.

Finally, there are what might be called the *militantly* fragmentary novels. B. S. Johnson's *The Unfortunates* (1969) consists of 27 chapters, or sections, unbound and delivered in a box. Though the beginning and ending are identified as such, the 25 sections in between are designed to be read in any order. Johnson was insistent that novels must be real, not given to "lying," and his scheme for *The Unfortunates* was chosen to undo the false coherence of the traditional novel. Although he was not entirely satisfied with his approach, he argued that "it was still a better solution to the problem of conveying the mind's randomness than the imposed order of a bound book" (qtd. in Coe, "Death"). J. G. Ballard may also have attempted to convey "the mind's randomness" in *The Atrocity Exhibition* which consists of "chapters," each of which is made up of disconnected paragraphs. In the revised edition the text is further broken up by marginal comments added by Ballard, and in one of them, he explains that the many lists in this novel were produced by free association (9). Free association is thus the explanation given by Ballard for the structural principle in *The Atrocity Exhibition*, and, though it may be an instance of the "mind's randomness" that Johnson hoped to capture, free association is still a principle of connection, one grounded in a mentalistic theory.

For almost pure randomness and fragmentation, we might consider the "cut-up technique" of William S. Burroughs in the 1950s and 1960s (one of Ballard's inspirations). This aleatory combination was not entirely original, since the Dadaists did something similar with poetry in the 1920s and 1930s. In employing it, Burroughs used shears to cut up passages of prose by himself or by others and then pasted them together randomly. He elaborated a theory underlying his practice; according to him, just as the body could be controlled by drugs and sex, so the mind was controlled by conventional uses of language. The cut-up technique, then, was an act of liberation. Burroughs's cut-ups seem to be much more frequently discussed than read; and I can report that when I heard him speak, in the late 1970s, he admitted that he sometimes overrode the randomness of the cut-up, changing the results in order to arrive at something more interesting, or to intervene when the cut-up technique had accidentally resulted in something that looked too intentional.

Both Ballard and Burroughs are among those mentioned by Ted Gioia, in an essay called "The Rise of the Fragmented Novel" (2013). Gioia refers to these artists as "relying on fragmentation as a means of disjunction and dissolution," and contrasts them with more recent works, declaring that "the new fragmented novel is holistic and coalescent. It resists disunity, even as it appears to embody it." That provocative distinction could also apply to the three categories of fragmentation fiction which I propose as representative of some fragmentary practices in contemporary British and American literature: the braid, the bricolage and the mosaic. For each category, I will propose a definition and refer to earlier examples in literature, before focusing on a shortlisted book in the 2016 Man Booker Prize competition to examine how its fragmentary modes and processes are related to the identified category.

The braid

In the variety of fiction I refer to here, the fragments can be called the braid, as they function like discrete narrative projects which are presented interwoven rather than in strict sequence. These may be, among other possibilities, different plot developments with different characters; or plot developments which illustrate the same characters in action in different times; or a story and the story of how it was discovered.

One of the most brilliant instances of the braided fragmentary novel is Flann O'Brien's *At Swim-Two-Birds* (1939). In its first paragraph, the narrator announces "One beginning and one ending for a book was a thing I did not agree with" (9). There follow three opening paragraphs, one of which has to do with "the Pooka McPhellimey, a member of the devil class"; the second is an introduction to Mr. John Furriskey, whose one distinction was that "he was born at the age of twenty-five and entered the world with a memory but without a personal experience to account for it"; and the third launches the story of Finn Mac Cool, "a legendary hero of old Ireland" (9–10). For the remainder of the novel, until its three closing paragraphs, these three narrative strands will be braided and combined with a fourth, the story of the narrator, a shabby university student involved in spare-time literary activities, who is the source of the other three.

Similar braided novels include Mikhail Bulgakov's *The Master and Margarita* (written between 1928 and 1940 but censored and only first published in Paris in 1967), which interweaves a story set in Moscow in the 1930s with one set in first-century Jerusalem, focused on Pontius Pilate. Another example is Doris Lessing's *The Golden Notebook* (1962) in which writer Anna Wulf keeps four notebooks, color-coded to different aspects of her life (the red notebook, for instance, reports on her Communist experiences) and tries to synthesize all these in a golden notebook. The story of her life, her writing, her family and friends in the "present day" of the novel constitutes yet another strand, called "Free Women." Jonathan Coe's *The House of Sleep* (1997) produces a different kind of braid. The Author's Note explains: "The odd-numbered chapters of this novel are set mainly in the years 1983–84. The even-numbered chapters are set in the last two weeks of June 1996" (Coe, *House*). The alternating chapters are fragmentary, too:

on a grammatical level, many of them end in mid-sentence, with the next chapter picking up the sentence fragment and completing it, but with an entirely different application.

Among the shortlisted books in the 2016 Man Booker Prize competition, the critical and betting favorite was Madeleine Thien's *Do Not Say We Have Nothing* (2016), which is a carefully constructed braid. The novel is narrated by Marie Jiang, a young Asian woman, living in British Columbia in the recent past. The appearance in her life of another Chinese girl, a refugee named Ai-ming, launches the plot. Marie investigates and finds out about her father's life in the People's Republic, why he left Canada and the role of music in his life. Eventually, there are three main strands of plot. One is the ongoing life of Marie Jiang in Canada, as she attends university, majoring in mathematics. The other two are narratives of Chinese events at two moments of world-historical crisis: the first, the Cultural Revolution under Mao Zedong in the 1960s, the second, the student revolt leading to the events in Tiananmen Square in 1989. These three strands are artfully interwoven, though unevenly so: it is hardly surprising that the life and experiences of a Canadian university student are less gripping than life-and-death events in China.

The novel makes much of music, particularly classical music and the performances of Canadian pianist Glenn Gould, part of the reason for which is that Marie's father was a classical performer in China. Early in the book Marie is struck by the sound of Gould in a recording – a recording, we later learn, that the musicians in China have also treasured – when she hears it coming from a record store, and she thinks, "The counterpoint, holding together composer, musicians and even silence, the music, with its spiraling waves of grief and rapture, was everything I remembered" (4). Perhaps counterpoint is as good a metaphor as braid for the kind of interrelationship of multiple narrative strands Thien is undertaking. As reviewer Stephanie Boland wrote, "the counterpoint of Johann Sebastian Bach" invited comparison to Thien's "finely-balanced composition" through "the intricacy of its storytelling." The invocation of counterpoint should remind us of Aldous Huxley's *Point Counter Point* – also something of a braid – published in 1928, in which a novelist discusses "the musicalization of fiction":

> Not in the symbolist way, by subordinating sense to sound.... But on a large scale, in the construction. Meditate on Beethoven. The changes of moods, the abrupt transitions.... Get this into a novel. How? The abrupt transitions are easy enough. All you need is a sufficiency of characters and parallel, contrapuntal plots. (293–94)

Counterpoint, which in its original sense interweaves disparate strands of music, rather than of narrative, is another useful metaphor for this particular variety of fragmentary fiction.

The bricolage

The second category in my taxonomy of fragmentation fiction is the bricolage, which applies to novels made up of fragments of very disparate materials. An early bricolage novel is John Dos Passos's *USA* (1938), a very long three-volume work which includes multiple narrative modes, newspaper clippings and song lyrics, as well as biographies of both fictional and historical characters. Dos Passos's fragmentation is influenced by modern technology as some sections of the novel are called "Newsreel," and others, "Camera Eye."

In the second half of the twentieth century, the classic example of the bricolage novel is Julian Barnes's *Flaubert's Parrot* (1984). Though it has two main narrative projects – one of them an exploration of the life of Gustave Flaubert, the other an account of the Flaubert-admiring retired physician Dr. Geoffrey Braithwaite – they are divided out into fifteen chapters. Among these are some that follow relatively normal narrative procedures, but there is also a chronology, which is actually two chronologies, differing in the positive or negative light they shed on Flaubert's life, followed by a third one made of quotations by Flaubert himself; an examination paper; a chapter about all the animals that are to be found in Flaubert's writing; "The Train-spotter's Guide to Flaubert"; "The Flaubert Apocrypha" – books mentioned but not written; a chapter on coincidences, called "Snap!"; and "Braithwaite's Dictionary of Accepted Ideas."

Barnes's reviewers called *Flaubert's Parrot* a collage; "a tour de force of fiction, criticism, and biography"; a "compendium of genres"; a Menippean satire; an "intellectual whodunit" and "a thing" (qtd. in Guignery 38). Joyce Carol Oates called it "a gathering of prose pieces, some fiction, others rather like essays" (13), while in France it won an award given to a book of essays (Guignery 38–39). Despite all these suggestions that it is something other than a novel, Barnes insisted that a novel is "an extended piece of prose, largely fictional, which is planned and executed as a whole piece" (Sexton 42) – a definition which *Flaubert's Parrot* clearly meets.

Among more recent examples is Lee Siegel's *Love in a Dead Language* (1999), which includes a translated Indian sex manual, movie posters, undergraduate essays, a board game and a CD-ROM, a passage of opera with sheet music, passages printed upside down, newspaper articles, a scientific study of snails' sexual slime, and much more. Nicola Barker's *The Cauliflower* (2016), in turn, intersperses its story of a nineteenth-century

Bengali holy man with random haikus, a quiz about the goddess Kali, an inquiry into the nature of farina pudding, fables, dreams, and a bizarre imagined tour of a Kolkata temple by means of a miniaturized camera attached to a swift. The narrative pauses for "ten slightly irrelevant answers to nine slightly irrelevant questions you didn't even know you'd asked" (231). It is, as one reviewer wrote, "a book of shards and fragments, with the narrative intercut by haikus, questionnaires, playlets and found documents" (Kelly). Its author calls it "a painstakingly constructed, slightly mischievous, and occasionally provocative/chaotic mosaic" (Barker, *Cauliflower* 287).

Robert Grudin is a more obscure novelist – undeservedly obscure, I think – whose novel *Book* (1992) is a fascinating and multifarious collection of documents in what is, overall, a satire on modern developments in the late-twentieth-century university mashed up with a crime thriller. It is built up, alongside stretches of quite conventional narration, from passages from the 11th edition of the *Encyclopedia Britannica*, letters from and to the characters, pages from their journals, newspaper accounts, transcripts of medical investigations, transgressive and revolutionary footnotes, a glossary of modern literary theory terms, minutes of a faculty meeting in the form of a script, "nine bagatelles," computer error messages, and questions posed by readers to the writer: these constitute, Grudin explains, "extratextuality," or "things readers won't ever know unless they ask the author personally" (170). Grudin is clearly embarked on a mission to discover how miscellaneous the contents of his novel can be without becoming something else. According to my understanding, it is a bricolage novel.

His Bloody Project (2016), Graeme Macrae Burnet's Booker-shortlisted novel, tells the story of a series of injustices leading to a horrific murder in the nineteenth-century Scottish Highlands. It is also a bricolage, though without quite so extravagant a range of materials. Subtitled "Documents Relating to the Case of Roderick Macrae," it begins with a preface by Burnet, carefully footnoted, which pretends to vouch for the authenticity of the documents that follow and declines any role except in punctuating and paragraphing. The contents consist of statements from villagers; a map of the area where the events took place; the (first-person) account of Roderick Macrae, the murderer; a glossary; medical reports; an extract from a brutally insensitive psychiatric report by an unsympathetic, benighted Englishman who helped to doom Roderick Macrae; an account of the trial attributed to contemporary newspaper coverage and an 1869 book; and an epilogue.

The comparison of Burnet's bricolage to Grudin's is instructive. Though clearly without any real intent to deceive practiced readers, Burnet's materials are all of the sort that buttresses verisimilitude. They are the class of materials that might appear in a non-fiction book – contemporary journalism, maps, interviews with witnesses; his own preface, in fact, is quite similar to that of Daniel Defoe in *Moll Flanders* (1722), who also declared the ensuing work authentic non-fiction and said he had only cleaned it up a bit, as editor. Grudin, by contrast (and like Lee Siegel), works to explode the pretense of verisimilitude or naturalism, to flaunt the fictionality of his fiction. While Burnet's epilog gives the aftermath of the trial, in sober prose, Grudin's postscript is by Adam Snell, *Book*'s protagonist, and relates the disappearance of Robert Grudin, *Book*'s author, in an involution reminiscent of O'Brien's *At Swim-Two-Birds*. Despite these differences, both books have the same subtitle printed on the cover: "a novel."

The mosaic

For the third category, I use the term "mosaic" to describe a novel composed of fragments each of which is a narrative effectively complete in itself. Clearly, the dividing line between the mosaic novel and the collection of short stories is a blurred one, and the right of such mosaic novels to be considered novels at all is sometimes challenged. An extreme case may be found in Julio Cortázar's *Hopscotch* (1963), made up of many fragmentary chapters which are not necessarily to be read in sequence or in their entirety. The author's instructions explain that there are two ways of reading what amounts to two books. First, "in a normal fashion," beginning at the beginning and reading through chapter 56 (about a third of the book), ignoring the rest (making the novel fragmentary in one way). Alternatively, "The second should be read by beginning with Chapter 73 and then following the sequence indicated at the end of each chapter. In case of confusion or forgetfulness, one need only consult the following list: 73 – 1 – 2 – 116 – 3 – 84 – 4 – 71 – 5 – 81 – 74 – 6 – 7 – 8 – 93 - 68 [etc.]" (Cortazar, unnumbered preface).

One of the most extreme examples of the mosaic is the practice of David Markson,[1] the tesserae of whose novels consist not of chapter-long fictions or even of fragments that are primarily narrative in intention or function, but of individual chunks consisting of a sentence or two. Here is a typical passage from *Vanishing Point* (2004):

> In his comick scenes he is seldom very successful. Said Johnson of Shakespeare.
> Spurinna.
> Charlotte Brontë was four feet nine inches tall.

---

[1] See Wojciech Drąg's essay in this volume.

Sara Bernhardt was illegitimate.
Marseilles, Rimbaud died in.
Wondering if youngsters still in fact read Marco Polo. (35–36)

What then *does* justify calling Markson's *Vanishing Point* or *The Last Novel* (2007), or Barnes's *History of the World in 10 ½ Chapters* (1989), a novel rather than an anthology of smaller, disparate parts? Jonathan Coe's review identified *A History of the World in 10 ½ Chapters* as "10 short stories," to which Barnes responded with the declarations that "it was conceived as a whole and executed as a whole" and that "things in it thicken and deepen" (qtd. in Cook 21). Presumably, in the mosaic novel there is some overriding order, whether of construction of leitmotiv or symbolic resonance or thematic continuity – as in Sebastian Faulks's *A Possible Life: A Novel in Five Love Stories* (2012). The widely separated stories in David Mitchell's *Cloud Atlas* (2004) are linked through their Russian-doll structure as well as through verbal echoes and a common theme of human exploitation of the weak. Barnes's *History* chapters, in turn, connect through such themes as salvation and such properties as ark-like vessels, and even apparently throwaway elements such as woodworms and reindeer.

David Szalay's *All That Man Is*, featured on the 2016 Booker shortlist, is also a mosaic novel and, as such, is vulnerable to the charge that it is not a novel at all. In the *Irish Times* Eileen Battersby dismissed it as "really a collection of ponderous stories, amounting to nine glimpses of the male experience" (8), and the reviewer in *The Guardian* said "it's more a short story collection rather than a novel (despite being marketed as the latter)" (Skidelsky). The Man Booker jury obviously felt otherwise as that prize is reserved for the year's best original novel in English. *All That Man Is* consists of nine sections, or chapters, or portions, or fragments if you will, each of them depicting a short segment in the life of a European man. Several depict moments of crisis. That the man in the last section is the grandfather of one of the young men in the first section is the only connection between characters, plots, or settings (it is a very cosmopolitan book, with events set all over Europe).

When challenged by an interviewer about his claim that the book is a novel, Szalay responded, "The novel consists of nine segments. The basic structure is that the central character in each segment is five to ten years older than the central character in the previous one" ("Writing"). So, though none of these are the same characters, one may argue that these fragments make a whole because they proceed chronologically through the ages of man – nine rather than seven in this case. Szalay seems to have written this book (his fourth novel) in this style because he had become dissatisfied, or as he says, "disaffected with the form." "What's a novel?," he asks, "You make up a story and then you tell that story. I didn't understand why or how that could be meaningful" ("Writing"). The juxtaposition of apparently unrelated narratives appealed to him as an alternative; as he explains, "It occurred to me that a kind of meaning could be achieved by the relation of one story to another – by the structure in which they're set, by echoes between them, by a dialog they have among themselves" ("Writing").

This is the kind of relationship that helps to justify the term "mosaic" rather than "anthology" or "collection" or just "some short stories in one volume" for this kind of work. The individual pieces of a mosaic create no picture; in Szalay's terms, they have no meaning by themselves; they derive meaning by their relation to one another, as Szalay claims happens with his segments. One may wonder what this overall meaning to which the fragmentary sections contribute is. The title of the book is the clearest guide. These men, in their frustrations, inadequacies, compromises, their thralldom to their desires, illustrate all that man is. This is manhood and the crisis of masculinity about which we have heard so much in recent years. The title is also a line from W. B. Yeats's "Byzantium" and invites us to ponder the lines that follow: "All that man is, / All mere complexities, / The fury and the mire of human veins." "Byzantium" is one of Yeats's poems that express impatience with the condition of being a man, with fury and mire, with complexities, and (in "Sailing to Byzantium") particularly with the paltriness of being an old man, which is also the topic of Szalay's novel.

Szalay's disaffection with the novel form aligns him with other authors of fragmentary novels such as William S. Burroughs, B. S. Johnson and J. G. Ballard. Most of them have become impatient with what they see as the falsity of fiction – that exquisite geometry which James praised but which modernist and postmodernist authors disdain. Johnson rather helplessly objected to novels because they *were* fiction – in his explanation, they were lying. But novelists like Burroughs and Ballard, like Donald Barthelme and Gilbert Sorrentino, object to the falsification involved in pretending that wholeness is possible. Szalay's practice puts him in this group.

Conclusion

To conclude my modest attempt to identify three important kinds of fragmented fiction (the braid, the bricolage, the mosaic), I need to insist that there are far more members of these groups than I have named; moreover, an overlap among them is possible. An example of such a hybrid is Jonathan Coe's *What a Carve Up!* (1994), which contains a braided combination of two major stories – that of the horrible Winshaw family and that of their biographer, Michael Owen, two stories that become increasingly intertwined, or braided – while also, in the miscellaneous nature of its contents, partaking of the bricolage.

I return to the notion that essentially all fictions are fragmentary in some real sense, the differences among them arising from the *degree* of fragmentation (so that a book by Johnson or Markson presents a spectacle of profound fragmentation when compared to a more traditional kind of novel); and the *flagrancy* of that fragmentation. Modernist and postmodernist practitioners decline to attempt the Jamesian geometry required to achieve the pretense that a fiction is a smooth, unified, continuous, linear, and complete whole. Consistent with recent practices which bare the device, many of them flaunt and celebrate their work's fragmentation.

Besides, it is not just modernist and postmodernist authors that present us with fragmentation. In *The Modes of Modern Writing: Metaphor, Metonymy, and the Typology of Modern Literature*, David Lodge identifies, as one of the keynotes of postmodernist fiction, "discontinuity," his discussion of which shows it to be what I have been calling fragmentation (231–33). His examples come from Beckett and Borges, Barthelme and Richard Brautigan. But what is more discontinuous than a collection of occasional letters? Or spasmodic entries in a journal? We can expect that a novel like Nicola Barker's *Burley Cross Postbox Theft* (2010), consisting of apparently random letters stolen from a postbox and stuffed into a bin bag, will be radically discontinuous and fragmentary; but even Samuel Richardson's *Pamela* (1740) consists of irregularly written and dispatched letters, some of them delayed and presented out of order and others stolen, along with journal entries, and thus is a pre-modernist work of discontinuity. In one of Ezra Pound's later *Cantos*, themselves highly fragmented poetic works, the speaker laments, "I cannot make it cohere!" David Szalay, Madeleine Thien and Graeme Macrae Burnet, in their 2016 Booker Prize shortlisted books, solved the problems of coherence, in their different ways, successfully. If my understanding of the term is correct, fragmentation is the bedrock condition of fiction; it is its *donnée,* and the differences between one text and another consist in how the novelist recognizes that condition, what he or she chooses to do about it and how elegantly the chosen solution works: matters which are particularly highlighted in self-consciously fragmentary fiction, and decisions on which constitute the art of the fragmentary.

Works Cited

Ballard, J. G. *The Atrocity Exhibition.* 1970. New Revised Edition. San Francisco: Research, 1990.

Barker, Nicola. *Burley Cross Postbox Theft.* 2010. London: Open Road Media, 2012.

---. *The Cauliflower.* New York: Henry Holt, 2016.

Barnes, Julian. *Flaubert's Parrot.* New York: Vintage, 1984.

---. *A History of the World in 10 ½ Chapters.* New York: Vintage, 1989.

Battersby, Eileen. "US Satire Undeservedly Wins Man Booker." *The Irish Times*, 26 Oct. 2016: 8.

Baum, Kelly, Andrea Bayer, and Sheena Wagstaff. *Unfinished: Thoughts Left Visible.* New York: Metropolitan Museum of Art, 2016.

Boland, Stephanie. "Why Do Not Say We Have Nothing Should Win the Man Booker." *New Statesman*, 17 Oct. 2016, https://www.newstatesman.com/culture/books/2016/10/why-do-not-say-we-have-nothing-should-win-man-booker. Accessed 24 Oct. 2016.

Bulgakov, Mikhail. *The Master and Margarita.* 1967. Trans. Richard Pevear and Larissa Volokhonsky. London: Penguin, 1997.

Burnet, Graeme Macrae. *His Bloody Project.* 2015. New York: Skyhorse, 2016.

Coe, Jonathan. "Death by Naturalism." *Prospect*, 20 Feb. 2003, https://www.prospectmagazine.co.uk/magazine/deathbynaturalism. Accessed 23 Mar. 2017.

---. *The House of Sleep.* New York: Vintage, 1997.

---. *Like a Fiery Elephant: The Story of B. S. Johnson.* 2004. New York: Continuum, 2006.

---. "A Reader-Friendly Kind of God." *The Guardian*, 23 June 1989, https://www.theguardian.com/books/1989/jun/23/fiction.history. Accessed 29 Mar. 2017.

---. *What a Carve Up!* London: Penguin, 1994.

Cook, Bruce. "The World's History and Then Some in 10 ½ Chapters." *Conversations with Julian Barnes.* Eds. Vanessa Guignery and Ryan Roberts. Jackson: UP of Mississippi, 2009. 20–22.

Cortázar, Julio. *Hopscotch.* 1963. Trans. Gregory Rabassa. New York: Pantheon, 1966.

Cunningham, Guy Patrick. "Fragmentary: Writing in a Digital Age." *The Millions*, 24 Jan. 2012, https://themillions.com/2012/01/fragmentary-writing-in-a-digital-age.html. Accessed 20 Dec. 2016.

Daniels, J. D. "Rules for Consciousness in Mammals." *The Paris Review*, 26 May 2017, https://www.theparisreview.org/blog/2017/05/26/rules-for-consciousness-in-mammals. Accessed 26 May 2017.

Dos Passos, John. *U.S.A.* New York: Harcourt, Brace, 1938.

Ewen, Paul. *London Pub Reviews.* London: Shoes With Rockets, 2007.

Faulks, Sebastian. *A Possible Life: A Novel in Five Love Stories.* New York: Picador, 2012.

Gioia, Ted. "The Rise of the Fragmented Novel: An Essay in 26 Fragments." *Fractious Fiction*, 17 July 2013, http://fractiousfiction.com/rise_of_the_fragmented_novel.html. Accessed 11 Jan. 2017.

Grudin, Robert. *Book: A Novel.* New York: Penguin, 1992.

Guignery, Vanessa. *The Fiction of Julian Barnes: A Reader's Guide to Essential Criticism.* Basingstoke: Palgrave Macmillan, 2006.

Huxley, Aldous. *Point Counter Point.* 1928. Normal: Dalkey Archive, 1996.

James, Henry. *Roderick Hudson.* 1875. New York: Scribner's, 1907.

Kee, Thuan Chye. "The Best of British." *New Straits Times,* 14 Aug. 1996: 11.

Kelly, Stuart. "*The Cauliflower* by Nicola Barker Review – Unclassifiable Genius." *The Guardian,* 13 Apr. 2016, https://www.theguardian.com/books/2016/apr/13/the-cauliflower-nicola-barker-review-novel. Accessed 3 Apr. 2017.

Johnson, B. S. *The Unfortunates.* London: Panther, 1969.

Lessing, Doris. *The Golden Notebook.* New York: Simon and Schuster, 1962.

Lodge, David. *The Modes of Modern Writing: Metaphor, Metonymy, and the Typology of Modern Literature.* London: Edward Arnold, 1977.

Mackenzie, Henry. *The Man of Feeling.* 1771. London: Oxford UP, 1967.

Markson, David. *Vanishing Point.* Washington: Shoemaker and Hoard, 2004.

McCarthy, Tom. "Writing Machines." *London Review of Books* 36 (18 Dec. 2014): 21–22.

Melville, Herman. *Moby-Dick; or, The Whale.* New York: Harper & Brothers, 1851.

Nabokov, Vladimir. *Pale Fire.* New York: Putnam's, 1962.

Nance, Kevin. "'Moonglow' Reflects Chabon in Rich Layers of Light." *USA Today,* 8 Dec. 2016: D5.

Oates, Joyce Carol. "But Noah Was Not a Nice Man." *New York Times Book Review,* 1 Oct. 1989: 13.

O'Brien, Flann. *At Swim-Two-Birds.* 1939. New York: Penguin, 1976.

Pavić, Milorad. *Dictionary of the Khazars: A Lexicon Novel in 100,000 Words.* 1984. Trans. Christina Pribicevic-Zoric. New York: Vintage, 1989.

Perec, Georges. *Life: A User's Manual.* 1978. Trans. David Bellos. New York: David R. Godine, 1987.

Rimell, Victoria. *Petronius and the Anatomy of Fiction.* Cambridge: Cambridge UP, 2004.

Sexton, David. "Still Parroting on About God." *Sunday Telegraph,* 11 June 1989: 42.

Siegel, Lee. *Love in a Dead Language.* Chicago: U of Chicago P, 1999.

Skidelsky, William. "*All That Man Is* by David Szalay Review – Tales of Love and Money." *The Guardian,* 3 Apr. 2016, https://www.theguardian.com/books/2016/apr/03/all-that-man-is-review-david-szalay-short-story-collection. Accessed 29 Mar. 2017.

Szalay, David. *All That Man Is.* Minneapolis: Graywolf, 2016.

-----. "Writing *All That Man Is*: An Exchange." *Paris Review* 217 (2016), https://www.theparisreview.org/miscellaneous/6478/writing-iall-that-man-is-i-an-exchange-david-szalay. Accessed 29 March 2017.

Thien, Madeleine. *Do Not Say We Have Nothing.* New York: Norton, 2016.

Waugh, Evelyn. *Vile Bodies.* London: Chapman and Hall, 1930.

Chapter 2

Fragmentary writing and polyphonic narratives in twenty-first-century fiction

Mariano D'Ambrosio,
University Paris 3 – Sorbonne Nouvelle

Readers of contemporary fiction are frequently exposed to novels which employ a fragmented form. Besides the use of hybrid material and non-linear plot, one of the strategies adopted to achieve fragmentation in a novel is the employment of a variety of voices. The choice of polyphony, in such works, is the principal agent of the collapse of the traditional single authoritative voice of the narrator, still predominant in realist fiction. The fragmentation of the text, thus, corresponds to the fragmentation of the self, as well as the fragmentation of reality, whose manifold, complex, plural experience is considered impossible to render in a sequential, unitary text. The adoption of disparate standpoints and identities in relation to a chaotic and problematic reality may spring from the search for a more appropriate representation of life and the ways it is experienced. The result, despite these presumably mimetic intentions, is a dismissal of the sequential form typical of the tradition of the realist novel. Thanks to polyphony, the form of the novel undergoes a radical rethinking: the disparateness of the textual material, instead of being concealed within a coherent narrative, is explicitly made visible. The coexistence of different textual installments depending on various narrative voices is often highlighted through an array of formal and typographical devices, exploring the many possibilities offered by the space of the page and the book.

Polyphonic novels are, thus, materially fragmented, as a natural consequence of the dispersion of the disparate voices assembled within the text. Sometimes the textual sections depending on several voices may be physically distanced (for example, through endnotes), while some other times they may coexist in the same space (within the main text itself or, for example, through marginal notes or footnotes). These alternative modalities of textual arrangement reshape the reading experience: such polyphonic fragmented novels require each reader to be proactive in choosing a unique order of reading, to assemble the disparate parts and try to realize a unity which is never stable. Multiplicity is, therefore, the critical aspect of these novels: a multiplicity of voices, a multiplicity of textual fragments juxtaposed within the novel, a multiplicity of forms and of possible readings. /

While the use of fragmentation and multiplicity represents a stable trend in the contemporary novel, fragmentary writing and polyphonic narratives cannot be considered solely as prerogatives of twenty-first-century fiction. It may be said, in fact, that the exploration of non-linear forms has constituted a parallel tradition in the history of the novel. This tradition, which has been defined by some scholars as "nonaristotelian" (Orr 13) or "nonmimetic" (Richardson 38), seems to be cyclically rediscovered and appreciated whenever fragmentation and multiplicity return to fashion, often in opposition to the predominance of totalizing narratives and realist models. Postmodernist author Ronald Sukenick proposed to refer to this trend in fiction as a "new tradition," pointing out that it "coexisted with the old tradition from the beginning, not as the exception but as an alternative rule," as exemplified by Laurence Sterne's *Tristram Shandy* (1759–67) (37). The relation between the exploration of fragmentation and polyphony in contemporary novels and their antecedents may therefore be considered in terms of both continuity and renewal. Continuity is often explicitly acknowledged by contemporary authors through direct references and homages to non-linear models from the past, but these writers are also intent on offering new modes of fragmentation.

Before examining several contemporary fragmentary and polyphonic novels, I shall sketch, in the first part of this essay, a theoretical frame as a starting point for later textual analysis. These preliminary observations will focus on three authors from different eras and different cultures who can help to address the questions raised by fragmentariness and polyphony in the twenty-first-century novel: Sterne, Mikhail Bakhtin and Italo Calvino. I will also introduce the notion of *liberature*, which will prove useful in analyses of typographical experimentation. In the second part, some recent examples of fragmentary polyphonic novels, spanning from 2000 to 2013, will be discussed. This survey of contemporary examples of fragmentary and polyphonic writing will aim at showing the formal continuity with the literary tradition of non-linearity and multiplicity, whose main classic model is *Tristram Shandy*, but will also point out the specific ways in which contemporary fiction works to engage with this lineage.

Sterne's *The Life and Opinions of Tristram Shandy, Gentleman* has been celebrated as a precursor of postmodernism and of experimental literature. The novel establishes a close connection between fragmentary writing, polyphony, the loss of centrality of the narrative of the self and the idea of a fragmented reality experienced through appositive mental processes. These features are often supposed to be typical of contemporary fiction, though *Tristram Shandy* can serve as proof that they have been explored since the origins of the novel as a genre. Sterne's novel is a perfect example of a plural approach to reality: while the book's title announces the biography of a character named Tristram Shandy, the reader soon becomes aware that little will be said about the life and opinions of the protagonist, while a great deal will be revealed about the lives and opinions of many other people. For the most part, in fact, the novel incorporates the voices of Tristram's relatives. Furthermore, by virtue of a bold and very skilful use of intertextuality and incorporated genres, Tristram composes his narrative borrowing (occasionally even appropriating) other people's oral and written voices. Moreover, he decides to arrange all this disparate material in a form that refuses coherence; the traditional sequential order of the narrative seems to have been splintered and shuffled, to the point that paragraphs appear almost randomly juxtaposed. The form taken by the novel supports the theory of appositional thinking championed by Tristram: his book is a "history-book … of what passes in a man's own mind" (Sterne 61).

It must be stressed that in *Tristram Shandy* both reality and the self are composite, and irreducible to a unit: that is why, to the seemingly simple question "who are you?" Tristram cannot but reply, "Don't puzzle me" (369). This awareness of multiplicity is also the result of fully taking into account heteroglossia within the novel. Heteroglossia, a notion developed by Mikhail Bakhtin in his 1935 essay "Discourse in the Novel," lies at the core of the definition of the novel as a genre:

> The novel can be defined as a diversity of social speech types (sometimes even diversity of languages) and a diversity of individual voices, artistically organized … this internal stratification present in every language at any given moment of its historical existence is the indispensable prerequisite for the novel as a genre. The novel orchestrates all its themes, the totality of the world of objects and ideas depicted and expressed in it, by means of the social diversity of the speech types and by the differing individual voices that flourish under such conditions. Authorial speech, the speeches of the narrators, inserted genres, the speech of characters are merely those fundamental compositional unities with whose help heteroglossia can enter the novel. (Bakhtin 262–63)

According to Bakhtin, heteroglossia is a "basic distinguishing feature of the stylistics of the novel" (263), as well as an intrinsic feature of any living language. However, only such novels that refuse to operate in an authoritative unitary language, and consciously incorporate and draw attention to heteroglossia, are able to fully realize the possibilities of the novelistic hybrid, defined by Bakhtin as "an artistically organized system for bringing different languages in contact with one another, a system having as its goal the illumination of one language by means of another, the carving-out of a living image of another language" (361).

The ideal type of novel addressed by Bakhtin, then, is defined by its embracing of multiplicity (of languages and voices). Thanks to its composition, such a novel can substitute the centrality of the self with a full acknowledgment of the plural nature of experience. Calvino, in his lecture in *Six Memos for the Next Millennium*, takes a very similar stance, praising the "manifold text which replaces the oneness of a thinking 'I' with a multiplicity of subjects, voices, and views of the world, on the model of what Mikhail Bakhtin has called 'dialogic' or 'polyphonic' or 'carnivalesque'" (Calvino 117). To the centripetal tendencies of the unitary form, Calvino opposes the centrifugal force of those novels which can display a plurality of interpretative methods, modes of thought and languages:

> the modern books that we love the most are the outcome of a confluence and a clash of a multiplicity of interpretative methods, modes of thought, and styles of expression. Even if the overall design has been minutely planned, what matters is not the enclosure of the work within a harmonious figure, but the centrifugal force produced by it – a plurality of languages, as a guarantee of a truth that is not merely partial. (116–17)

Sterne's example, as well as Bakhtin's and Calvino's observations, all seem to stress how the heteroglot manifold text is intended to be, in the first place, a tool to better grasp the disparateness of experience and the composite nature of the self. Individual identity, these authors suggest, is the result of a combination of experiences, languages, books read and other people's lives. Calvino lucidly explains this shift from the self to the plural when he claims that "each life is an encyclopedia, a library, an inventory of objects, a series of styles, and everything can be constantly shuffled and reordered in every way conceivable" (124). This multiplication of possibilities, characteristic of the manifold, polyphonic novel, is enhanced by the fragmentation of the text and the refusal of an organic, totalizing form. In order to supplement these observations about the heteroglot text, I will consider the typical features of fragmentary writing as they have been observed in contemporary literature, with the purpose of confronting them, later in my essay, both to twenty-first-century novels and to their former models.

Wojciech Drąg, in an article titled "Heteroglossia and Fragmentariness in *The Absent Therapist* by Will Eaves," outlines a description of the features of fragmentary writing, providing a list of its common ingredients, based on the analysis of contemporary fiction but, in my opinion, retroactively relevant for fragmentary writing in general. Among its traits, the author lists heteroglossia, the democratic arrangement of disparate parts, non-linearity, lack of chronological order, metatextuality, frequent use of cita-tions, repetitions and lists, and the lack of a cause-and-effect relationship between consecutive passages, which "forces the reader to focus maxi-mum attention on the scattered formal or thematic connections" (Drąg 61–62). This list proves fully applicable to a novel such as *Tristram Shandy*. Besides, two specific features highlighted by Drąg deserve closer examina-tion: the notion of a democratic arrangement of disparate parts and me-tatextuality.

The stress on composition is typical of the fragmentary and polyphonic novel. This kind of writing relies on the assumption that reality cannot be rendered by a sequential form, because it is disparate and plural; moreo-ver, a single authoritative voice is not considered adequate to represent the fragmentariness of the self. Therefore, the unity of the text is shattered and torn to pieces, as the fragments permit infinite possibilities of arrange-ment. Two main consequences ensue: the first is the adoption of metatex-tual writing, which continually reflects on the organization of the text itself. The best-known example of this textual self-consciousness is proba-bly the episode of *Tristram Shandy* in which the narrator draws on the page graphs supposed to correspond to his story-line, and opposes them to the straight line representative of traditional sequential storytelling. The second consequence is the possibility to fully exploit the space of the page to compose the many different voices and arrange the disparate narrative material in non-sequential layouts. The choice of fragmentariness, thus, as noted by Katarzyna Bazarnik, affects the material structure of the book, subverting the default space of the page in an exploration of unconven-tional spatial and typographical arrangements of the text (Bazarnik 47–48).

Polyphonic and fragmentary fiction, in this regard, is often akin to the literary genre called liberature, a notion introduced in 1999 by Polish au-thor Zenon Fajfer to describe a kind of literature "in which the text and the space of the book constitute an inseparable whole" (Fajfer 43), and further developed by Bazarnik, especially in her work *Liberature: A Book-bound Genre*. For the proponents of liberature, despite the fact that the term was deliberately coined to describe their works of fiction (the first one being

Fajfer and Bazarnik's 2009 triple-codex novel *Oka-leczenie*), "liberature is simply a distinct literary genre or type of literature, or, to put it still differently, it constitutes a separated kind of or trend in literature, a trend whose generic distinctness is established by an organic bond between a text and its material book form" (Fajfer 136). This means that liberature as a genre is applicable, *a posteriori*, to refer to "the (paradoxically) very rich tradition to which liberature belongs, which extends back to antiquity and which can boast such masterpieces as Laurence Sterne's *Tristram Shandy* and Stéphane Mallarmé's *A throw of dice*" (Fajfer 136). Besides, Fajfer has often paid homage to Sterne, whom he considers a "liberatic writer" (121), and to *Tristram Shandy*, referred to as "the muse of liberature" (115).

According to Bazarnik, *liberature* may also be defined as the kind of literature which is aware of its spatial nature and the semantic dimension of the material form: this is why the liberatic novel is often self-reflexive (Bazarnik 43) and displays features considered typical of metafiction. The close link between typographical experimentation and the metareferential dimension has also been observed by Grzegorz Maziarczyk, who considers it a "visible tendency in contemporary fiction," even though, significantly, he acknowledges *Tristram Shandy* as the first effort to extensively explore the material dimension of the novel through the use of devices disrupting the conventional page layout (Maziarczyk 169).

As the space of the page and the materiality of the book assume a new meaningful dimension, the fragmentary and polyphonic novel realizes what Joseph Frank defined as a "spatial form," namely the predominance of space over time in the composition of the text. The work that adopts a spatial form, instead of being conventionally based on narrative sequence, attempts to present its constitutive parts in juxtaposition, as in the plastic arts, and ideally requires to be apprehended spatially by the reader. Bazarnik has also pointed out how the liberatic book is often perceived as an architectural structure, and how productive the conceptual metaphor of the book as a building has been in the last decades (Bazarnik 65–70). Among the most notable examples are *The Unfortunates* (1969) by B. S. Johnson, *The Castle of Crossed Destinies* (1973) by Italo Calvino and *Life: A User's Manual* (1978) by Georges Perec. More recently, *House of Leaves* (2000) by Mark Z. Danielewski has embodied even more explicitly the conceptual metaphor of the book as a building.

Each fragmentary and polyphonic novel adopts different textual and compositional strategies to address a recurrent set of themes that includes the representation of a disparate and disjointed reality; the portrayal of a fragmented, often traumatized, self; the rethinking of the conventional biographical narrative; the questions raised by the increasing distrust in the possibilities of mimesis. Of the variety of contemporary novels that could be labeled as polyphonic, I have decided to focus on Danielewski's *House of Leaves*, *The People of Paper* (2006) by Salvador Plascencia, *The Body* (2002) by Jenny Boully, *S.* (2013) by Doug Dorst and J. J. Abrams, and *The Absent Therapist* (2014) by Will Eaves. These novels will serve to illustrate the main characteristics of twenty-first century fragmentary and polyphonic writing and its engagement with the earlier examples of this literary tradition. The thesis of the continuity of these novels with a tradition of non-linearity in fiction will be defended, highlighting, on occasion, the formal similarities with former models of fragmentariness and polyphony, as well as the explicit acknowledgments of the literary influence of predecessors such as Sterne. At the same time, though, it will also be stressed how each one of these novels has been able to find specific ways to renew fragmentary and polyphonic writing, exploring new formal strategies through which to address issues relevant to our contemporary world.

House of Leaves and *The People of Paper* are two typical examples of novels which are at the same time fragmented, polyphonic and liberatic. In both novels text is arranged in unconventional layouts, exploiting the spatial and typographical possibilities offered by the page. *House of Leaves* is probably one of the most radical examples of creative typography, with its use of embedded texts and extensive footnotes, columns and windows of text, marred words and paragraphs, an unusual arrangement of words and single letters on the page, different colors and many other ingenious typographical tricks. *The People of Paper*, by contrast, displays a less copious array of typographical inventions, which includes side-by-side columns taking into account many different narrators, marred words, incorporated images, black pages and black squares superimposed on the text, blank pages, words singled out and left alone in the middle of a page, and even the repetition of the title-page within the novel, suggesting it starts over after 140 pages. Both novels are polyphonic, though in different ways.

In *House of Leaves* the reader can recognize at least three distinct voices: that of Zampanò, the author of the splintered manuscript entitled *House of Leaves*; that of Johnny Truant, who finds, reconstructs and annotates the manuscript with footnotes (which supplement other footnotes already provided by Zampanò); and that of Pelafina, Johnny's mother, whose letters appear in the appendix. However, while reading the book, the reader cannot but acknowledge that those three voices often cross the ontological narrative frames and blend in such a way that it is impossible to untangle them and compose distinct embedded but linear threads. The novel takes on a highly metafictional dimension, which obliges the reader to accept the impossibility of unraveling identities, voices and memories, as the narrative becomes paradoxical and uncanny. Even the name of the author, Danielewski, appears within the novel, but ciphered through an acrostic, hidden in a text supposed to be the invention of a fictional character, Zampanò. To stress this ontological ambiguity, the resort to cipher is formally and thematically prominent in one of the many subplots: Johnny is explicitly required by his mother to read her letters between the lines, in order to discover secret messages. Moreover, Pelafina's ciphered sentences contain the name of Zampanò, a mysterious reference that complicates, even more, the intricate web of ontological levels, whose hierarchy is impossible to establish. This multiplication of utterers is exacerbated by the overabundant intertextuality, both explicit and hidden (often even apocryphal, as in Jorge Luis Borges' fiction), and by the use of incorporated genres and literary pastiches. *House of Leaves* is therefore a novel that radically embodies heteroglossia, in such an extreme way that every utterance can be attributed, simultaneously, to a whole community of identities, voices, traumatized selves supposed to live in distinct layers of reality.

Danielewski seems to purposefully complicate, with his novel, a model of fragmentary polyphonic writing previously employed by Vladimir Nabokov in *Pale Fire* (1962) – the manuscript of a fictional author annotated by another fictional character. Invasive annotation, in both texts, encourages a fragmentary reading, which interrupts the linear flow of the main text. Fragmentariness is more radical in *House of Leaves* than in *Pale Fire*, not only because Johnny's footnotes – in contrast with Kinbote's endnotes in *Pale Fire* – physically break the continuum of Zampanò's text, but also because Zampanò's manuscript itself, as found by Johnny Truant, is described as fragmented and chaotic. It is, in fact, made of "endless snarls of words, sometimes twisting into meaning, sometimes into nothing at all, frequently breaking apart, always branching off into other pieces I'd come across later – on old napkins, the tattered edges of an envelope, once even on the back of a postage stamp," and it displays words "layered, crossed out, amended; handwritten, typed; legible, illegible; impenetrable, lucid; torn, stained, scotch taped" (Danielewski xviii). As he tries to edit this chaos and recompose the fragments into a meaningful whole, Johnny is confronted with the proliferation of polyphony and fragmentariness, expanding over every layer of reality, in a process which mirrors the very nature of Johnny's traumatized mind. While Danielewski has dismissed the "so-called originality" attributed to his book, claiming that "anyone with a real grasp of the history of narrative can see that *House of Leaves* is really just enjoying the fruits of a long line of earlier literary experimentation," including Mallarmé, Sterne and B. S. Johnson (qtd. in McCaffery and Gregory 106), yet his novel has undoubtedly represented a turning point for fragmentary and polyphonic fiction. Through its ever-expanding multiplicity of voices and incorporated genres, as well as its turmoil of inter-twining fragmented narratives, *House of Leaves* has brought the tradition of non-linear fiction into the twenty-first century and the World Wide Web era. In this respect, Danielewski's novel addresses such topical issues as remediation (as observed by N. Katherine Hayles), the impossibility to establish authenticity in the digital world, and the way the overload of information can affect memory and identity.

Similarly, in *The People of Paper*, the polyphony of the numerous charac-ters speaking directly through the columns of its pages takes an unex-pected metaleptic turn. The characters of the novel, all struggling with histories of sorrow, wounds, decay and sadness, go to war against the planet Saturn, which is constantly gazing on them in a sinister way. They will discover that the malevolent planet is the omniscient narrator himself, Salvador Plascencia, dramatized as yet another character within the novel. Saturn/Plascencia is responsible for their unhappiness because he has decided to unload on his fictional creatures all his sorrow, frustration and anger during the lacerating end of a love story. After a strenuous battle with the narrator, the main characters – whose strategies vary from cover-ing one's utterances under big black squares of ink to filling the pages with a multitude of voices – have only one choice left, which is to "walk south and off the page, leaving no footprints that Saturn could track" (Plascencia 245).

In both *House of Leaves* and *The People of Paper*, thus, the polyphonic, fragmentary, non-linear, multimodal and metafictional writing displays an obstinate resistance of the fragments to cohere into a whole, and a pro-found distrust of the possibility of reassembling a unitary meaning, narra-tive and identity. Wholeness, which has been lost as a result of trauma, is impossible to recover. The battle fought in the space of the page between Saturn and the community of characters represents, also graphically, an opposition between the linearity of the omniscient narrative, correspond-ing to a conventional layout of the page, and the fragmentariness intro-duced by polyphony. Columns of text appear in the book to give voice, on the same page, to as many as six characters at the same time. This typo-graphical device also emphasizes the opposition between a solipsistic narrative and a narrative which takes into account more effectively the existence of multiple experiences, voices and lives. The wounded pride of the author/narrator is contrasted with the power of the community to speak up collectively, despite its sometimes dramatic heterogeneity: the battle between the narrator and his characters is a fierce competition be-tween two distinct narrative models.

In its style, *The People of Paper* recalls the literary tradition of magical realism and, more broadly, a visible tendency to heteroglossia in Latin American fiction, stretching from *Pedro Páramo* (1955) by Mexican author Juan Rulfo to *The Savage Detectives* (1998) by the Chili-born Roberto Bolaño. Besides featuring polyphony, these novels also share the theme of crossing the border – an experience which, in *The People of Paper*, implicates both a spatial frontier, between Mexico and the United States, and an ontological one, the line which should separate the narrator from his fictional creatures, the eponymous "people of paper." Through this double border-crossing, Plascencia addresses the necessity, for the contemporary writer of fiction, to acknowledge a world in which cultures regularly interact, blend and modify each other, affecting individuals' lives and identities. Plascencia's novel demonstrates that fragmentary and polyphonic writing in the twenty-first century could take on a more distinct political and ethical dimension. The dynamics of power between a totalizing model of narrative and a more democratic reattribution of voices to many characters in search of recognition is explicitly depicted as a war. This battle seems to imply that world literature in the age of crossed borders, traumatized selves and communities struggling to have their voices heard, cannot but be fragmentary and polyphonic.

Another characteristic feature of *House of Leaves* and *The People of Paper* is their poetics of alternation of excess and absence, saturation and emptiness. This is a rather common trait in liberatic fiction, noticeable as early as in *Tristram Shandy*, a novel which plays extensively with the opposition between a narrative of missing information and an extreme version of exhaustive storytelling. As in *Tristram Shandy*, both *House of Leaves* and *The People of Paper* include all-white and all-black pages, as supplementary instruments of fragmenting narrative material, as well as graphical representations of the paradoxes of totalizing narration.

This alternation between absence and saturation is also vital in fragmentary polyphonic writing, as illustrated by two antithetical recent examples: *The Body* by Jenny Boully and *S.* by Doug Dorst and J. J. Abrams. These novels employ two different strategies to achieve the fragmentation of the text: the abolition of the text itself and the expansion of textual supports within the book. These approaches to fragmentariness, absence and saturation lead to an exploration of new possibilities of the compositional space of the page and to a rethinking of the book as an object – an endeavor that, especially in the case of *S.*, is sustained by the existence of new technical possibilities in volume design. Literary practices that go back to the Sternean and Scriblerian traditions are thus updated in the attempt to reflect the specificity of the contemporary world.

In Boully's highly unconventional novel, the body of the text is missing, and most pages are either entirely or almost entirely blank. The only exception are footnotes which, however, do not help to fill in the gaps or to reconstruct even the skeleton of a possible plot. They do provide at least some thematic clues for this enigmatic, cryptic book: through many intertextual references, they engage with the textual void to suggest a story dominated by a sense of incompleteness, trauma, separation, absence and loss. The loose fragments of text resist a unitary interpretation also because of their polyphony. The alternation of footnotes written in the first and third person precludes a clear understanding of who is speaking. Identity appears impossible to be fixed because even the name of the supposed main character is continually shifting. Besides, the footnotes are riddled with quotations from other works, especially poetic and philosophical, in a heteroglot blending of genres (the book's subtitle identifies it as *An Essay*). The materiality of the page, enhanced by its blankness interrupted only by few strings of text on the bottom of the page, takes an important dimension, whereas the compositional space of the volume contributes to creating a persistent sense of incompleteness and ineffability. As information is mainly concealed, discourse survives only in fragments coming from different voices, emerging like islands of meaning in a sea of void.

Despite many differences between *S.* and *The Body*, the two novels share some formal features, including the use of annotation and of devices characteristic of polyphony and fragmentary writing. *S.* is somewhat comparable to the model set by *House of Leaves*, as evidenced by their shared adoption of a poetics of excess, proliferating stories and voices. Like Danielewski's novel, *S.* requires from the reader a physical engagement with the book, as he or she must manipulate the many artifacts found between the pages: letters to unfold and read, postcards, a map drawn on a napkin, pictures and facsimiles of documents. It is also a *tour de force* of metafiction, as its external and internal paratexts mimic an old novel found in a library, while the marginalia scribbled by two readers are rendered in a typeface imitating handwriting. In a blending of genres, four layers of text are established: a novel titled *The Ship of Theseus*, written by the mysterious V.M. Straka; an introduction and copious footnotes provided by his translator, F.X. Caldeira; the handwritten text in the margins provided by two readers, Eric and Jen (young scholars who discuss extensively upon the real identity of Straka), and the artifacts they leave to each other between the pages of the book. Such a multilayered and fragmented structure forces the reader to read back and forth in order to re-establish the plot, a method of reading made necessary also by the fact that the inscriptions in the margins are not chronologically ordered. Besides, similarly to

House of Leaves, many ciphered messages are left within the text, some of which are solved by the two intradiegetic readers, while others are left unsolved or concealed. While being a boldly polyphonic, ergodic, multimodal and liberatic novel, *S.* does not seem to embrace non-linearity as radically as other fragmentary works, because most of the fragmented plot can be patiently reconstituted by the reader, and the possibilities of representation are not renounced altogether. Nevertheless, the thematic alternation of presence and absence, of proliferation and lack of information, constitutes the framework for the emergence of the theme of collective identity, signaled by the reference to the famous paradox of the ship of Theseus, and also embodied within the subplots. In this respect, the choice of polyphony and fragmentariness stems from an interrogation of the relations between identity and multiplicity.

The last novel I will take into account, Will Eaves's *The Absent Therapist*, seems less radical, especially with regard to multimodality (which is here missing), but it still constitutes an extraordinary example of fragmentary and polyphonic writing. The themes of multiplicity and polyphony are stressed as early as in the book's epigraph – a quotation from the First Epistle to the Corinthians: "There are, it may be, so many kinds of voices in the world, and none of them is without significance." Saint Paul's words placed at the beginning of the novel may suggest to the reader an effort to embrace this multitude of voices, all worthy of being transcribed. *The Absent Therapist*'s narrative endeavor may be inscribed, indeed, along these guidelines, through the use of unconventional form. Divided into five sections, the book comprises 150 miniature monologs which are deprived of any context and cannot be attributed to any specific speaker. The utterances are juxtaposed without any recognizable logic, while the thematic links are quite loose.

Among the few elements which grant the work a degree of unity and could justify its status as a novel are several metatextual commentaries coming from a possible narrator, a handful of cross-references, as well as some recurring motifs and names. What is entirely missing is a narrative frame. This appositive and discontinuous narrative, instead of conveying meaning, seems to aim at triggering a multitude of interpretations. Besides, it may be said that this kind of writing is an extreme example of the formalist idea of "lay[ing] bare the device" of the novel, a formula made famous by the observations of Victor Shklovsky regarding *Tristram Shandy* (Shklovsky 147). In a way, these textual fragments could either be the debris of a larger dismantled encyclopedic novel or the raw building material for a future novel that may or may not be written, similarly to bricks that need to be assembled. The conceptual metaphor of the book as a building appears towards the end of the book, perhaps offering a key for a possible interpretation:

> You have to look behind the contents of houses ... You must penetrate all of this drift and dreck to get to the soul of the building, to what it is thinking and saying, in many voices – the voices of everyone who has ever lived or died or stayed there, all of whom go on talking after they have moved on with a sort of calm but intangible insistence like the sound of a radio being reasonable in an empty room. (Eaves 108–09)

The Absent Therapist probably realizes the ultimate fantasy of the polyphonic fragmentary novel: the disappearing of the self, absorbed into a multitude of voices, dispersed in a vast non-hierarchical net of loose fragments, available for rearrangement: a collective, heteroglot biography. Fragmentary writing and polyphonic narrative combined, then, seem to aim at the acknowledgment of the plural nature of human experience, in order to apply it to the narrative of the self, which therefore definitely loses its presumed centrality.

To conclude, it can be said that the twenty-first-century fragmentary polyphonic novel challenges the conventional model of mimetic realist fiction, in which a protagonist and its unique self are central. It does so in order to draw attention to the variety of life, identity and reality. The stress on fragmentation, moreover, as well as the disruption of the sequential presentation of the narrative material, reflect the refusal of a totalizing narrative, in order to embrace heteroglossia and multiplicity. The brief survey attempted by this essay may suggest that this alternative model can take two different directions: it can be turned inward, towards the self, following the suggestion that every life narrative should encompass all the disparate voices and experiences constituting the composite biography of a single individual; or it can be turned outward, towards society, trying to compose a collective narrative where many lives incessantly interact, intertwine and blend, or even hinting at the possibility of a plural identity. The main preoccupation of this kind of novel is epistemological because fragmentary polyphonic writing mainly stems from a reflection on the nature of the self and the world. As a consequence, the novel adopting this viewpoint tries to overcome the classical mimetic model, which is considered inadequate, and suggest new models of representation of the relations between the self and the world. Nevertheless, it should also be stressed that this kind of writing often assumes an ethical dimension, because of its effort to embrace a multitude of lives, to give voice and dignity to a diversity of characters. Whether this empathic, democratic stance is a dominant trait of the fiction of our times is debatable. Its permanent vitality, though, is in my opinion praiseworthy and necessary, as a much-needed tool to grasp the complexity of the globalized, fractured, plural world we live in – with its mutations, tensions, its constant flux of people and its infinite web of interactions, experiences and voices.

Works Cited

Bakhtin, Mikhail. "Discourse in the Novel." 1934–35. *The Dialogic Imagination: Four Essays*. Trans. Caryl Emerson and Michael Holquist. Austin: U of Texas P, 1981. 259–422.

Bazarnik, Katarzyna. *Liberature: A Book-bound Genre*. Kraków: Jagiellonian UP, 2016.

Boully, Jenny. *The Body: An Essay*. Athens: Essay, 2007.

Calvino, Italo. *Six Memos for the Next Millennium*. Trans. Patrick Creagh. Cambridge: Harvard UP, 1988.

Danielewski, Mark Z. *House of Leaves*. New York: Pantheon, 2000.

Dorst, Doug, and J. J. Abrams. *S*. Edinburgh: Canongate, 2013.

Drąg, Wojciech. "Heteroglossia and Fragmentariness in *The Absent Therapist* by Will Eaves." *Studia Anglica Posnaniensia* 51.4 (2016): 53–65.

Eaves, Will. *The Absent Therapist*. London: CB Editions, 2014.

Fajfer, Zenon. *Liberature, or Total Literature: Collected Essays 1999–2009*. Kraków: Korporacja Ha!art, 2010.

Frank, Joseph. "Spatial Form in Modern Literature: An Essay in Three Parts." *The Sewanee Review* 53.2–4 (1945): 221–40, 433–56, 643–53.

Hayles, N. Katherine. "Saving the Subject: Remediation in *House of Leaves*." *American Literature* 74.4 (2002): 779–807.

Maziarczyk, Grzegorz. "Print Strikes Back: Typographic Experimentation in Contemporary Fiction as a Contribution to the Metareferential Turn." *The Metareferential Turn in Contemporary Arts and Media: Forms, Functions, Attempts at Explanation*. Ed. Werner Wolf. Amsterdam: Rodopi, 2011. 169–93.

McCaffery, Larry, and Sinda Gregory. "Haunted House. An Interview with Mark Z. Danielewski." *Critique* 44.2 (2003): 99–135.

Orr, Leonard. *Problems and Poetics of the Nonaristotelian Novel*. Lewisburg: Bucknell UP, 1991.

Plascencia, Salvador. *The People of Paper*. London: Bloomsbury, 2005.

Richardson, Brian. "Narrative Poetics and Postmodern Transgression: Theorizing the Collapse of Time, Voice and the Frame." *Narrative* 8.1 (2000): 23–42.

Shklovsky, Victor. *Theory of Prose*. 1925. Trans. Benjamin Sher. Elmwood Park: Dalkey Archive, 1991.

Sterne, Laurence. *The Life and Opinions of Tristram Shandy, Gentleman*. 1759–67. New York: Norton, 1980.

Sukenick, Ronald. "The New Tradition in Fiction." *Surfiction: Fiction Now and Tomorrow*. Ed. Raymond Federman. Chicago: Swallow, 1975. 35–45.

Chapter 3

The short story: fragment and augment

David Malcolm,
SWPS University of Social Sciences and Humanities in Warsaw

1.

The defining feature of the short story is shortness (Liggins, Maunder and Robbins 1). If this is so, brevity inevitably carries with it associations of fragmentariness. Indeed, the notion of fragmentariness has accompanied the discussion of the short story for much of the past century. For example, Viorica Patea writes of the "brief, fragmentary, inclusive form" of "the modernist short story," and sees this brief fragmentariness as an expression of "the limits of human knowledge in a world that holds no absolutes" (19). Although she refers here to modernist short fiction, Patea clearly sees abridgment and omission as constitutive of all short stories (13–15). Contraction and compression have been a focus in classic discussions of the form. Frank O'Connor famously notes that "the short story remains by its very nature remote from the community – romantic, individualistic, and intransigent" (21). H. E. Bates argues that the short-story writer must "master the art of implication" (177). Separation from a whole – fragmentariness, albeit a suggestive fragmentariness – is central to their observations. Ivan Reid, too, considers this quality integral to short fiction. For example, with regard to attitudes within the nineteenth-century French literary world, he writes, "Mostly it could be left to the novel to delineate those large-scale social patterns which were so amply extended within urban life; the short story seemed especially suitable for the portrayal of regional life or of individuals who, though situated in a city, lived there as aliens" (24). He extends this observation to Russian short fiction (24–25). He also sees the emergence of the short story in the United States as conditioned by the atomistic nature of North American society (29); a fragmented society favors a fragmentary fiction. Mary Louise Pratt uses terms like "fragment" and "a piece of a mosaic" when she sets out her first proposition as regards the short story's relationship with the novel (99–100). Suggestive incompletion is also key to Cynthia J. Hallett's consideration of "minimalism" in short fiction (487–95). Indeed, there are many such examples in the canon of literary analysis of the short story – for example, in the work of Clare Hanson and Valerie Shaw – and I have written at some length about their views elsewhere (Malcolm, *British and Irish Short Story* 37–39). V. S. Pritchett is in good company when he sees the short story as "the glancing form of fiction" (qtd. in Head 190).

Some commentators disparage fragmentariness; others laud it. G. K. Chesterton writes scathingly in 1906 that the contemporary interest in the short story indicates that "[w]e have no instinct of anything ultimate and enduring beyond the episode" (qtd. in Shaw 17). I have noted elsewhere how Arnold Bennett and Graham Greene are both abusive about the spatial and semantic restrictions of short fiction (Malcolm, *British and Irish Short Story* 37). Thomas Gullason notes Leon Edel's disdain for Hemingway's short stories because they are not long. "The short story," Edel writes, "by its very nature demands simplification... Hemingway is an artist of the small space, the limited view" (qtd. in Gullason 222).

But elision has its advocates too. Viorica Patea clearly thinks that "brief, fragmentary, inconclusive form" gets to the truth of things (19), an observation Hanson would concur with (26). Elizabeth Bowen is a forceful proponent of tenuity. In the introduction to *The Faber Book of Modern Stories* (1937), she admires the short story because it is not part of a whole. It is "an affair of reflexes, of immediate susceptibility, of associations not examined by reason; it does not attempt a synthesis" (7). It is free of the longueurs and conclusiveness of the novel; "it may thus more nearly than the novel approach aesthetic and moral truth" (15). In May 1945, she still celebrates the fragmentariness of the short story:

> The short storyist shares – or should share to an extent – the faculties of the poet; he can render the significance of the small event. He can take for the theme of his story a face glimpsed in the street, an unexplained incident, a snatch of talk overheard on bus or train.... Wartime London, blitzed, cosmopolitan, electric with expectation now teems, I feel, with untold but tellable stories, glitters with scenes that cry aloud for the pen. (qtd. in Beachcroft 212)

James Lasdun admires the short story for a fragmentary quality, for "omission, occlusion, cropping: the ability to cultivate a kind of force-field of negative space within a narrative" (Lasdun 23). In her study of short fiction from 2007, Renate Brosch argues that the elision of the short story is constitutive of the form and demands of readers an intellectual, imaginative, and emotional engagement that is different from those suggested by the novel. The fragmentary nature, the constraint of the short story prompts exercises in extrapolation and extension. Brosch argues that "the reading of short stories almost always means a confrontation with insuffi-cient information; an experience that calls forth extrapolation on the part of the reader or the construction of analogies, and thus reacts to the limi-tation of short narration" (19–20).[1] Junot Diáz also advocates the short story for its brevity and its fragmentary incoherence. He writes that "the short story's colossal power extends from its brevity and restraint" (xii). The benefits of the "form's defining limitation" include an ability to enact transience and existential incoherence (xii-xiv).

2.

Thus, fragmentariness is integral to short fiction. However – or perhaps therefore – writers, editors and publishers of short stories continually attempt to augment the fragment. Chapter Four of Reid's classic study of short fiction is entitled "Brevity Expanded." In it, he points out the variety of fictional texts that lie – in terms of length – between the novel and the short story: the novella, the cycle, the framed miscellany (Reid 43–53). Besides the long short story (the novella, Henry James's "blest nouvelle" [Scofield 5], which is arguably just that – a longer short story, still fragmen-tary, but just longer), there are three ways in which those involved in the production of short fiction expand the individual example of the short form.

The first is through epiphany and epiklesis. This is a well-known tech-nique in short-story writing and a well-known principle in short-story studies. The method is that of synecdoche. A brief moment in a character's life allows the character or/and the reader to understand something about an entire life, mentality, or social configuration. I have discussed this else-where (see, for example, Malcolm, *British and Irish Short Story* 39), and it has been discussed by many commentators on short fiction (see, for ex-ample, Adrian Hunter's remarks in Hunter 44–45; see also Head [110, 205]). Particularly good examples of this kind of resonant fragment are James Joyce's "An Encounter" and Virginia Woolf's "Kew Gardens."

The second way of expanding the short story is to turn the text into a kind of compressed novel. A clear example of this is Julian MacLaren-Ross's short story "My Father Was Born in Havana" (published in *The Nine Men of Soho* [1946]). In approximately 4,500 words, the author offers up a condensed family saga novel, in which incident after incident piles up breathlessly to form an absorbing, entertaining, and strangely expansive text that de-automatizes both short-fiction and novel narrative techniques

---

[1] This is part of the substance of Gérard Genette's comments on "Ellipse" in *Discours du récit* (103–06). Translated from German by David Malcolm.

(Malcolm, "The Short or the Long" 102–03). An example of a different but similar type of expansion can be seen in John McGahern's collection *High Ground* (1985). In it, three linked stories – "Old Fashioned," "Eddie Mac," and "The Conversion of William Kirkwood" – all approach the topic of Protestants who return to or stay on in the independent southern part of Ireland. Coherence of topic, recurrence of characters and locales, and proliferation of related story materials, *inter alia*, lead to a cohesive and coherent group of stories that push against the limits of the single brief narrative. McGahern certainly produces condensed fragmentary texts that resonate as synecdoches of broader matters (see, for example, his celebrated story "Korea" from *Nightlines* [1970]), but especially in "Eddie Mac" and "The Conversion of William Kirkwood" aim an enacted expansion of the fragment, realizing at least some of the implications of a single text (Malcolm, "The Short or the Long" 104–05).

The third way of augmenting the fragment is in the collection. As Pratt notes, "A short story is always printed as part of a larger whole, either a collection of short stories or a magazine, which is a collection of various kinds of texts. Except in schools, perhaps, individual short stories are usually read as part of a larger reading experience" (103–04). The short text may be a fragment, but its context adds an extra semantic dimension to that individual text. It takes on resonances because of the texts among which it is placed. This is usually a matter of its collection context, although in principle, in the case of magazine publication it might be worthwhile examining the fragment as it is augmented by the gallimaufry of other texts in which it is embedded – with respect to a *New Yorker* story, for example, the cartoons, advertisements, dance reviews, and political-social essays and articles that wrap up the short story so published. An analysis of the story's codicological environment is at least theoretically possible, although I am not aware of any attempt to do so. However, semantic amplification of the individual short story through its placement in a collection is well-documented. Examples spring readily to mind: George Moore's *The Untilled Field* (1903), James Joyce's *Dubliners* (1914), Ernest Hemingway's *Men without Women* (1927), Angela Carter's *The Bloody Chamber* (1979), and Tim O'Brien's *The Things They Carried* (1990), among many others. I have discussed this with reference to work by Rudyard Kipling, J.G. Ballard, and William Trevor in *The British and Irish Short Story Handbook* (43–47). Emma Liggins, Andrew Maunder, and Ruth Robbins point to the expansiveness and range of the collection when they argue that many North American writers have "helped to establish the collection as a valid alternative to the modern novel" (15).

3.

A simple typology of collections will serve to make distinctions among them, and how the relations differ among their component texts – their fragments – and, thus, the status of the augmentation the collection offers.

1. Edited collections with little connection among fragments, except, for example, nationality or domicile of author, or place or time of publication. Among the many examples of such are *Best Irish Stories* (2013) or *The Best American Stories* (2016). Augmentation here may exist, but it is unlikely to be authorial.

2. Edited collections organized round homogeneity of subject matter, for example, boxing stories or animals stories. Although these are very *post hoc* congeries, they can produce interesting and revealing semantic relations among writers and texts. For example, the genre diversity of Kipling's work might become apparent if a story of his were included in a collection of utopian writing, or science-fiction texts, or the historical short story (a much-neglected genre in short-story studies).

3. Edited collections prepared by an editor who is someone other than the author of the texts in question. Examples abound: Hubert Crackanthorpe's *Last Studies* (1897), published after the author's death; Mollie Panter-Downes's *New Yorker* short stories, published in *The New Yorker* between 1939 and 1944, and only published in a collection in 1999 by Persephone Books, with a preface by Gregory Lestage; and Lucia Berlin's *A Manual for Cleaning Women*, published in 2015, and edited by Stephen Emerson, in which Berlin's separate collections are combined and their particular contents undesignated. The status of the mutual relations among texts of this kind is intriguing. Is it authorial or imposed by an outside hand?

4. Authorial collections, in which the stories included, in fact, have little in common but are a set of short stories from a specific period or a specific point in the author's career. A cultural and publishing imperative may be at work in such a collection too. The publisher needs a collection of x number of stories to make a commercially viable book. Examples of such collections are David Constantine's *Under the Dam* (2005) and David Foster Wallace's *Brief Interviews with Hideous Men* (1999). It should be stressed that a lack of coherence and cohesion in contents does not diminish the quality of individual stories or the collection as a whole, which is manifestly so in the case of Constantine's and Wallace's fiction.

5. Authorial collections which are highly integrated and in which individual texts enter into complex, modifying, and amplifying semantic relations with each other. Clear examples of such collections are John Berger's *Pig Earth* (1979) and Graham Swift's *England and Other Stories* (2014) (Malcolm, Review of *England* 21). In my view, the short-story cycle – exemplified by Sherwood Anderson's *Winesburg, Ohio* (1919), Eudora Welty's *The Golden Apples* (1949), or Tim O'Brien's *The Things They Carried* – does not differ in principle from such collections.

4.

In what follows, I consider two collections of short fictions which, while courting and foregrounding the inherent fragmentariness of the short form, manifest a drive to augment the fragment on the level of the collection, and become in consequence highly coherent and cohesive texts.

Alan Garner is the author of enigmatic fictions on the border between young adults' and adults' prose. *The Stone Book Quartet* consists of four separate texts: "The Stone Book" (1976), "Granny Reardun" (1977), "The Aimer Gate" (1978), and "Tom Fobble's Day" (1977). The parts were published separately, and the entire collection came out in 1979. The title of the collection suggests coherence, but fragmentation initially strikes the reader. Four separate narratives make up the volume. Although no specific dates are given, they are considerably separated in terms of time. "The Stone Book" must take place in the first half of the nineteenth century, for Old William is weaving silk at home, his work and livelihood not yet displaced by power-loom weaving. "Granny Reardun" must take place after the 1850s; the Crimean War is referred to as being in the past (67). "The Aimer Gate" is full of references to the Great War (81, 83, 113, 117, 121); the most obvious reference is Uncle Charlie's being present with his rifle, and his imminent return to the front. "Tom Fobble's Day" is set in the early 1940s. The German air force is bombing Manchester (133–34, 166–67).

Ellipses in action and information abound. The reader continually wants to ask what happens to various characters, what the relations among them are, why Joseph is brought up by his grandparents, why Joseph is so upset by the Allmans' forced removal, why Joseph and Charlie are so antagonistic towards each other, why Charlie calls Robert Dick-Richard, what the Aimer Gate is, what became of Robert, whom Grandfather married (160), and where William's father and mother are in "Tom Fobble's Day." This fragmentariness of narrative is emphasized by the recurrent presence of abandoned artifacts, broken parts of larger units. These are present in the bad ends of silk in Old William's room (21), in the dismantled Allmans' house (63–64), in the stones that Robert gathers for Faddock Allman, which he will break down further (85–87), in the shrapnel that falls from the sky during the German air raids (133–34), and in the lumber room full of old broken things that someday might be useful (153).

This fragmentariness (the enigmas, the detritus) is real, and powerful observation of how the world is. But the fractured and limited is contained within a strong coherence and cohesion. Narrational technique – third-person but highly focalized – is consistent throughout. The point of view in all stories is that of a young person. The syntax is persistently that of simple and compound sentences. Where subordination occurs, it is of the simplest kind. Parataxis is widespread. Lexis, too, is informal to neutral or drawn from dialect. Stories are linked by characters' use of Cheshire dialect forms. The lexis of work is omnipresent – of stone working, of iron working, of building (63), and of reaping (83). Coherence is also maintained by unity of setting; all stories are set in the vicinity of Chorley; the same fields, hills, expanses of land, and landmarks recur. The stories are held together, too, by the recurrence of family names (Allman, Leah, Latham), and by the evident relationships among the principal characters. Joseph in "Granny Reardun" is the son of Mary in "The Stone Book" (although there appears to be no father), and he reappears in "The Aimer Gate" and "Tom Fobble's Day." Objects link the stories too. For example, Mary's father drops a pipe in the garden (20); William finds it (152). William's wonderful sledge is constructed partly from his namesake's broken loom (154). Transience marks all the stories – of people, things, features of landscape – but things endure in fragmented form, can be put to use through labor, and link generations. The skill and craft of the stonemason and the ironworker recur throughout the texts and bestow a type of endurance on people and things. Mary sees the hand mark of the prehistoric painter deep underground (30); Robert sees his grandfather's mark in the clock tower (100). The amplification of the fragmentary is precisely what Garner wishes to communicate in the collection.

Lydia Davis is well-known as a writer of enigmatic and short or shorter short fictions. (She is a winner of a MacArthur Fellowship and the International Man Booker Prize, and she is a *Chevalier de l'Ordre des Arts et Lettres*.) Her first collection *Break it Down* (1986) suggests disintegration and segmentation in its title, and, indeed, the volume enacts fragmentariness. This is apparent on the level of narration. The collection presents a range of narrators and narrational strategies. For example, "Story," "Extracts from a Life," "The House Plans," "A Few Things Wrong with Me," and "The Housemaid" are first-person narrations. "The Fears of Mrs Orlando," "Liminal," "Break It Down," "In a House Besieged," "Sketches for a Life of Wassilly," and "Once a Very Stupid Man" are third-person narrations. Often such third-person narrations are focalized: for example, "The Letter" and "Once a Very Stupid Man." At times, the third-person narration morphs into a first-person one: for example, "Break It Down." The stories continually (and surprisingly) edge towards or embrace omniscience: for example, "Liminal," "Mothers," "Two Sisters," and "Problem." "Le Meurtre" is narrated in the voice of a language-teacher, and might be classed first-person, third-person, third-person omniscient, or even third-person restricted (it is hard to say finally – which is the point). The use of tenses in narration is also fragmented. The volume contains thirty-four stories. Of these, fourteen predominantly use present tenses to recount events; twenty predominantly use past tenses, particularly past simple (although these may be combined with the present, as "The Mouse" or "Extracts from a Life"). There is no coherence, either on the level of narration or of narrative tense.

On other levels, too, the texts continually court the fragmentary. Many are very short indeed, comprising only a few hundred words, if so many. Examples are: "What She Knew," "The Fish," "Mildred and the Oboe," "How W.H. Auden Spends the Night in a Friend's House," "The Mother," "Safe Love," and "Problem." But even longer stories are attenuated, elliptical, and off-focus in their presentations of story material. The contrast between *fabula* and *sjuzet* is pronounced. It is easiest to demonstrate this through one particular very short text. In "The Fish," a woman has cooked a fish. It lies before her filleted and skinned. The woman looks at the fish "with a weary eye" and reflects on the mistakes ("irrevocable" ones) that she has made this "troubling day," among which preparing the fish thus belongs. Clearly many things of substance have occurred to bring the character to this point, but the reader learns of none of them. The actual events of the story are at the border of narrativity (Abbott 24–25). Little actually happens. The focus of the story is not on momentous occurrences, even on a personal level, but on a trivial cooking disappointment (an odd disappointment because the fish has been cooked skillfully and well). But the suggestiveness of this fragment of action is considerable – "irrevocable mistakes," "troubling day," "fleeced" and "violated" (of the fish), "weary eye," and "latest mistake" – all suggest something unpleasant and damaging. Such a strategy of attenuation, ellipsis, and off-centeredness runs through all the texts of the collection. The stories do not usually even read as synopses of longer texts, but rather as fragments of those texts.

Characters, too, are fragmented isolates. In many stories, characters have no names. The strategy of anonymity in "The Fish" is typical. Characters are, thus, unconnected with larger units, for example, families or ethnic or national groups. Even when characters have names – for example, "Mr

Burdoff's Visit to Germany," "Mildred and the Oboe," and "The Letter" – the allocation of names is perfunctory and limited. For example, Mr Burdoff's possible Jewishness or Central European background are never amplified on; we never know his first name; nor do we know the family name of the Norwegian and blond Helen with whom he falls in love. The names cry out for contextualizing or elaboration, which the story resolutely denies the reader. Fragmentation is everywhere in the collection.

But fragmentation itself paradoxically lends a striking coherence to the collection. Indeed, the fragmentary stories in the volume become in the context of the collection amplified parts of a whole. Attenuation becomes plenitude. Indeed, one of the coherent functions of tenuity in the stories in *Break It Down* is to de-automatize traditional story materials. Thus, for example, "Mr Burdoff's Visit to Germany" is a disjointed and abbreviated reworking of a tale of foreign travel, romance, and alien encounters. "The Brother-in-Law" and "The Bone" are cunningly defocused gothic stories, and "Two Sisters" reads like a generalized synopsis of a dark family novel. Further, at the level of narrative (the organization of the story material and its realization), texts are consistently linear. They may be elliptical, but they follow a logical and chronological progression. Exceptions are "Extracts from a Life," which is highly non-linear; "Mr Burdoff's Visit to Germany," which within an overall linear progression contains prolepses and analepses; and "Cockroaches in Autumn," which is nearly a zero-narrative, and is, in fact, a text in the lyric mode.

Vocabulary and sentence structure are consistent throughout the collection. Sentences are either compound ones ("and . . . and," for example) or ones that are relatively simple combinations of compound structures and some subordinate clauses ("when," "if" etc. clauses). Parataxis is widespread. Lexis, too, is never formal, but is constantly at an informal to neutral level. Thematically, the stories are also remarkably homogeneous. Ineptitude and lassitude mark so many of the characters. Wassilly in "Sketches for a Life of Wassilly," unable to organize his life, failing to deal with his dead brother's artifacts, or the narrator in "Five Signs of Disturbance," unable to choose two quarters from a group of three, are typical. Characters are isolated, nameless, divorced, and separated from others, for example, the narrator in "House Plans" (mostly) or "A Few Things Wrong with Me" (persistently). Incomprehension and unknowing runs through stories (on the level of both character and reader), for example, the narrator's mistrust of her lover in "Story," or the man and woman who hear different things in "In a House Besieged."

All the above is set and embodied in a world of consistent drab quotidian banality, for example, urinating, misplacing a glove, bumping into people on the street, and eating an orange (without noticing one is doing so) in "Visit to My Husband." However, despite the tawdriness, the stories almost all involve intense emotions, even obsessions. The title of "The Fears of Mrs Orlando" speaks for itself. The emotions in "Two Sisters" are no less intense for being enacted within what is banal, and the eponymous narrator of "The Housemaid" is a woman with an *idée fixe* and much *ressentiment*. "Le meurtre" is a tale of *crime passionnel*. The collection may be broken down into tesserae, but those shards can be made to form a coherent and cohesive image of the world.

Thus, even short fictions that argue for, and enact, fragmentariness in experience and its recounting within the context of a collection may encourage a vision of wholeness and completion. Brosch is right. Noncohesiveness encourages a perception of coherence, and the fragment is duly amplified. Narrational technique, linguistic configurations, recurrent settings, characters, and motif all offer coherence and breadth that underlie the fragmentary in Garner's collection. Davis's methods are similar: patterns of language and narrative technique, and an underlying homogeneity of character and environmental traits bring cohesion and coherence. Finally, of course, the very fragmentariness of individual experience is – besides an achieved coherence and plenitude – what both these collections have in common. Both have it both ways – and are all the more complex and interesting for that.

Works Cited

Abbott, H. Porter. *The Cambridge Introduction to Narrative.* 2nd ed. Cambridge: Cambridge UP, 2008.

Bates, H. E. *The Modern Short Story: A Critical Survey.* Boston: Writer, 1941.

Beachcroft, T. O. *The Modest Art: A Survey of the Short Story in English.* London: Oxford UP, 1968.

Bowen, Elizabeth. Introduction. *The Faber Book of Modern Stories.* Ed. Elizabeth Bowen. London: Faber, 1937. 7–19.

Brosch, Renate. *Short Story: Textsorte und Leseerfahrung.* Trier: Wissenschaftlicher Verlag, 2007.

Davis, Lydia. *The Collected Stories of Lydia Davis.* London: Penguin, 2009.

Diáz, Junot. Introduction. *The Best American Short Stories – 2016.* Ed. Junot Diáz. Boston: Mariner Books/Houghton Mifflin Harcourt, 2016. xii-xx.

Garner, Alan. *The Stone Book Quartet.* 1983. London: Harper Perennial, 2006.

Genette, Gérard. *Discours du récit.* 1972. Paris: Éditions du Seuil, 2007.

Gullason, Thomas A. "The Short Story: Revision and Renewal." *Studies in Short Fiction* 19.3 (1982): 221–30.

Hallett, Cynthia J. "Minimalism and the Short Story." *Studies in Short Fiction* 33.4 (1996): 487–95.

Hanson, Clare. "Things out of Words: Towards a Poetics of Short Fiction." *Re-Reading the Short Story.* Ed. Clare Hanson. Basingstoke: Macmillan, 1989. 22–33.

Head, Dominic. *The Modernist Short Story: A Study in Theory and Practice.* Cambridge: Cambridge UP, 1992.

Hunter, Adrian. *The Cambridge Introduction to the Short Story in English.* Cambridge: Cambridge UP, 2007.

Lasdun, James. "A Genius for Misery: William Trevor and the Art of the Short Story." *Times Literary Supplement*, 23 Sept. 1996: 23.

Liggins, Emma, Andrew Maunder, and Ruth Robbins. *The British Short Story.* Basingstoke: Palgrave Macmillan, 2011.

Malcolm, David. *The British and Irish Short Story Handbook.* Malden: Wiley-Blackwell, 2012.

---. Review of *England and Other Stories.* By Graham Swift. *Times Literary Supplement*, 26 June 2015: 21.

---. "The Short or the Long of It: How Can Short Stories Do Human Life?" *From the Cradle to the Grave: Life-Course Models in Literary Genres.* Eds. Sabine Coelsch-Foisner and Sarah Herbe. Heidelberg: Universitätsverlag Winter, 2011. 97–106.

O'Connor, Frank. *The Lonely Voice: A Study of the Short Story.* 1962. Cleveland: Meridian, 1965.

Patea, Viorica. "The Short Story: An Overview of the History and Evolution of the Genre." *Short Story Theories: A Twenty-First-Century Perspective.* Ed. Viorica Patea. Amsterdam: Rodopi, 2012. 1–24.

Pratt, Mary Louise. "The Short Story: The Long and the Short of It." *The New Short Story Theories.* Ed. Charles May. Athens: Ohio UP, 1994. 91–113.

Reid, Ivan. *The Short Story.* The Critical Idiom. London: Methuen, 1977.

Scofield, Paul. *The Cambridge Introduction to the American Short Story.* Cambridge: Cambridge UP, 2006.

Shaw, Valerie. *The Short Story: A Critical Introduction.* London: Longman, 1983.

Part Two

The fragment and the whole

Chapter 4

The architectural fragment: ruins and totality in J. G. Ballard's fiction

Marcin Tereszewski,
University of Wrocław

Though ruins and fragmentary imagery can be found pervading twenty-first century media culture, architecture and literature, the fascination with these tropes is certainly not an exclusively twenty-first century phenomenon, as there is a distinct history of the fragment that can be traced to the eighteenth-century Gothic tradition through its nineteenth-century Romantic iterations, especially in poetry, and then later with Modernist aesthetics and the postmodern critique of totality. Andreas Huyssen emphasizes this trajectory as one that has been spurred by a "catastrophic imagination":

> If in the late twentieth century, as Lyotard has claimed, architecture and philosophy lie in ruins, leaving us only with the option of a "writing of the ruins" as a kind of micrology, then the question arises whether the tradition of modernist thought all the way into postmodernism is overshadowed by the catastrophic imagination and imagery of ruins that has accompanied the trajectory of modernity since the eighteenth century. (19)

The image of ruins and ruination also has a parallel and intertwining history with that of the fragment, manifesting itself especially clearly in Gothic imagery, which, in turn, is seen to cast a long shadow on even our modern images of ruins (e.g., the World Trade Center).

What follows is not an attempt to provide a diagnosis of why fragmentary aesthetics and ruination have had such a long hold on Western aesthetics; neither is it an attempt to present reasons for this fascination today, though, of course, political and cultural disintegration, anxiety, global warming, etc. come readily to mind and are always mentioned in almost every study of this subject to the point of having become almost cliché. What this paper will attempt to do is address the relationship of the fragment as ruination to the concept of totality, a point that may go some way towards distinguishing the contemporary fragment from its Romantic predecessor. In order to do so, I would like to frame my article within the context of Maurice Blanchot's considerations regarding the fragment before moving on to an analysis of J. G. Ballard's particular usage of ruins and fragmentation as an extension of Gothic preoccupations with similar matters and aesthetics.

In *The Infinite Conversation*, Blanchot argues that, although the word "fragment" is a noun, it "possess[es] the force of a verb that is nonetheless absent" (307), thus indicating a unique dynamics, or force, that resides within the concept itself. This, in turn, leads to a consideration of precisely what kind of force resides in the fragment. To answer this question, Blanchot develops the idea that fragmenting itself has a power that is far from destructive, like "interruption in speech does not arrest being but, on the contrary, provokes it in the rupture that belongs to it" (307). Momentary gaps of silence, interruptions, breaks, and lacunae are, for Blanchot, semantically charged events which engender meaning, and are at the heart of poetics. However, what is crucial here is the understanding of meaning not as a part of a whole, but as a break from totality: "Whoever says fragment ought not say simply the fragmenting of an already existent reality or the movement of a whole still to come" (307). Blanchot concedes that doing so is difficult given that comprehension is usually based on apprehending the whole, as a unity, which is why a fragment from this point of view is always a part of something that used to be whole or will be whole in the future.

As was mentioned earlier, for Blanchot, it is poetry, always fragmentary in nature, that has this dislocating energy able to shatter the specter of totality. It is possible to see that this approach to the fragment is dangerously reminiscent of a kind of apocalyptic provocation which would find liberation and salvation in undermining the stability of structure seen as a totality. And it is precisely this understanding of the fragment that has become a staple in Ballardian criticism, though it is an approach that should be deployed with caution to avoid oversimplifying Ballard's ambiguous stance on the subject of transgression, perhaps one of the most interesting aspects of his work.

Fragmentation is a constant aspect of Ballard's prose manifesting itself in numerous ways, which is why a brief introduction to how his work manifests fragmentary aesthetics is important before embarking on an analysis of his imagery of ruins. Fragmentary writing is most visible in *The Atrocity Exhibition*, which was for Ballard perhaps the most explicit foray into experimental writing. Greatly influenced by the cut-up technique of William S. Burroughs, Ballard attempts to convey the fragmentary nature of modern culture as it would appear on the flickering screen of a television set. The book is a collection of scenes and tidbits painting a mosaic picture of modern culture, which has become increasingly disintegrated as a result of media technology. Ballard, however, never followed up these experiments with any other longer work except a few short stories that employed fragmentary plotting, such as "Passport to Eternity" and "The Voices of Time." The vast majority of his writing, following and preceding *The Atrocity Exhibition*, was cast in traditional prose and style. Surrealism, which was to have a profound and long-lasting influence on his writing, was incorporated in the imagery and thematics of his fiction, even the most overtly realistic, such as *Empire of the Sun*. Throughout much of Ballard's work, therefore, the fragment manifests itself not only in the form of stylistic choices but also in terms of the themes, scenery, and references employed, the most salient being ruins.

Ballard's various instantiations of fragmentation, regardless of whether they take on the form of social withdrawal, destruction of high-rises, ruins of defunct cities, or psychological disintegration, have been presented as a convenient exit strategy from what appear to be dehumanized, technocratic constraints imposed by modern capitalist culture. This approach would constitute the transgressive reading of Ballard's fiction. It is a reading that is sensitive to the anarchic and the liberatory, if not libidinal, elements of entropy; however, it is an approach that all too easily ignores the critique that Ballard levels at modern culture, at the totality that it is meant to represent. An important question to consider in reference to this approach is whether the fragment is to be construed as a manifestation of loss, a fragment intimating a whole, plentitude, which would naturally entail discourses of nostalgia and grief. Or, conversely, should we consider the fragment as a means to celebrate the liberation from an imposed totality, always a totalitarian and imperialistic notion effectively limiting the autonomy of its subjects? To answer this question, it is important to define how totality is intimated in Ballard's work and in the representations of ruins.

What makes ruins especially provocative are their double trajectories mirroring the above-posed question. On the one hand, ruins point to the irretrievability of the past, the implacability of time, giving rise to discourses of melancholia and nostalgia. The fragmented ruin would here be approached as a piece of an incomplete whole, viewed with reverence as the absolute, harmonious perfection, a utopia of sorts. This trajectory marks the interplay in the Romantic fragment between the "unfinished" poetry written between 1790 and 1830 and the "cult of ruins and of fragmentary relics that has been part of European thought since the Renaissance and was assimilated into British thought as inherently 'Romantic' in the eighteenth century" (Harries 360). In the first instance, totality, that is the image of a coherent, though perhaps irretrievable past, is presented as something that existed and could function as a kind of utopian blueprint, a "shadowy 'ground' of the possible 'finished' work" (Harries 361). This is a totality that has served as the underlying principle of a colonial hegemony or a technocratic order regulating social life.

The second trajectory will focus on the transgressive aspect of ruins with regards to totality. In her study on the critical function of ruins, philosopher Sophie Lacroix writes that ruins "reduced to a fragmentary condition are often incoherent and uncertain" (28). The fragmentary form of ruins focuses "towards the absent" (31) as a way to undermine all forms of totality, thereby providing a "critical message" (81) against all forms of totality. What is more, this reading also insists that totality is an impossible project, wherein only the fragment is nothing more than an intimation and source of poetic energy in a vein similar to Blanchot's notion of fragmentary poetry. One can discern here a certain similarity between this particular approach to totality and apophatic speech, or negative theology, which similarly, through breaks, silences and negations attempted to intimate the existence of what by definition must remain outside of language, i.e., God.

I think it is possible to posit that Ballard's ruins combine these two concepts (ruins and fragment) in relation to totality (or in this case completion). Though ruins in Ballard's fiction do represent a part of a whole that can be remembered or reconstructed through the imagination, a similarity between these two seemingly different concepts can be drawn – a similarity based on Ballard's tacit insistence on the underlying unreality, or disconnectedness, that underpins our representation of external reality. Ballard's earlier catastrophe novels depicting various post-apocalyptic worlds are replete with ruins: *The Wind from Nowhere* (1961), *The Drowned World* (1962), *The Burning World* (1964), *The Drought* (1965) and *The Crystal World* (1966). These catastrophe novels of Ballard's earlier period also represent the aftermath of some cataclysmic event which has rendered the earth uninhabitable for a variety of reasons (heat, flooding), thereby reducing a once industrialized society to savagery, condemned to fight for their survival amidst the ruins of their former glory. The post-apocalyptic world depicted therein is seen as riddled with ruins of the past piercing through the worlds laid to waste, a reminder of an irretrievable past.

Ballard's so-called "urban novels," *Crash* (1973), *Concrete Island* (1974), *High-Rise* (1975), tend to portray the singular instances of disintegration within the context of a fully-functioning modern society. The eponymous high-rise deteriorating from what was once a high-tech, perfectly harmonious building catering to every whim of its residents to an incoherent array of corridors and isolated rooms illustrates the societal breakup resulting from the implementation of vast government projects based on social engineering. *Concrete Island*, on the other hand, has an interesting scene depicting the main character, stranded in an urban wasteland surrounded by motorways, who at one point comes across ruins, remnants of an old cinema, Edwardian houses, remains of a civil defense post.

Furthermore, in line with the Gothic tradition, many short stories tend to represent houses falling into ruin as reflections of the disintegrating minds of their inhabitants – "The Enormous Space," portraying the slow and methodical lapse into solipsism, is a case in point. These "fragments are really versions or symptoms of the extreme otherness of the Gothic sublime, which emerges, in these fragments, as the embodiment of what Slavoj Žižek has aptly called the "void, the emptiness created by the symbolic structure implicit in the fragments" (Mishra 83). This definition ties in perfectly with Ballard's penchant for surrealist imagery, which only enhances the aesthetic value of the fragment, presenting reality as a collection of fragmented images or spatially distorted scenes, very often alluding to Surrealism in the visual arts.

The repetitive imagery of ruins – dilapidated modern high-rises, discarded modern technology, abandoned aerodromes – is so prominent that it has been incorporated into the adjective "Ballardian." From seeing these images appear and reappear in different contexts, from his most surrealistic to his most realistic instantiations, a pattern does emerge, one that may provide insight into the ideological backdrop of this recurring theme. For Alex Watson, who employs a postcolonial reading of Ballard, this disintegration can be seen as a response to or a reflection of the socio-economic shift characterized by a "reformulation of global power" (Watson 273). More specifically, he continues to explain that "the overtly hierarchical and Imperialist style of nineteenth-century European capitalist hegemony yielded to the apparently more libertarian ethos of twentieth-century American consumer capitalism" (273). The result of this shift – to elaborate on Watson's observation – is the fragmentation of what was once held to be a stable, hegemonic, ordered world view, though this understanding might imply that Ballard was somehow mournful for this loss, representing these ruins elegiacally, nostalgically as pieces of a greater whole that is the memory of the past. This is, however, not the case. In fact, Ballard's representation of ruins brings him closer to the transgressive element of the Gothic tradition than to the anxiety-ridden representation of post-war Britain.

To illustrate this point further, I would like to refer to Ballard's perhaps most popular novel, the semi-autobiographical *Empire of the Sun*, published in 1985, which depicts a fictionalized account of Ballard's own childhood experiences in the Lunghua internment camp during World War II. Departing from his science-fiction roots, Ballard casts *Empire* in a traditional and realistic mode, gaining him further mainstream recognition with a Booker Prize nomination. Beneath the realistic veneer of a supposedly autobiographical work lie interesting aesthetic decisions that reveal ideological assumptions. *Empire* refashions the Gothic imagery of ruins to represent the disintegration of the old-world order in postcolonial terms. Because the historical and cultural connections are more discernible in a text like *Empire*, this novel has consequently come to serve as the go-to text for postcolonial analyses of Imperial disintegration as experienced by post-war Britain (Watson, Paddy). The war itself already frames the book within a postcolonial discourse. Specifically, the Second Sino-Japanese War depicted in the novel effectively not only thwarted the colonial ambitions of the Japanese Empire but also brought an end to Britain's economic and political influence on the Chinese east coast.

The ruins of the wartime landscape are reminiscent of many of the already mentioned tropes found in his earlier works: the drained swimming pools, the downed aircraft, abandoned aerodromes, burial grounds, destroyed stockyards, the empty houses, the burned outer shell of an English country club; all of these tropes are present in *Empire*. And if we are to take a closer look at these images, it will become clear that they are evocative of how a former empire – in this case, post-war Great Britain – could be metaphorically depicted as a graveyard of its former power and glory.

It has not gone unnoticed that Ballard's aesthetics is cinematographic in its portrayal of scenes – aestheticized images of ruin and destruction – which are laid out for the viewer in much the same way a movie panes through the scenography. The power of cinematic representation to defamiliarize war-torn imagery is noted by Watson, who writes that "[i]n the association these images create between ruin and cinema, Ballard highlights how ruination transforms real landscapes into fantastical images" (274). The editing, cut-frames, snapshot imagery of the ruins are visual forms of the fragment, which along with the icon of ruins, transfer post-war crisis into an aesthetic of fragmentation.

All this, even the aestheticizing of these ruins, would not be remarkable or especially poignant were it not for how Ballard contextualizes these ruins. All of these images refer to a past that was manifestly not real in the sense that it was recreated from memories. That the past is always fictionalized, devoid of objectivity and direct empirical verification, is a postmodern notion that Ballard takes one step further by making it clear from the very beginning that Jim, the protagonist whose experiences depicted in the book are based on Ballard's childhood, has no way of verifying the historical veracity of the encountered ruins of war. On his return to Lunghua, Jim finds a discarded issue of *Life* magazine with Joseph Rosenthal's famous 1945 photograph of American soldiers heroically raising the flag in Iwo Jima. The glory and boldness epitomized in this photograph is juxtaposed with the stark brutality of his wartime experience with Jim remarking "the Americans in these magazines had fought a heroic war, closer to the comic books that [he] had read as a child" (Ballard 314).

This poses an interesting problem, because the totality to which the ruins are in contradistinction is manifestly a construct, an illusion of Englishness propped up next to Chinese paddy fields, thus amplifying the air of unreality that pervades Jim's understanding of Englishness, so when war breaks out shattering these illusions, Jim is left with only ruins of a place that was a recreation of London, of Englishness, an illusion of a totality. The British prisoners at Lunghua defiantly attempt to regain symbolic control over their environment by putting up their own signs "Regent Street," "Piccadilly," "Knightsbridge." These were nothing but "relics of an imaginary London – which many of the Shanghai-born British prisoners had never seen" (Ballard 167). Because Jim had never lived in England, having grown up in a British colony where he attended an English school, having read English books and magazines, he had been immersed in English culture and language, and later he was sent to an internment camp, which gave him access only to a simulacrum of the Empire.

This idea of ruins referring to a whole that was never real is but one of the features of Ballardian ruins. Applicable to Ballard's representation of disintegration and ruination is the notion of creative destruction, a phoenix-like element which Watson regards as implicit in eighteenth-century discourses, especially in relation to the sublime. He quotes Edmund Burke's example of the sublime in his remarks about the destruction of London: "What numbers from all parts would crowd to behold the ruins" (Watson 77). Ballard takes these images of destruction to a new level in his fantasies of wrecking which stem from the belief in "the transgressive potential of sites unencumbered by the norms weighing on encoded, regulated space" (Watson 274). This liberation from societal norms and ideological determinations is precisely what Brian Dillon was referring to in his article for the *Guardian*, where he described Ballardian landscapes as the "landscape of a decidedly post-romantic sublime."

In conclusion, the transgressive potential of ruins seems to inform Ballard's aesthetics with regard to ruination in the physical form and psychological disintegration. Blanchot's statements about the fragment being the basis for poetic thought are predicated on the idea that fragmentary writing opposes hegemonic order in the sense that it opens up the possibility of multiple perspectives and epistemological orderings. Ruins are the physical symbolic manifestation of past hegemonic structures, past ways of seeing and understanding, succumbing to the Hegelian notion of History, a force which moves from despotism to freedom. It seems that Ballard's fiction questions the validity of this order and totality, often casting it in a dystopian light or in terms of grand narrative conspiracy theories. And it is precisely because order and totality in Ballard's fiction are often presented as inimical to the freedom of the individual that his novels tend to acquire an anti-utopian aspect, portraying totality as a utopia that by definition limits the individual. What is more, the ideological disintegration attached to ruins strikes one in this context as being more real, more immediate than that manufactured state of wholeness, which only serves to conceal the underlying state of fragmentariness. Whatever glue is used to unite all these parts into a neat totality is presented as an ideology (e.g., patriotism, as sense of nation, civilizational superiority, or the idea of Empire), all of which are manifestations of what Sartre would term "bad faith." Whereas the Romantics utilized the fragment as a strategy to avoid the impossibility of expressing the infinite within the finite material of poetry, Ballard presents the fragment in the form of ruins to undercut the false image of totality imposed by nations, history, or culture. In the first case totality is the unattainable goal, in the second it is little more than a false image.

Works Cited

Ballard, J. G. *Empire of the Sun*. London: Grafton, 1989.

Blanchot, Maurice. *The Infinite Conversation*. 1969. Trans. Susan Hanson. Minneapolis: U of Minnesota P, 1993.

Dillon, Brian. "Ruin Lust: Our Love Affair with Decaying Buildings." *The Guardian*, 17 Feb. 2012, https://www.theguardian.com/artanddesign/2012/feb/17/ruins-love-affair-decayed-buildings. Accessed 12 Sept. 2017.

Harries, Elizabeth Wanning. "'Unfinish'd Sentences': The Romantic Fragment." *A Companion to European Romanticism*. Ed. Michael Ferber. Malden: Blackwell, 2005. 360–75.

Huyssen, Andreas. "Authentic Ruins: Products of Modernity." *Ruins of Modernity*. Eds. Julia Hell and Andreas Schönle. Durham: Duke UP, 2010. 17–28.

Lacroix, Sophie. *Ruine*. Paris: Editions de la Villette, 2008.

Mishra, Vijay. *The Gothic Sublime*. New York: State University of New York Press, 1994.

Paddy, David I. *The Empire of J.G. Ballard: An Imagined Geography*. Canterbury: Gylphy, 2015.

Watson, Alex. "Ruins of Empire: Refashioning the Gothic in J. G. Ballard's *Empire of the Sun* (1984)." *Gothic Landscapes: Changing Eras, Changing Cultures, Changing Anxieties.* Eds. Sharon Rose Yang and Kathleen Healey. Palgrave Macmillan, 2016. 271–91.

Chapter 5

Fragmentary transtextuality: David Mitchell and his novel

Gerd Bayer,
University of Erlangen-Nuremberg

In his first published novel, *Ghostwritten* (1999), David Mitchell was already dazzling readers with his innovative narrative style. The work relies substantially for its aesthetic effect on the manner in which Mitchell creates superficially disjointed micro-narratives that, ultimately, are revealed to be connected by the very disembodied voice that the novel's eponymous ghostly narrator has evoked. This contrast between fragmentation and cohesion forms a response to the poetological sense of exhaustion that followed upon the literary mode of postmodernity (itself famously defined by John Barth as a "literature of exhaustion"), and it resurfaces in many of Mitchell's subsequent novels, including both *Cloud Atlas* (2004) and *The Bone Clocks* (2014). While this contrast dissolves the absolute rupture that fragmentation employs as its essential gesture, Mitchell's engagement with fragmentation includes another, even more radical aspect.

This essay argues that what sets Mitchell's novelistic output apart from that of many other contemporary writers is not so much his employment of fragmentation as an aesthetic device that echoes and comments upon the perceived loss of coherence his readers experience in their actual reality; rather, what Mitchell supplies in his writing, here presented as consisting of one single novel only materially (but not aesthetically and effectively) broken up into a sequence of individual publications, is instead a themed engagement with the fact that this transtextual technique, which transcends the singularity of individual novels, deflates the at-times defeatist ethics of fragmentation. While an ethical-poetological commitment to fragmentation – as for instance encountered in such modernist texts as James Joyce's *Ulysses* (1922) and Virginia Woolf's *To the Lighthouse* (1927) – often results from a nostalgic feeling of loss, Mitchell's sublation of fragmentation subscribes to a more optimistic outlook. In Mitchell's novels, fragmentation ceases to relate to a sense of rupture or loss, the nostalgia diagnosed by Fredric Jameson as a central concern of postmodernist aesthetics (279–96), and instead signals towards connection, timelessness, and, ultimately, to what Maurice Blanchot has envisioned as "the book to come" (224–44). This poetological (if not to say, utopian) gesture supplements fragmentation with transtextuality, and by doing so poses the impossibility of fragments.[1]

Fragmentation: which way to go?

One way of thinking about the fragment is as a finished form: unlike the fragmentary or the unfinished, the kind of work that an author kept hidden in the back of some drawer and never really meant to publish in its incomplete state, the fragment as a finished form is elder sister to smaller forms such as the paradox or the aphorism. What all three genres share is an ostentatious engagement with the paucity of language: they highlight and emphasize that any form of literary representation cannot but fall short in its attempt at giving a reliable picture of the complexity of life. And these forms accordingly decide to elevate this shortcoming to an aesthetic principle. In other words, and paradoxical as it may sound, to write a fragment is to produce a higher form of reliability and veracity precisely because such a text reveals its partiality as it confronts actual totality. The fragment, seen this way, succeeds in reaching a higher level of truthfulness. And in doing so, it underlines the postmodern impetus to disrupt and segment what hitherto had been taken for complete and coherent. To cite Nietzsche, from *Twilight of the Idols and the Anti-Christ* (1889), "I mistrust all systematizers and avoid them. The will to a system is a lack of integrity" (35).

An honest reading of Nietzsche's quote clearly reveals that it is at odds with my initial statements and my overall claim, which after all argues that what Mitchell does across his entire oeuvre is not so much abandon the system of the novel, but rather replace the limitations of the individual book with the communication that ensues when various books relate to each other through "a machinery directed towards both destruction and resurrection" (Barthes 38). This corresponds to what Barthes, in discussing a writer's unique style or form of writing, would probably call *écriture*. Seen this way, Mitchell's principle of the fragment is precisely what Nietzsche chastises as a "will to a system"; yet it also resists the system of the book and as such is a form of avoidance.

---

[1] See Edwards.

The two trajectories with which I have started take two rather opposite views of what a fragment is, or can be. While some see in the fragment a means of reaching beyond the limitations of any form of conventionalized representations, others will see in the fragment itself a form that systematizes, and thus falls short of, the openness and complexity of extra-textual reality. Or seen differently, the fragment as text tries to have its cake and eat it: it sets out to undermine the text by establishing its own textuality.

Frankfurt School critic Theodor Adorno, too, in his *Ästhetische Theorie* (1970), emphasizes this inner tension when he notes that in the form of the fragment, art achieves to console its desire for truth through the admittance that it cannot be what it represents. One of Adorno's aphorisms accordingly begins with Proust, famously struggling to move his writing from concept to final form (see Cano), and ends with the claim: "The whole is the false" (Adorno, *Minima Moralia* 50). When the whole is indeed "the untrue" (Adorno's original reads "das Unwahre"), yet the fragment remains ultimately incapable of persisting in a state of resistance towards conventional forms, what, one could ask, is a text to do? How is a writer to avoid this impasse and nevertheless follow a progressive and maybe even radical vision of textual creation?

The principle of avoidance that rules Mitchell's aesthetics I here view through the notion of transtextuality, building on some of the concepts presented by Jonathan Walker. This term has been used by scholars in queer studies to speak about textual realities in a transsexual textual environment (Marshall); and by media scholars to evoke the non-reality of virtual textuality (Ruffino). The way in which I would like to think about transtextuality, a term that goes back to Gérard Genette's cladistic reflections in *Palimpsests* and there stands as the most abstract and wide-reaching form of a text's connection to other texts, is more humble and simply takes the physical object of the text, in the shape of a single novel, as an entity that, at least in the case of Mitchell's writing, obsessively signals beyond its boundaries. I would like to suggest that it is through the principle of transtextuality that the mutually incompatible notions of fragmentation can be resolved. The solution, as practiced by Mitchell, is to reach beyond the book; in other words, to reach for fragmentation not on a level below the individual or finite text but instead beyond the textual singularity.

Mitchell's writing engages in this counter-intuitive form of fragmentation, and in doing so reveals how transtextuality allows writers to escape the limitations both of the principle of textuality as a form of communication that eventually reverts back to the author and of the materiality of the book. When Gilles Deleuze and Félix Guattari theorize about the radical and revolutionary potential of what they term in *A Thousand Plateaus* "the root-book" (5) – "le livre rhizome" in French – they signal in a similar direction yet appear to take too reduced a view of what the book is, even within its rhizomatic embeddedness. Yet their insistence that a book is always already composed of lines of flight, a form of assemblage reminiscent of Jacques Derrida's supplement, signals towards an understanding of textuality that, in my reading of Mitchell's series of novels, I would see as transtextuality, akin to what Deleuze and Guattari describe as "an immediate, indefinite multiplicity of secondary roots" (5) that attach to the book; and the two critics go on to observe that, in such a rhizomatic context, "a book" can become "all the more total for being fragmented" (6). One advantage of the biological metaphor they belabor rests in the fact that a living organism continues to change even after its moment of creation, thereby evading the determinism that resides in genre and in the finality of conventional forms of textuality.

Mitchell, fragmenting

In the spirit of my essay, what follows will not be a detailed reading of one particular novel by Mitchell, but rather an engagement with the transtextual sphere of his oeuvre. Mitchell now easily counts amongst the most respected younger contemporary writers. Born in 1969, Mitchell published his first novel, *Ghostwritten*, in 1999, making of him just about a late twentieth-century writer, yet his breakthrough followed upon the release of *Cloud Atlas* in 2004, later also adapted into a major film directed by the Wachowskis and Tom Tykwer, whose *Lola rennt* (1998) in turn marked a crucial turning point in German postmodern film narratives. In 2009, Mitchell's work was the focus of a two-day conference held in St Andrews and run by Sarah Dillon, who subsequently published a collection of essays that marks something of a foundational moment of what has since then turned into a real David Mitchell industry of scholarly publications. While this joint research is very diverse, attesting to the richness of Mitchell's fiction, much has been made in this body of work of the narrative structure in particular of Mitchell's first three novels, including in addition to the two novels already mentioned *number9dream* from 2001. These first novels shared an interest in a somewhat segmented and non-directional narrative structure that can be described as a composite novel or even short story cycle.[2]

Most of Mitchell's novels indeed consist of more or less independent smaller units – including the two most recent publications, *The Bone*

---

[2] See Bayer, "Short Narrative Form."

Clocks (2014) and its sequel, *Slade House* (2015) – that congeal into a larger novelistic narrative as the reader progresses, forming the essential realm of a Mitchell narrative.[3] Yet, as Sarah Dillon and others have pointed out, Mitchell's oeuvre can and perhaps even should be thought of as what she calls a "macronovel" (9), that is, as a literary entity that exists at a level higher than the singular text. What this observation calls up is an investment in matters of textuality, and indeed totality, akin to the notion of transtextuality. And it is at this point, also, that the matter of fragmentation takes on importance. While the question of fragmentation mostly addresses how an individual work somewhat falls short of its own potential or the conventions usually associated with a particular genre (an aspect whose specific temporality is revealed in the word's frequent collocation with "remain," as in a text "remained a fragment"), in Mitchell's case the matter of fragmentation plays out not within the individual text but across the writer's entire literary output. Whereas individual short narratives within a particular novel are placed in more or less lucid connections in works like *Cloud Atlas* or *Slade House*, various features establish connections beyond individual books, be it characters that appear in more than one text or narrative ideas that are being recycled. While an overly academic tutor may accuse Mitchell of self-plagiarizing when the author brings back a literary character invented for text A again in text B, Mitchell himself views this approach as doing justice to the kind of literary world that he is creating, where characters take on a life of their own that simply transcends the limitations of particular texts.

Mitchell here clearly echoes the likes of James Joyce, whose Stephen Dedalus puts in appearances in various publications; or fellow Irish modernist Flann O'Brien, whose characters in *At Swim-Two-Birds* (1939) actively resist the controlling function as conventionally claimed by any author and eventually stage their own revolution as an act of fictional emancipation. These (late) modernist experimentations have also been picked up by postmodernist writers like John Fowles, whose infamous chapter 13 in *The French Lieutenant's Woman* (1969) stages the supposed independence of the work's character from control even by the faux-Victorian novel's omniscient narrator,[4] himself a metaleptic avatar of Fowles, the author. Mitchell's fictional universe also frequently seems to exist at a diegetic level that is metaleptically resisting the restrictions that conventions have set up as being attached to the covers of an individual book. And when I use Genette's term "metalepsis," which in its original use

---

[3] See Hopf.

[4] See Isekenmeier.

speaks about transgressions across extra- and intradiegetic boundaries (*Narrative Discourse* 234–37), I am intentionally moving it beyond the physical boundaries of the actual book and into the actual reality of both author and reader. Or, to be perhaps more accurate, what I am suggesting is that transtextuality exists in its own ontological sphere, one that may not be identical with "our" reality but is nevertheless active beyond the actual individual book. Not wanting to quibble about details here, the critical point I want to make, however, is that the feature of transtextuality provides a text with a dimension that is not, like most fragmentation, a reduction of its potentiality but instead reaches for, and, in doing so, establishes an additional and transgressive layer of its existence.

Another aspect of Mitchell's literary program is revealed in the aesthetic process that has led to the publication of his latest novel, *Slade House*. On many counts this novel is a sequel to *The Bone Clocks* and as such raises the level of fragmentariness of the earlier novel, which becomes retroactively less complete through the publication of *Slade House*. The later novel, however, itself grew not only out of the far longer earlier novel but also out of an experiment in a very short literary form, a Tweet.[5] The beginning of *Slade House*, in fact, goes back to the publication of a short story over a few days in mid-July 2014, running to 280 Tweets. Each published text clearly remains a mere fragment of the full short story, which itself would end up as the opening chapter of the novel, which in turn is a sequel to *The Bone Clocks* and furthermore has a number of characters that have already appeared in earlier Mitchell novels, most importantly Dr Marinus from *The Thousand Autumns of Jacob de Zoet* (2010).

All these links, fragments, palimpsestic and metaleptic auto-references beg the question of what the smallest unit is that one should take in order to think about Mitchell's engagement with parts and totality. To reflect on the role played by fragments requires us to agree on the quality of any totality; and in Mitchell's case – as well as in works by other contemporary writers – the role played by genre takes pride of place. The Mitchell trademark collection of quasi-independent yet markedly interconnected mini-narratives is remarkable only when contrasted with more conventional forms of literary publications: the novel, the short story, the short story cycle.

Seen from this angle, Mitchell's writing is less an intervention in the supposed totality, wholeness or even holiness of the novel than an investigation in how the nature of genre predetermines forms of representation that accordingly become limited in terms of their truth-value and ability to

---

[5] For further discussion of this aspect, see Bayer, "Right Sort of Form."

relate to reality more substantially. By subverting the principle of genre – or rather, the consequences that arise from taking stable genericity for granted beyond being merely "a function of reading" (Frow 102) – Mitchell's literary oeuvre does not so much reduce the novel as a stable form as enlarge our understanding of how conventions are always already forms of reduction. In an almost paradoxical twist, Mitchell's fragmentary approach to the postmodernist novel reveals the well-made novel to have been a mere fragment of lived totality.

Author function

My reflections on Mitchell's novels and the way they engage in matters of fragmentation is clearly inspired by Michel Foucault's writing about the author function. Foucault's reminder that, for legal reasons, texts needed and need authors highlights the fact that the author function is a form of negotiation in which readers engage in order to relate a text to the world; and, in another step, to allow for the discussion of an author's work that is essentially built around the notion of the author as a unifying (and, at times, even signifying) instance in the production of the readerly text. It is the author through whom each individual text from within an oeuvre attains a meaningful relationship to other texts; and it is through this process that each text becomes a part of something larger. In other words, each novel becomes more meaningful in and of itself precisely by being situated in an author's oeuvre. What Mitchell sets out to do in his cross-connected novels merely makes more visible this general principle, built as it is on the two-fold and self-contradictory nature of fragmentation as a force that holds the promise to signal simultaneously towards a lost wholeness and an as-yet unattained complexity.

While I see Foucault's author function as a crucial element in establishing the idea of transtextuality with which I am currently toying, his focus on the author as the point of connection nevertheless is a more modest vision. Transtextuality is closer in quality to Barthes's notion of *écriture* yet remains restricted to the actual world-making that relies on specific textual connections as we know them from critical work on intertextuality or the palimpsest. So, Mitchell's transtextual sphere would accordingly include elements and aspects that he has taken over from writers like Joyce and Fowles, but also from contemporary inspirations like Haruki Murakami.[6] But rather than thinking of these connections as reduced borrowings, fragments in the strict sense, I would want to see them as extensions of both works that signal to their transtextual means of connection.

---

[6] See Machinal.

Outcome: post-text and post-book

The aesthetic principle that speaks through Mitchell's work, as well as those of writers like Kazuo Ishiguro, Haruki Murakami or Roberto Bolaño, thus directly affects our understanding of the novel on at least three fronts: first, it once again puts the format of the novel as a generic constant into play, thus extending the legacy of a form that, at least since the seventeenth century, has taken pride in its commitment to reinvent itself, and doing so more excessively since the modernist and postmodernist moments. Secondly, Mitchell invites his readers to situate the book as a textual entity that reaches beyond its physical limitations. To speak of the novel as a singular event makes even less sense after Mitchell, and he thus continues the kind of work to which Barthes and Blanchot have made significant contributions. The book itself, and certainly each novel by Mitchell, becomes a mere crossroad at which literature as *écriture* reaches for an ever-elusive book-to-come that will then also be a mere episode in a larger textual scheme. This already signals towards the third element, something one could call the post-book. Such a post-book exists not behind an ISBN or library call number – it cannot be shelved and definitely not owned. A post-book – of which another example is clearly J. J. Abrams and Doug Dorst's experimental novel *S.* (2013) – transcends the limitations of the object formerly known as the book. One side effect of seeing Mitchell's writing as an example of such a post-book means that there will never be a final work that can be related clearly to the author. Like Jorge Luis Borges's playful discussion of Franz Kafka's precursors, Mitchell's author function will essentially remain incomplete. What incompletion precludes, of course, is fragmentation, which necessitates some form of essential stability from which to break off. And at this point, my essay ends, in fragments.

Works Cited

Adorno, Theodor. *Ästhetische Theorie*. Frankfurt am Main: Suhrkamp, 1970.

---. *Minima Moralia: Reflections on a Damaged Life*. 1951. Trans. E.F.N. Jephcott. London: Verso, 2005.

Barth, John. "The Literature of Exhaustion." *The Atlantic Monthly* 220.2 (1967): 29–34.

Barthes, Roland. *Writing Degree Zero*. 1953. Trans. Annette Lavers and Colin Smith. New York: Noonday, 1993.

Bayer, Gerd. "The Right Sort of Form for 'The Right Sort': David Mitchell's Tweet-Story." *The Epistolary Renaissance: A Critical Approach to Contemporary Letter Narratives in Anglophone Fiction*. Eds. Maria Löschnigg and Rebekka Schuh. Berlin: DeGruyter, 2018. 277–88.

---. "The Short Narrative Form in David Mitchell's *The Bone Clocks.*" *Constructing Coherence in the British Short Story Cycle.* Eds. Patrick Gill and Florian Kläger. New York: Routledge, 2018. 245–59.

Blanchot, Maurice. *The Book to Come.* 1959. Trans. Charlotte Mandell. Stanford: Stanford UP, 2002.

Cano, Christine M. *Proust's Deadline.* Urbana-Champaign: U of Illinois P, 2002.

Deleuze, Gilles, and Félix Guattari. *A Thousand Plateaus: Capitalism and Schizophrenia.* 1980. Trans. Brian Massumi. Minneapolis: U of Minnesota P, 1987.

Dillon, Sarah, ed. *David Mitchell: Critical Essays.* Canterbury: Gylphi, 2011.

Dillon, Sarah. "Introducing David Mitchell's Universe: A Twenty-First Century House of Fiction." *David Mitchell: Critical Essays.* Ed. Sarah Dillon. Canterbury: Gylphi, 2011. 3–23.

Edwards, Caroline. "'Strange Transactions': Utopia, Transmigration and Time in *Ghostwritten* and *Cloud Atlas.*" *David Mitchell: Critical Essays.* Ed. Sarah Dillon. Canterbury: Gylphi, 2011. 177–200.

Foucault, Michel. "What is an Author?" Trans. Josue v. Harari. *The Foucault Reader.* Ed. Paul Rabinow. New York: Pantheon, 1984. 101–20.

Frow, John. *Genre.* New York: Routledge, 2006.

Genette, Gérard. *Narrative Discourse: An Essay on Method.* Trans. Jane E. Lewin. 1979. Ithaca: Cornell UP, 1980.

---. *Palimpsests: Literature in the Second Degree.* Trans. Channa Newman and Claude Doubinsky. 1982. Lincoln: U of Nebraska P, 1997.

Hopf, Courtney. "The Stories We Tell: Discursive Identity Through Narrative Form in *Cloud Atlas.*" *David Mitchell: Critical Essays.* Ed. Sarah Dillon. Canterbury: Gylphi, 2011. 105–26.

Isekenmeier, Guido. "John Fowles's Neo-Victorianism in *The French Lieutenant's Woman.*" *Recollecting John Fowles / Wiedererinnerungen an John Fowles.* Eds. Guido Isekenmeier and Gerd Bayer. Münster: Lit, 2018. 83–111.

Jameson, Fredric. *Postmodernism, or, The Cultural Logic of Late Capitalism.* Durham: Duke UP, 1991.

Machinal, Hélène. "*Cloud Atlas*: From Postmodernity to the Posthuman." *David Mitchell: Critical Essays.* Ed. Sarah Dillon. Canterbury: Gylphi, 2011. 127–54.

Marshall, Nowell. "Beyond Queer Gothic: Charting the Gothic History of the Trans Subject in Beckford, Lewis, Byron." *TransGothic in Literature and Culture.* Ed. Jolene Zigarovich. New York: Routledge, 2018.

Mitchell, David. *The Bone Clocks.* London: Hodder and Stoughton, 2014.

---. *Cloud Atlas.* London: Hodder and Stoughton, 2004.

---. *Ghostwritten.* London: Hodder and Stoughton, 1999.

---. *number9dream.* London: Hodder and Stoughton, 2001.

---. *Slade House.* London: Sceptre, 2015.

---. *The Thousand Autumns of Jacob de Zoet.* London: Sceptre, 2010.

Nietzsche, Friedrich. *The Twilight of the Idols and the Anti-Christ.* Trans. R.J. Hollingdale. 1889. London: Penguin, 1990.

Ruffino, Paolo. "A Theory of Non-Existent Video Games: Semiotic and Video Game Theory." *Computer Games and New Media Cultures: A Handbook of Digital Games Studies.* Eds. Johannes Fromme and Alexander Unger. Berlin: Springer, 2012. 107–24.

Walker, Jonathan. "The Transtextuality of Transvestite Sainthood: or, How to Make the Gendered Form Fit the Generic Function." *Exemplaria: Medieval, Early Modern, Theory* 15.1 (2003): 73–110.

Chapter 6

Fragmentary writing and globalization in Ali Smith's *Hotel World*

Alicia J. Rouverol,
University of Manchester

In "Narrating Remainders: Spectral Presences in Ali Smith's Fictions," Stephen M. Levin claims that "[Ali] Smith invents a narrative form that emerges decidedly from the era of globalization" (36). Levin makes his charge in the context of an analysis of Smith's work as a critique of late capitalism, and examines Smith's writing, specifically *The Accidental* (2005) and *Hotel World* (2001), through the vantage point of spectrality, drawing on the work of Jacques Derrida's *Specters of Marx* (1994). Levin argues that Smith's breaking of continuity in narrative forms exemplifies the intrusion of spectral presences (38), offering the "potential to disrupt the dominant narratives of globalization," which manifests itself in "the dissolution of language" (43). In this article, I investigate Smith's narrative forms in *Hotel World* with the aim of isolating Smith's "inventiveness" to determine how these forms may be said to "emerge" from globalization. I consider her use of non-linear narratives and this "dissolution of language" not simply as breaks in narrative continuity but as illustrative of fragmentary writing – a vantage point from which her work is not generally explored. I argue that *Hotel World* features fragmentary writing in a variety of forms: in the novel's braided structure, in non-linear narrative excerpts juxtaposed in mosaic form, and in individual sentence and word fragments. As such, Smith's writing may be less an "invention" of narrative form than a carefully devised application of fragmentary writing as a strategy by which Smith articulates her perception of the impact of globalization.

Leslie Hill, in *Maurice Blanchot and Fragmentary Writing: A Change of Epoch*, notes that the "spectre of fragmentary writing, of the text as fragment and the fragment as text," has haunted literature over the past two hundred years (197). "Since the early nineteenth century," he writes, "the list of literature's fragmentary artists is at any event a long one: Schlegel, Hölderlin, Keats, Novalis, Coleridge, Büchner, Nietzsche, Mallarmé, Pound, Eliot, Kafka, Valéry, Proust, Musil, Artaud, Char, Bataille, Beckett, among many others" (1–2). As Blanchot recognizes, fragmentary writing can take many different forms (Hill 27): fragmentary work that is intentionally incomplete (Strathman 197); narratives that are braided, i.e. interwoven, in mosaic or bricolage form (as argued by Moseley in this volume); non-linear narratives; and fragments of text on the page, i.e., language that has been elided, broken or fractured. Hill posits that attention to the fragment is correlated to "break[s] in continuity" and "new episodes in cultural history," and that this kind of writing "bears witness to the trials and tribulations, birth-pangs as well as death-throes, of literary, historical, and cultural upheaval" (27) – to which I add, economic upheaval. Hill also suggests that much of the assessment of fragmentary work is framed negatively, in terms of "the continuity it interrupts, the unity it breaks" (2). By contrast, *Hotel World* offers ample critique of globalization (as it also critiques late capitalism),[1] yet Smith departs from Hill's decided norm by using fragmentary forms to express connectivity and cohesiveness of community, even within the constraints, challenges and ugliness of a globalized world. Thus Smith's use of fragmentary writing presents a counter-narrative of globalization that is more nuanced and more complex in its interpretation and stance than a wholesale critique of the effects of global capital. In my article, I will first consider the novel as a "novel of globalization," then isolate examples of the fragmentary (in structure, non-linear narratives and language) as illustrative of narratives that depict globalization, and I will conclude by examining the "relationality" between Smith's characters as indicative of her fictionalized vision of what it means to live in a globalized world.

Globalization and the "novel of globalization"

Globalization has been defined as "a transnational process in which diverse cultural flows are mediated by the exchange of goods, capital, people, information, knowledge and images" (Featherstone 1). Smith, described variably as a Scottish, lesbian and innovative author, is rarely re-

---

[1] For an excellent discussion of *Hotel World* as a critique of late capitalism, see Alissa G. Karl's "Things Break Apart." Karl's reading focuses on the use of language, especially word play, as it pertains to illustrations of global capital in the novel, in particular on the "body" as imperiled in the neoliberal state. She highlights the use of empty space to designate "unavailable language," but the emphasis is more on the narrative "breaking apart" and the language "slipping away" than on Smith's perception of globalization (81, 83).

garded as a writer depicting the contemporary experience of globalization. Yet her novels and stories demonstrate, among other contemporary themes like non-space and the supermodern, the daily effects of living in a globalized world. Marc Augé defines "the supermodern" as a form of modernity that produces "non-places," which in turn dominate contemporary culture: spaces that are passed through but not lived in, that are experienced transitionally (78, 109–11). "The passenger through non-place," Augé comments, "retrieves his identity only at Customs, at the tollbooth, at the check-out counter," and proposes that "[t]he space of non-place creates neither singular identity nor relations; only solitude, and similitude" (103). Such "non-places" frequently appear in Smith's work, especially in *Hotel World*, in which key transactions between characters – like Else, homeless outside the Global Hotel – occur in liminal settings. These meetings at once interrogate the experience of contemporary life and illustrate the transitional world that many of Smith's narrators inhabit. The transitional world Smith invokes in *Hotel World* is a world re-made through the impact of globalization; as such, the work is exemplary of a "novel of globalization."

The "novel of globalization" is frequently discussed alongside the "neoliberal novel," which, according to Emily Johansen and Alissa G. Karl, is "particularly attuned to the economic rationalities of its time" (203). Johansen and Karl see neoliberalism as constitutive of both economic dogma and political rationale over the past forty years, featuring an emphasis on privatization, curtailment of welfare, trade deregulation and weakening of organized labor (203). They define the "novel of globalization" as one that "reproduces the everyday realities of globalised life" (206), drawing their assessment from Suzanne Rohr and James Annesley. Rohr argues that the novel of globalization evinces "a fictional reality of disorientation, insecurity and imbalance within the bounds of a seemingly known and familiar world" (99), featuring the "tension between collapsing systems of order within the encompassing structures of global networks" (92). Annesley claims that the novel of globalization "involves not a simple process of measuring the accuracy of the representations, but an analysis of the ways in which it engages with the globalization debate" (113). My reading of the novel of globalization aligns closely with Annesley's, for *Hotel World* demonstrates measures of disorientation and insecurity in existing "structures of global networks" (e.g., the Global Hotel), alongside implied and stated critiques of the social and psychological costs of such global networks.[2]

---

[2] Annesley problematizes the term "globalization," recognizing the degree to which

Hotel World charts the stories of five individuals, each connected to the Global Hotel, set in one of its affiliate locations in an unidentified (Northern) British city – "any town," Smith's omniscient narrator announces in the final pages of the book (229), as if to suggest the ubiquity of capital mobility (Karl 79). Smith establishes themes of globalization and its discontents through key passages such as the one in which the homeless Else meets a Global Hotel staff member:

> Else can see her head and the side of her face, quite close to Else's own eye; up close in the light from the hotel the surface of the white of the woman's eye is pitted and unhealthy. Else braces herself. But the woman is not looking at Else at all; instead she is staring out across the road into space. The embroidered badge on the lapel of the uniform says, in browns and greens, *GLOBAL HOTELS*. Stitched in white on the breast pocket there are small words. The top half of the circle says: *all over the world*. The bottom half says: *we think the world of you*. (55–56)

Else's description of the woman's eye as "pitted and unhealthy" is an implied critique of the ill effects of the global hotel on worker health. Moreover, Else notices this "in the light from the hotel," which places the global chain as central to that condition. "I work in the Global," the woman says, announcing her traffic in the global economy and defining herself not by name but in relation to globalism (57). The embroidered GLOBAL HOTELS badge suggests a link between homelessness and globalization: the ironic tone of "*we think the world of you*" stitched on the breast pocket – in an exchange in which a representative of the Global Hotel reaches out to a homeless person – highlights the hypocrisy inherent in the idea that the hotel holds its clients in genuine esteem. Further, the remainder of the passage refers to the "little bits of broken glass and grit in the crease where the hotel wall and the pavement meet," indicating the inhospitable, liminal space in which these individuals interact (56). While the hotel worker proceeds to offer Else a room in the hotel, she initially is not looking at Else at all, but rather "staring out across the road into space," evoking Augé's concept of "non-places" and evincing the lack of "singular identity and relations" and the sense of "solitude ... and similitude" in the encounter. The passage shows Else's homelessness as illustrative of the "daily effects" of globalization, but also the concomitant sense of dislocation and disconnection accompanying the experience of being homeless on the door-

---

it is used to encompass wide-ranging phenomena (from mass migration and international brands, to tourism and trans-national media conglomerates); as such, the term can be overstretched (112). In this article, I emphasize economic forms of globalization, utilizing the term "globalization" alongside, sometimes synonymously with, "global capital."

step of the Global Hotel. Moreover, the predominance of global capital is illustrated spatially in the novel, when Else remarks that "[i]t's like the street exists just for the hotel to be there in it"; "up-lights spaced all along its front make it look rich, expensive and strange" (i.e., "strange," as in foreign or not belonging, evincing the problematics of its presence) (64). Else likens the hotel building to a face: "The awnings are the eyelids, the word GLOBAL scarred across them both" (64). Here, again, sight is used as a metaphor for global capital's scarring influence, conveying its capacity to negatively affect how we "see" (or perceive) and suggesting that globalization's impact is not merely economic and social but also psychological.

Fragmentary writing through braided narratives in *Hotel World*

Hotel World begins with the tragic incident in which Global Hotel employee Sara Wilby dies in a dumbwaiter accident, after accepting a £5 bet from a hotel co-worker. The novel's five narratives, told from five different points of view, feature, in turn, Sara (worker/ghost, recounting the accident); Else (homeless and panhandling outside the Global Hotel); Lise (Sara's co-worker); Penny (the journalist reviewing the hotel); and Clare (Sara's sister); with the final chapter featuring an omniscient narrator.[3] The chapters constitute a braided narrative, as they represent multiple narrative strands that eventually come together to illustrate crucial points in the novel. Each constituent chapter refers to the hotel and the character's relationship to it, placing the hotel – and by extension the global chain – as central to the novel's story.

Each narrative also points either centrally or obliquely to the inciting incident (Sara's accident), and in some instances, references are made to the coins or money (the latter found at the base of the dumbwaiter, where Sara fell), as if to imply that global capital cannot be separated from each narrator's experience (or body), evident in the death of this central character. For instance, Penny, who "works on the *World*" (169), comes to the aid of Sara's teenage sister Clare in loosening the door of the dumbwaiter shaft, where Clare seeks to locate her sister's place of death and to throw coins

---

[3] Typically referred to as a novel, *Hotel World* has been called a short story cycle by Valerie O'Riordan, who argues in "Traumatic Cycles" that the "gap or rupture between its constituent stories in the short story cycle is significant to its form," situating her study of trauma within it (181). O'Riordan envisions the collection effectively as a cycle of trauma narratives, linked to the inciting dumbwaiter accident. I would extend this argument further, to query whether the book's inciting traumatic "incident" may be the presence of the Global Hotel itself. See E. E. Smith for an insightful discussion of the multiple narration in the novel as a "democracy of voice" (84).

into the shaft to clock the exact length of time leading to her sister's death (142–54). "Out in the corridor," Penny notices, "there was money splayed over the carpet as if part of the carpet's design" (142). Coins feature throughout the novel, most prominently in Clare's narrative, where she recounts the events leading up to Sara's death, trying to learn precisely what happened to her sister in the Global Hotel. In this penultimate chapter, Smith weaves together Penny's and Clare's separate narratives, as Clare narrates the same hotel scene from her point of view. She describes how she was crying beside the lift shaft, when Penny brings her the Kleenex. "[S]he [Penny] said it looked like the wall was a giant slot machine & that I had hit the jackpot that kind of made me want to laugh because that was exactly what it looked like all that money had come spewing out of the wall or something" (203). Yet the wall (i.e., the "structure" of the hotel) remains a menacing force; for the screw holding the wood over the shaft "jutted out like white teeth in the mouth of the hole in the wall" (145), insinuating that the Global Hotel had swallowed Clare's sister. Here the novel's fragmentary form of braided narratives serves to highlight Smith's theme of the effects (costs) of globalization on daily life, heightening the fragility of individual lives in the "face" of ubiquitous, anonymous global capital.

Fragmentary writing and the language fragment

Critically, *Hotel World* opens with a fragment that serves to establish Smith's interest in, and perspectives on, globalization:

> Wooooooooo-
>   hooooooo what a fall what a soar what a plummet what a dash into dark
>   into light what a plunge what a glide thud crash what a drop what a rush
>   what a swoop what a fright what a mad hushed skirl what a smash mash
>   mash-up broke and gashed what a heart in my mouth what an end. (3)

The fragment features a typographic gap, with the text itself descending to the next line, as if to mirror Sara's fall in the dumbwaiter shaft; in turn, the gap is followed by a series of sentence fragments, with no punctuation or gaps, crammed together, or compressed, as if to demonstrate the speed of Sara's body in motion or the compression of that free fall.[4] The excerpt

---

[4] Here Smith seems to be paying homage to the incipit of Virginia Woolf's *Mrs Dalloway*, whose third paragraph opens with "What a lark! What a plunge!," as Mrs Dalloway is remembering how "she had burst open the French windows and plunged at Bourton into the open air" in her youth (1). In Mrs Dalloway's nostalgic memories, the prevailing emotion is one of elation and this is also what is deceptively conveyed in Smith's extract through the hypnotizing repetition of "what a." However, Smith's subversive rewriting of the modernist canon precisely consists in

does not directly address globalization or global capital, yet the novel focuses, as Levin has noted, "on subjects marginalized within the field of global culture" (43), with Smith's "semantic fragments … [evoking] a sense of dislocation associated with subalternity" (44). Launching the novel with a fragment illustrating a young woman worker's death in a global hotel chain clearly establishes this problematic. Levin rightly argues that the ghost represents an "arrival" of "the other" that disrupts dominant globalization narratives (43). "Lost in purgatorial space between worlds," Sara fades in and out of language (Levin 43), as such, "haunting" a symbolic "non-place" of global capital. Thus Sara's language fragments demarcate the degree to which she is outside dominant culture or the culture of the global.

If displacement outside the dominant/global culture represents a subtheme of the novel, the sentence fragments in Else's chapter characterize this narrator's dislocation and marginal role, camped out in front of the Global Hotel, another liminal space. There, homeless Else suffers from a persistent cough (suggesting illness as another cost of globalization). In her interior monologue, Else responds to the comments she receives from passers-by, who critique Else for her homelessness and joblessness:

> To stop herself shaking, to stop herself thinking of it, she thinks of them instead, all the gd jb secretaries over time, row after row of
> (Spr sm
> (pause to cough
> too long, person's gone)
> ch?)
> shorthanders, 100-word-per minuters. Think of them nearly filleting the words, and their wastepaper baskets overflowing with the thrown-away i's and o's and u's and e's and a's. But they're all redundant now, she thinks, all those scrtries. They're history. (46–47)

Here fragmentary writing serves multiple purposes. Else pauses for the immediate task at hand – to secure change from passers-by – but the fragments also foreground her physical challenge, the cough we presume she has developed while living on the streets. The language itself is a fragment. Elsewhere in the novel, words are elided; here individual letters are erased. Smith has dropped vowels and consonants in Else's dialogue, resulting in clipped language. The elided letters find their way into Else's thoughts: the "gd jb secretar[y]" has "thrown-away" her own letters. References to being "redundant now" and "overflowing waste basket" suggest that people living as Else does are themselves "redundant," just as the

---

conveying a sensation of exhilaration through the fast rhythm and the repetitions, when she is actually referring to a death.

secretaries (spelled "scrtries") are now "history." The discarding of letters epitomizes the fact that women on the street like Else have themselves been discarded. Such excerpts bolster Levin's argument that in *Hotel World* Smith offers a focused "indictment" of the legacy of Adam Smith and an "exploration of both the economic and epistemic cruelty of late capitalism" (36). Else herself, in a self-reflexive moment, "imagines the pavement littered with the letters that fall out of the half-words she uses (she doesn't need the whole words)" (47). According to Karl, Else's language and body "diminish in accordance with her irrelevance in capitalist labor and consumer markets, her body persists in and through its illness and the social and economic marginalization that is its purported cause" (81). The shorthand language offers a shorthand to Else's own circumstances. Referring to the secretaries, Else reflects, "They're probably on the street now, the scs, doing the same day's work Else does" (47). The abbreviated words illustrate how Else – and women like her – have been "abbreviated" or eclipsed by the globalized world.

Fragmentary forms: non-linear narratives and the mosaic chapter

The focus on globalization through the fragmentary is more explicit in Lise's chapter, "Future Conditional," where Smith uses non-linear narrative forms. The narrative comprises a series of fragments – from the bureaucratic questionnaire Lise is completing about her undiagnosed illness, to the brief clips describing her night's work at the hotel. Lise's physician has charged her to make a note of her symptoms, while the government health form, "Incapacity for Work Questionnaire," requires filling in (86). Additionally, Lise's poet-mother Deirdre, writing a poem titled "Hotel World," has urged her daughter to "write down the things [she] can remember" (94) about the hotel. The resulting chapter forms a mosaic, initially of Lise's free indirect discourse, followed by the fragmented responses to the form and lastly Lise's re-constructions of her work life for her mother's project. Collectively, these fragments draw attention to the dislocating or disorienting aspects of globalization and the degree to which the "illness" Lise is experiencing may be rooted in something more systemic and problematic than a physical condition. Here the fragmentary is exemplified in form, rather than exclusively through language, as Lise moves from narrating fragments that describe, variably, the musak played in the hotel lobby and staff badges, to the "Global Hotel" lingo, alongside frequent references to clock time.[5]

---

[5] Smith uses literary time-elements in the work to express her concerns about the effects of capitalism and globalization on individual lives. Tense names for chapter

The chapter begins with Lise, in bed, responding to the questionnaire's request: "Tell us about yourself" (81). Faced with the task of articulating her identity, Lise struggles for the language to do so: "I am a (   ) person" (85). But the language has devolved over several pages; four pages earlier, she has written, "I am a nice person," then "I am a sick person" (81). Now Lise leaves a gap in the text, experiencing a failure of language or discomfort in naming precisely her circumstances. Karl argues that the "use of empty space to designate language that is unavailable recalls the dilemmas of the dead chambermaid and ill homeless woman who quite literally lose self-representation when they are extraneous to capital's norms" (81). Jean-Luc Nancy writes in "Elliptical Sense" of what has been left out, or what I call the "unnarrated," and how it underscores constitutive meaning: "the text says or it writes or it ellipses something else as well, something we cannot know. It lets us know that we are truly missing something" (186). What is missing cannot be named, it seems. This unnaming is featured also in one of the non-linear fragments Lise narrates about her work at the hotel; each of the fragments begins with an excerpt of text, usually an action, in bold, followed by an elaboration on that event:

> **Thanks, Duncan, Lise says:** Most of the Global staff at this branch, at least those who were working here then, are protective of Duncan and his habits.... Everybody who works there knows Duncan saw what happened, he heard it, he was on the top floor with Sara Wilby when she did it. Newer staff members tell each other in low voices that he should leave or be asked to leave. They discuss the rumour that he refused compensatory redundancy. They discuss what it must have been like, to be there. They discuss suicide.... They implicate Duncan....
>
> **She puts her finger in her mouth:** The body's logical urge towards natural antiseptic.
>
> **The finger is reddened:** The local inflammatory response of the body's coagulation system.
>
> **She walks across the room with brisk purpose:** In six month's time, Lise will be incapable of walking across a room with brisk purpose. She will be almost incapable of walking across a room.... (106–07)

Duncan, it would seem, is the hotel worker who offered Sara the £5 note as the dare. Elsewhere in the book he remains unnamed; here the incident

---

titles announce each chapter's time frame within the book. Implicit in this is a kind of interrogation of "capitalist time," suggesting capitalism's inherit time-construct and, further, implying the question of where we are within the trajectory of global capitalism (Rouverol 322). Lise's frequent references to clock time, specifically her charting a four-minute stretch of time at the reception desk, show the degree of time regimen she and other global hotel workers face (Karl 82). Such non-linear fragments illustrate more broadly the sense of time/work-time as shaped by capitalism.

itself is unnamed, perhaps because even the other hotel workers do not hold him fully to blame. Lise's sore finger is linked to the pinprick received from throwing her badge in the trash (an indictment of its own), several minutes earlier, but also implies her unidentified illness. After writing these excerpts, the events will become, the narrator notes, unremembered: "Light and fevered, Lise's world spun; in its spinning the names of all its places were loosened and jettisoned off the sides of it, leaving seas and countries nothing but blanks, outlines waiting to be rediscovered and renamed, their longitudes and latitudes stretched and limp as done elastic" (119). Lise's work life has been parsed in this chapter, stripped down to its bare components; language itself seems to have "loosened." This "loosening" of language, "leaving seas and countries nothing but blanks" – surely a metaphor for the global – illustrates the ways in which language and its parts have broken down, mirroring too the stripping away of Lise's parts as a worker in the global hotel economy now that she is no longer able to participate in it fully. The non-linear fragments themselves serve a thematic component in this chapter, as they become representative of what Lise is leaving behind. Moreover, she too – like the Global Hotel's "Left Behind Room," which houses random objects forgotten by the guests – will become "left behind" as someone too ill to engage in the global economy.

Fragmentary writing, gaps and connectivity

Thus far my analysis might suggest, as Hill forewarns, that fragmentary writing focuses exclusively on the negative, the discontinuities or lack of unity in the text, and in this case, as reflective of the problematics of living in a globalized world. Smith's particular invocation of the fragmentary belies this concern, however, for fragmentary writing also serves to illustrate connectivity and community in the novel as a strategy to counter the stultifying impact of globalization. Levin argues for the stance of "radical hospitality" in *Hotel World*, "as an 'event' that creates the conditions for new modes of attachment and love" (46); and that "an unexpected visitation [Sara] unravels the synchronic time of globalization and, at least potentially, 're-worlds' the global through acts of love and hospitality" (47). Yet these reparations are not reflected simply in the characters' actions but through Smith's implementation of fragmentary writing to highlight these interactions. One such act of reparation is apparent in Clare's chapter. Once again, the fragmentary takes the form of elision, if for a different purpose. Clare's narrative features a stream of consciousness in which key words are dropped, paralleling Clare's moments of extreme grief over the loss of her sister:

it was weird because usually she never told me anything she never usually said anything to me about anything & then after that it was on the Monday night after that that was the Monday night she never came home when she was supposed to she never came   every night ever since then since that night it has been the bits of her coming at me ... (186–87)

As in Sara's opening narrative, Clare's words tumble out, not to illustrate the speed of a fall, but rather the intensity of her emotional state. Yet the constitutive meaning remains, as Nancy has suggested, since "home" is strongly implied to be the missing word, and Clare's incapacity to say it merely underscores its meaning and hence the depth of her loss. Here the gap serves to connect Clare to her emotional center rather than take her further from it; in this sense, Smith's use of fragmentation not only sustains meaning but establishes it. With "bits of her coming at me," Clare references her sister's graphic death at the bottom of the lift-shaft. In a following excerpt, Clare extends this bodily concern and fixates on the literal presence of her sister's skin:

maybe it came off you Sara it is possible like when your skin peels off in summer maybe I have some of her skin from spring 1999 in the top drawer God   fuck sake one minute there is   & the next you are   you were just flakes of whatever   stuff   that you can't even see properly   God   now all of the chest of drawers is mine ... (191–92)

Gaps of this kind riddle Clare's narrative, illustrating the sense of dissociation and dislocation that parallels the novel's broader themes of the psychological costs of globalization. The elided words here represent Clare's attempts to understand what cannot be easily comprehended – loss. But the recollections, even with their inherent gaps in language, still enable Clare to manifest her relationship and deep attachment to her sister. Clare's closely focalized monolog shifts into sentence fragments ("& since") in which she recounts memories of their childhood and her sister's (brief) swim career, with the fragments evolving into a more direct discourse with Sara that names her:

& since in the end when you went ... still listen Sara even though you couldn't even though you couldn't move couldn't do anything about it listen to me you were fast you were really really fast I know because I went there to see tonight I was there & you were so fast I still can't believe how fast you were less than four seconds just under four three & a bit that's all you took I know I counted for you (220–21)

Here the braided threads of Penny's and Clare's narratives join as Clare references the timing of her sister's death; and Clare secures a connection to her deceased sister, the ghost who began the novel. The words "I counted for you" indicate a thematic shift for Smith, positing the importance of "relationality" to this novel of globalization.

In her exploration of Christian Moraru's concept of "relationality," Alison Gibbons posits that it "signifies our human connectedness in the globalizing world and consequently our ethical obligations to each other" (31). Obligation and connectedness in the novel are realized through key scenes in which characters engage, unexpectedly, in liminal spaces, such as when Lise, on the street in front of the Global Hotel, offers homeless Else a room. Yet, as E. E. Smith notes, *Hotel World*'s "comment upon the *social* structures of the hotel world is played out [also] through the markedly innovative *narrative* structure of its textual world" (82). This refers at once to the braided narrative structure, which E. E. Smith suggests features a form of "communal narration," but equally to the social structures/social relations that play out in the book. The novel's final chapter, "Present," begins with the word fragment, "Morning," isolated on the first line and repeated throughout this chapter, as the omniscient narrator references community members, one by one, going about their day, dimensions of community nonetheless existent (and thriving) in the face of globalization: "Morning. The lady who cleans the steps every morning, and the paving outside with the word *Global* tiled into it.... The checkout girls who work in the supermarket.... The people who bought prescriptions in Boots..." (231). Levin comments that "[a]pparitions intermingle in the spaces around Global Hotel with café owners and passers-by queuing at *Boots* pharmacy," illustrating Smith's uniting of the living with the dead (47). But, more importantly, the narrator's reflections effectively bring relationality into the novel's liminal spaces or Augé's "non-places." As such, the "intermingling" evokes the sense that the "non-places" of globalization have been, in some sense, if not redeemed, at least humanized.

The shift toward relationality is represented as well in the fragments that close the book, reiterating Sara's adage, "remember you must live/remember you most love/remainder you mist leaf" (237), indicating the crucial significance of connection to the other. This excerpt comes immediately after Clare's narrative, with the words centered in the middle of the page, one word per line with each sentence written in smaller print, as though announcing a progressive erasure. Indeed, the next page is almost blank and the consecutive ones are blank. This erasure could suggest the irrelevance of language or its incapacity to communicate effectively, but I would posit the opposite. The "remember .../ remember .../remainder ..." text serves as a coda for the novel while also echoing Sara's narrative (30). The first mention of this text concludes Sara's chapter: "Time me, would you?/You. Yes, you. It's you I'm talking to" (31). Presumably, Sara is addressing her sister with the charge that will drive Clare's decision to time, however retroactively, Sara's fall to her death. The absence of any text after the coda suggests that Sara's appeal has been resolved by the end of Clare's narrative. Beyond the typographical nuance, the language itself shape-shifts in this segment in ways that elucidate Smith's theme of connection. "Remainder" means a quantity or part left over, as well as a part that remains to come. Placed at the novel's ending, this excerpt illustrates how language, even in the face of potential erasure, remains a presence, if somewhat altered. "Leaf" can be defined as putting out new leaves – illustrating growth. The language evinces that Clare's apparent resolution with her sister's death – coupled with the imperative "remember to love" – links love and connection with growth. The focus on connection to others in the text allows a new interpretation of the novel's final fragment (in new typographic form). Like the "remember .../ remember .../remainder ..." text, the final fragment echoes an earlier reference to the novel's opening (3), this time offering instead a celebratory or joyful sound/falling:

WOoooo-
   hooooooo
      oo
       o (238)

In *Hotel World* Smith defies the notion of a totalizing experience of globalization, for the novel evades a simplistic vision of what it means to live in a globalized world. By making her points through fragmentation of the text, Smith shows how language remains an essential tool for challenging more confined perceptions of complex cultural and economic concepts like globalization. Her narrators, and indeed her novels, succeed at least in part by breaking through such categorizations, just as her language breaks with conventional norms, using fragmentation as a central strategy. In Sara's opening narration from the grave, she says: "Lost, I've, the word. The word for you. You know. I don't mean a house. I don't mean a room. I mean the way of the   . Dead to the   . Out of this   . Word" (30). Smith drops the "l" and in so doing she connects the "word" with the "world." Levin recognizes the proximity of "word" and "world" in this sentence, but takes his analysis in a different direction, seeing them as "separated by an irreducible gap" (44), whereas I see language as bridging the gap. That connection is made possible by Smith's use of the fragmentary. Ian James, analyzing Nancy's writing on the fragmentary, comments that the "experience of fragmentation not only makes demands on thought and on the writing of philosophy, it also makes ethical and pragmatic demands on us, and calls for a certain kind of decision or response on our part, as readers of philosophy and as participants in a shared world existence" (2). Similarly, Smith's fragmentary writing, depicting the life globalized in *Hotel World*, calls upon us to locate a "shared world existence" in the interstices of globalization.

Works Cited

Annesley, James. "Market Corrections: Jonathan Franzen and the 'Novel of Globalization.'" *Journal of Modern Literature* 29.2 (2006): 111–28.

Augé, Marc. *Non-Places: Introduction to an Anthropology of Supermodernity.* Trans. John Howe. 1992. London: Verso, 1995.

Featherstone, Mike. Introduction. *Global Culture: Nationalism, Globalization and Modernity.* London: Sage, 1990. 1–14.

Gibbons, Alison. "'Take That You Intellectuals!' and 'KaPOW!': Adam Thirlwell and the Metamodernist Future of Style." *Studia Neophilologica* 87.1 (2015): 29–43, https://doi.org/10.1080/00393274.2014.981959. Accessed 26 Sept. 2017.

Hill, Leslie. *Maurice Blanchot and Fragmentary Writing: A Change of Epoch.* London: Bloomsbury, 2012.

James, Ian. *The Fragmentary Demand: An Introduction to the Philosophy of Jean-Luc Nancy.* Stanford: Stanford UP, 2006.

Johansen, Emily, and Alissa G. Karl. "Introduction: Reading and Writing the Economic Present." *Textual Practice* 29.2 (2015): 201–14.

Karl, Alissa G. "Things Break Apart: James Kelman, Ali Smith and the Neoliberal Novel." *Reading Capitalist Realism.* Eds. Alison Shonkwiler and Leigh Claire La Berge. Iowa City: U of Iowa P, 2014. 64–88.

Levin, Stephen M. "Narrating Remainders: Spectral Presences in Ali Smith's Fictions." *Ali Smith: Contemporary Critical Perspectives.* Eds. Monica Germanà and Emily Horton. London: Bloomsbury Academic, 2013. 35–47.

Nancy, Jean-Luc. "Elliptical Sense." *Research in Phenomenology* 18.1 (1988): 175–90.

O'Riordan, Valerie. "Traumatic Cycles: Ali Smith and A. L. Kennedy." *Constructing Coherence in the British Short Story Cycle.* Eds. Patrick Gill and Florian Kläger. London: Routledge, 2018. 181–99.

Rohr, Suzanne. "'The Tyranny of the Probable': Crackpot Realism and Jonathan Franzen's *The Corrections.*" *Amerikastudien/American Studies* 49.1 (2004): 91–105.

Rouverol, Alicia J. "The Narrative Now: A Study of the Use of Time in Ali Smith's *The Accidental* and Jennifer Egan's *A Visit from the Goon Squad.*" Thesis. University of Manchester, 2017.

Smith, Ali. *Hotel World.* London: Penguin, 2002.

Smith, E. E. "'A Democracy of Voice?' Narrating Community in Ali Smith's *Hotel World.*" *Contemporary Women's Writing* 4.2 (2010): 81–99.

Strathman, Christopher A. *Romantic Poetry and the Fragmentary Imperative: Schlegel, Byron, Joyce, Blanchot.* Albany: SUNY Press, 2006.

Woolf, Virginia. *Mrs Dalloway.* 1925. London: Penguin, 2012.

Chapter 7

Lives, etc.: fragments of lives in short stories by Julian Barnes

Teresa Bruś,
University of Wrocław

> And was it, in any case, a necessary truth: in order to be a writer, you needed in some sense to decline life?
>
> Julian Barnes, *Cross Channel*

> It is the art of the short expectation of life.
>
> V. S. Pritchett

In his short stories, Julian Barnes is a master of "aggregative" forms of evaluation of life, especially of the knowable and tellable episodes from the lives of others. He is the sympathetic fragmentist allowing, within the fictional and disciplining integrity of the short story, concise though loosening fragmentals, non-fictional expressions intercrossing meanings of lived and imagined lives. These microscopic life stories are often his versions of biography. In this paper, I propose to consider the commitment to fragments of life scripts in Barnes's short stories. I will refer to Barnes's interest not in narrative coalescence but in calculated episodes, in a refreshed sense of *bios* that is episode-based.

A condition of experience, form captures diverse modalities, embraces specific categories, and naturalizes others. Thinking of "broken" forms – for such is the etymology of fragment – we think of "small pieces or parts," of a "remainder of otherwise lost or destroyed whole," of an "unfinished portion of writing or work of art" (*fragmentum* is "a part broken off") ("Fragment"). Such forms as blog posts, text messages, and sketches, modernist fragments, footnotes, aphorisms, free-floating gestures, episodes, dribbles, drabbles, nano tales, brief appearances which in life-writing glossaries sometimes are identified as compressed fragments (cameos, profiles, portraits in miniature or *historiettes*, and most recently microbiofiction) are composite constructs reflecting often contradictory meanings. Their prominence speaks to the immediacy of the age in which they were created but also relationships of "minimal scale to maximal intensity" (Botha 201). In *Essayism* (2017), Brian Dillon reflects on the power of tensions and disparities activated by accelerated pieces: "'Fragment' gives us 'fragmental' and 'fragmentals': geological terms for rocks and shales that are heterogeneous, composed of more than one substance." Fragments, notes Dillon, engage in traffic "between identity and dispersal, between formal, almost physical integrity and a fracturing or even pulverizing action" (68). In a modern short story, aesthetic hybridity merges with a crushing sense of immediacy and immanence. V. S. Pritchett is of the opinion that the agglomerative nature of contemporary forms like the short story

> owes much to the quickness, the objectivity and cutting of the cinema; it owes much to the poet on the one hand and the newspaper reporter on the other; something also to the dramatic compression of the theatre, and everything to the restlessness, the alert nerve, the scientific eye and the short breath of contemporary life. (123)

Barnes, as I will show, is attracted to such a conglomerate power of the fragment. It is what life declines into, the endless seizing and starting, informed by the acute awareness of the existence of broken pieces needing to speak to other pieces in constructed arrays that are irresistibly attracting.

The attraction resides in the reduced, minimal nature of fragments. Some of us may say that fragments tend to be small "in execution" or small "in vision" (Campbell 17). Edgar Allan Poe feared that in very careful handling they might "degenerate into epigrammatism" (4). "Minimal," however, may suggest a certain degree of indirectness or instability achieved through crafty narrative tactics resisting amplification because large story arcs have been eschewed (Campbell 17). Evasive, they may leave an enduring impression. Minimal, indirect, often nebulous particularities, tiny fragments are what Jean-Luc Nancy and Philippe Lacoue-Labarthe refer to as sub-work – only a small, detached piece (unlike the plural and complete super-work of the literary absolute) yet with the potential to decompose the very coherence of form (44). Deliberate fragmentalists are alert to such unvalued, dispersing elements and the relations of looseness and informality they activate, the "hiatuses and stoppages" (Lee, *Virginia* 18) they sustain, and the holes they cover. In the context of life-stories, what makes *bios* come alive is the literary practice that defends change and irreverence in form and content, struggling, nevertheless, to arrive at some resolution, some intelligible tying and ending. Relying on fragments, Barnes, the apologist of the essay and the short story, builds tense textual relations which are dialectical in their navigation between the sub-layer of design and super-layers of crisp particulars. Such relations "advancing by the simultaneous struggle and agreement between fragments," depend on the tense "struggle and disparities between the parts" (Dillon 73). By fusing quintessentially essayistic impulses with the exacting framework of the short story, Barnes creates in sharp viable fragments compelling glimpses of ways of life.

In his fiction and non-fiction Barnes demonstrates an attraction to large-scale subjects; he submits their past experiences in episodes and particularities, changing the internal temporal scale of the stories. Their selves are accessed through fragments; many characters we encounter not in their totality but as minimal selves. Philosopher Galen Strawson defines minimal subjects as "portions of live subjectivity" (254): minimal selves are not complete imperial subjects but rather a sequence of momentary conditions, a state of potential agency. According to Strawson, a minimal self is a unit of "metaphysics of awareness" or "metaphysics of consciousness" (262). It is a part of living subjectivity activated especially in moments of resistance or in "the unnoticed gaps in the experience of an ordinary human being during the normal waking day." Such an experience "involves the existence of many thin or minimal subjects" (10.6). Living moments of experience generate energy, sudden up-currents, surges alimented by minimal selves. In a story called "Pulse," Barnes identifies "stepping outside in the morning and sniffing the air" as the context for the figuration of a pulse (*Pulse* 202). In this story, we hear from The Father character that there is "the pulse of the heart, the pulse of the blood" but there are also other pulses. When they are checked, energy rises (211). The pulse here is the cipher for a feeling of what we may refer to as the minimal sublime, unexpectedly increasing pleasure by alerting the reader to the awareness of the presence of life. Perhaps such a diminutive form of the sublime is, as Botha argues, "the most radical pole of smallness, shortness and brevity in contemplating disappearance, absence, nothingness and the void," and perhaps "it informs an aesthetic movement towards the infinitesimal" (208). For a death-fearing character, a thanatophobe really, only such singular pulses can capture the antipodes of pleasure.

Reading *Levels of Life* (2013), Barnes's latest essay-story-memoir composite, made me think about biography and its evolving functions. In the first part of this extraordinary narrative (called "The Sin of Height"), Barnes brings into very sharp focus the liberating aeronautic experiences and extraordinary aerostatic photographs of Nadar (whose real name is Gaspard-Félix Tournachon). Nadar was the first to combine photography and

aeronautics, allowing him to experience, as Barnes says, "the silent im-
mensities of welcoming and beneficent space, where man cannot be
reached by any human force or by any power of evil, and where he feels
himself live as if for the first time" (*Levels* 13). The thrill was documented
in his pioneering photographs. Barnes animates Nadar's advances believ-
ing that they "allowed us to look at ourselves better, with increasing truth"
(*Levels* 26).

Nadar's *historiette* provides an account of the famous photographer's
passionate balloon explorations. In his unreliable autobiography *When I
Was a Photographer*, Nadar crafts the aura of his adventure around his
"great cause" of aerial navigation. In his narrative, it is around the point of
balloon ethics – the bourgeois creed of individual action, effort and risk –
that Nadar invents himself. With a great deal of sympathy for the character,
in a gesture of friendship that Richard Holmes's defining biography nicely
identified as "a handshake across time," Barnes constructs an affective
map of pulses defining Nadar's *idée fixe* not to confront Nadar with some
new determinations but to resolve Barnes's own realization, much needed
after the shattering experience of the death of his wife of 29 years. Grafting
the story of Nadar's love life onto his grief Barnes does more than perform
a historical animation. By opting for a knowable and tellable referential
character, he performs "the miraculous trickery of art." Writers, after all,
"believe in the patterns their words make, which they hope and trust add
up to ideas, to stories, to truths. This is always their salvation, whether
griefless or griefstruck" (*Levels* 85–86). Fragments of Nadar's singular experience penetrate Barnes's struggle with fractured life, intercrossing its sta-
sis to release some force, some "soaring" he knew was "the basis for fiction" (*Nothing* 244).

Indeed, Barnes's grafting pattern proves fertile. It assures the biodiversity
of an autobiographical narrative, expanding memoir conventions. Nadar's
balloonatic episodes are chosen to evoke a way of apprehending a life, a
way that in Barnes's writing is often dependent on parallel directions and a
way that sees enormous value in resonant interlopers – temporal, emotional, and discursive. Building a pattern towards some coherence if not
spatial resolution, Barnes foregrounds the pulsating minimal self, a self
full of the "dancingness" defining his essayistic subjects. But the inclusion
of Nadar's passionate adventures injects other properties. Losing his wife,
Barnes says he lost "shared ... tropes, teases, short cuts, injokes, sillinesses,
faux rebukes, amatory footnotes" (*Levels* 88). The substantial, self-
conscious list of fragments alerts to the desire to talk, to converse. And the
dialog form sustains a list. Schlegel explained it in the following terms:

A dialogue is a chain or garland of fragments. An exchange of letters is a dialogue on a larger scale, and memoirs constitute a system of fragments. But
as yet no genre exists that is fragmentary both in form and content, simultaneously completely subjective and individual, and completely objective
and like a necessary part in a system of all sciences. (qtd. in Dillon 70)

Barnes seems to be finding some compensation for the loss of that linguistic level in grafts from a narrative of marital intimacy as Nadar rendered it, a narrative abounding in nurturing references.

Hermione Lee, with whom Barnes shares a passion for life stories and a
weariness with the certainties of biography, objects to the all-knowing,
firm and "smoothing biographical process." (*Body* 3) Like Barnes, the ami-
cable inventor and assiduous researcher, Lee cherishes small anecdotes
and little details: "We all want stories and details and particulars in our
life-stories" (*Body* 2). Mapping the changing rhythms of biography in recent years, Lee – in a revealingly titled volume *Body Parts* – argues that
biography has "always directed us to the figure of a real person in all his or
her particularity, accidentalness and actuality" (4). After the life of a person has ended, what is left are relics, legends, fragments, parts, bits, and
gaps. For Lee writing a life is about piecing together, "making up," "making
over." It is about producing "versionings" of other people's lives (29).
Barnes in "Tunnel," a short story I am going to refer to later, suggests that
writing lives is based on "knowing and not knowing, on the fruitful mispri-
sion, the partial discovery and the resonant fragment" (*Cross* 206). He
invests a great deal of attention in various bits and pieces which create
multiple and opposing centers of meaning. Constructing lives, he is just as
concerned about "everything that got away, that fled with the last death-
bed exhalation of the biographee" (*Flaubert's* 38).

Leaning towards composite auto/biographical modes of writing, Barnes
is interested in staging life meaning, in seeing significance in experience
without imposing a false sense of unity. He infiltrates robust biographical
shards into the contents of his composite narratives, both non-fictional
and fictional. At the same time, he is interested in what completes life in a
final way. He is interested in death, boldly. His nosiness about it is fruitfully
satisfied by his fascination with biographical details. Biographies "are
death-haunted in the very literal sense that every page you turn takes you
closer to the end," closer to the final meaning of life. At the same time no
biography "can hope to avoid the relentless process of being superseded,
outmoded, and eventually forgotten – a form of auto-destruction which
has no equivalent in the novel" (Begley C8). Barnes's readers encounter his
mature connoisseurs and elderly characters who relate intensely to a life's
work and a need for some intelligibility. This great brooder on death de-

nies finality to any meaning. We try to seize the lives of people and yet, as Barnes says in a famous passage in *Flaubert's Parrot*, "a causal detail shifts everything" (90). It is those small details, resonant fragments, he notes, that we always need to watch. A "very, very tiny fragment" remaining from a body of "the total evidence that was there during the lifetime of most of humanity" is all we have, says Barnes (qtd. in Guignery 53). Lee, too, quoting Henry James, suggests that what is retained after life ends we should see not in terms of "a few estimated and cherished things" but something like a "swarm of possibilities," something that always stands "nebulously" (2), inviting re-consideration. Barnes is inclined to direct his attention to local connections and, like the character in his story "Tunnel," he is apprehensive about the overall structure of things (194). He likes to distill events into experiences and identify thin selves behind them, hint at the presence of minimal selves. Enormous perspectives silence us; they are "mute and muting" – "the bigger the matter, the less there is to say" (*Pulse* 222).

Considering Barnes's intriguing ways of infiltrating fragments of the lives of others in short stories such as those collected in *Cross Channel* (1996), *The Lemon Table* (2004), and *Pulse* (2011), we cannot fail to detect a certain pull towards experientially live subjects and towards their last days of life. Barnes's short stories are populated by the elderly with a strong sense of an ending, characters who are getting more sensitive with age, more resistant to accepting the inevitability of closure. It is the "imminence of the end" that according to Susan Lohafer marks the short story as genre. We recognize and process the short story always against "closural markers," through "putative stories" offering a sense of pre-closure. The short story handles time in a distinctive manner – Lohafer says that it is "end-directed." An end is always in sight. It represents time synoptically: "time with a period after it." Its time is *Kairos*: "a span of time with internal grounds for closure." *Chronos*, linear time "[w]ith dots before it and after it" (147), is tied to life-writing which always tries to retrieve the past experience from a present perspective. Barnes in his handling of death, of the possibility of resolution and meaning, leans on fiction.

Barnes's story fragments are agents of delaying closure-referencing. Fragments figured as pulses or pressures are diverse interlopers from the temporal, auditory, discursive realms. In *Cross Channel* they may be incomplete sounds of melodies ("broke like biscuit" ["Interference," *Cross* 20]); bits of history ("Junction," *Cross*); fragments of memories and shattered life after a beloved brother's death ("Experience," *Cross*); brief encounters with the Surrealist group – a "mere appendix" recorded among "preface, introduction, text, appendices, footnotes to text, footnotes to appendices, footnotes to footnotes" ("Experiment," *Cross* 61). Barnes notes the pulses and their pressures in often parallel short surges. Speaking of *Pulse*, Peter Childs says that they "resonate with a sense of different pulses: the rhythmical throbbing of the heart, a short burst of sound, or a musical beat." These are a kind of "an intimation of life and the measured pace of continuing living" (110). There are also rhythms of horticultural or "viticultural cycles" (*Cross* 185). Conscious living, like measured rhythms, is marked by rhythms of remembering and forgetting; it is sometimes like digging: "you toiled and you lifted, and each year's double-spitting brought something different to the surface... So you only uncovered that Guinness shard, filter-tip, bottle top and ribbed condom at the expense of digging in other stuff from previous years" (*Cross* 209). In his stories we bump into these figurations of the pulse; they produce a peripheral resistance, a sense of resistance to closure. They compensate for anxiety and fill in the gaps. Structurally, appearing suddenly, such palpable dispersed pulses, I think, subvert the short story's inherent determinations.

"Tunnel" in *Cross Channel* is a "retrospectively imagined" story in which "a gatherer and sifter of memories: his memories, history's memories" airs old scripts on a train crossing the English Channel (210). The gatherer and sifter is an elderly Englishman on a train to France, having traveled there on many previous occasions, having written many stories before. The stories in this volume are connected. We hear motifs taken from all of them and reworked into the final narrative. The character in "Tunnel" is conscious about the changes the Eurostar has brought, speculating about the diminishing distance between London and Paris, of the lightness of travel requiring only a plastic ID. Most of all, he is conscious about his old age – a stage of arrival at a final narrative form of life. Moving across the countryside, he is thinking of life: "Young, middle-aged, elderly, old, dead: this was how life was conjugated." This is followed by the realization that life is a noun and therefore should not be conjugated but declined: "Yes, that was better in any case, life *declined*" (194). Yet even though it did, thanks to progress in medicine "there was a lot of being old to look forward to" (194). So this declining character, "anecdotic, memorialist, rambly" (194), thinking about life is also imagining (wrongly) lives for his immediate compartment neighbors in the train. He is constructing some French counterpart of himself (208). The train ride produces a train of thoughts about the lives of others, about life's work and thoughts about the inevitable twists of memory. Not able to verify his versions with the travel companions, he tries to remember or retrospectively imagine how it was that travel companions in the past became acquaintances for the duration of the journey. He misses those spontaneous sub-plots and anecdotes; he misses resonant incidents. Tunneling "the private darkness of his past,"

(200) like a Wordsworthian thinker, he does not chat but recollects vulgar, banal episodes from previous train journeys. During this train ride, his mind is drawn back to a few compressed and chaotically retrieved anecdotes, also to thoughts of absent stories about his grandfather, who died in the war. Finally, our "old man lumpy and misshapen with memories," acknowledging the inevitability of loss and deletion, also the "cancerous growth" (210) of some memories, arrives at Gare du Nord, bidding farewell to his inexact memories, "life refused, life not fully grasped" (194).

The English traveler is a writer, a surrogate for the elderly Barnes; he does not think passing memories and grafting them onto others to perceive his own life story is a shameful act. "Put[ting] together ... things that have not been put together before" changes lives, Barnes notes (*Levels* 3). It also changes art. Feeling the pulse, Barnes connects fiction in which we model *how* we know, with life-writing in which we save *what* we know. The result constitutes a curious species of life-writing. A way to resist the decline of life, Barnes intuits, is to locate the sites of these pulses, feel them and, possibly, apprehend a "contended decline" (*Pulse* 202) – as Nadar did.

Works Cited

Barnes, Julian. *Cross Channel*. London: Picador, 1996.

---. *Flaubert's Parrot*. London: Picador, 1984.

---. *The Lemon Table*. London: Picador, 2004.

---. *Levels of Life*. 2013. London: Vintage, 2014.

---. *Nothing to Be Frightened Of*. 2008. London: Vintage, 2009.

---. *Pulse*. 2011. London: Vintage, 2012.

Begley, Adam. "The Empathy Artist." *The Wall Street Journal* 26–27 Aug. 2017. Accessed 30 Aug. 2017.

Botha, Marc. "Microfiction." *The Cambridge Companion to the English Short Story*. Ed. Ann-Marie Einhaus. Cambridge: Cambridge UP, 2016.

Campbell, Ewing. "How Minimal Is Minimalism?" *The Tales We Tell: Perspectives on the Short Story*. Eds. Barbara Lounsberry et al. Westport: Greenwood, 1998. 15–21.

Childs, Peter. "Matters of Life and Death: The Short Stories of Julian Barnes." *Julian Barnes*. Eds. Sebastian Groes and Peter Childs. London: Continuum, 2011. 103–17.

Dillon, Brian. *Essayism*. London: Fitzcarraldo, 2017.

"Fragment." *The Concise Oxford Dictionary*. Oxford: Clarendon, 1982.

Guignery, Vanessa, and Ryan Roberts, eds. *Conversations with Julian Barnes*. Jackson: UP of Mississippi, 2009.

Holmes, Richard. "7 Annual Leon Levy Biographical Lecture," biographersinternational.org, http://www.youtube.com/wtch?v+sdQaswzlfS4. Accessed 12 Dec. 2017.

Lee, Hermione. *Virginia Woolf*. New York: Vintage, 1999.

---. *Body Parts: Essays on Life-Writing.* London: Chatto, 2005.

Lohafer, Susan. *Reading for Storyness: Preclosure Theory, Empirical Poetics, and Culture in the Short Story Format.* Baltimore: John Hopkins UP, 2003.

Nancy, Jean-Luc, and Phillipe Lacoue-Labarthe. *The Literary Absolute: The Theory of Literature in German Romanticism.* Trans. Philip Bernard and Cheryl Lester. New York: State University of New York Press, 1998.

Poe, Edgar Allan. "On the Aim and Technique of the Short Story." 1842. *What Is the Short Story?* Chicago: Scott, Foresman and Company, 1961. 4–14.

Pritchett, V. S. "Short Stories." *What Is the Short Story?* Chicago: Scott, Foresman and Company, 1961. 123–25.

Strawson, Galen. "The Minimal Subject." *Oxford Book of the Self.* Ed. Shaun Gallagher. Oxford: Oxford UP, 2011. 253–78.

Chapter 8

"Make it new" to return as rupture and difference: a study of Jeanette Winterson's *The Gap of Time*

Maria Antonietta Struzziero

Jeanette Winterson's fiction is, by her own admission, "full of Cover versions" (*Weight* xviii) as she frequently reworks stories and myths from several sources, injecting fresh material into an existing text. One of her most recent novels, *The Gap of Time* (2015), is an instance of her dialog with William Shakespeare's late play *The Winter's Tale* (1623). Winterson dissects and reassembles it but leaves in place both its central themes and enough traces of the original story to provide evocative intertextual echoes for her readers. At the same time, she gives a different emphasis to its constituent elements while encompassing alternative perspectives to "make it new" (*Gap* 286). To borrow Winterson's words from her collection of essays *Art Objects* (1995), *The Gap of Time* may be considered as one of those "strong texts [that] work along the borders of our minds and alter what already exists," flouting received ideas and views, and opening "a way into other realities, other personalities" (26).

In this paper, I propose to analyze the specificities of Winterson's artistic transformation of Shakespeare's play and to explore the reasons why the writer encapsulates her narrative within the structural and stylistic choice of fragmentary writing while simultaneously aiming for a form of coherence and unity. While many scenes in the novel are punctuated with images of life in ruins, I will show how Winterson moves beyond and transforms these ruins of lives, marked by separation, loss and death, into a story of recovery and reunion.

Weaving timeless stories between appropriation and creativity

Winterson's cover version, whose subtitle is "The Winter's Tale *Retold,*" preserves the armature of the action in *The Winter's Tale* but is set in the present in London, Paris and New Bohemia, a fictional American city. King Leontes is now Leo – an alpha male and an arrogant banker who runs a hedge fund called Sicilia in post-crash London. King Polixenes, his best friend, becomes Xeno – a video game designer living in New Bohemia, whose ambiguous sexuality generates the tension that is at the heart of the main narrative. Leo, convinced that Xeno is having an affair with his pregnant wife Hermione, a Parisian singer better known as MiMi, sends their new-born baby, Perdita, off to New Bohemia. Here she is rescued from a hospital baby hatch by a black bar owner, Shep, who brings her up. Years later Perdita falls in love with Zel, Xeno's son, which will lead to a final reconciliation of the two families and MiMi's forgiveness of Leo.

Like Shakespeare's play, Winterson's novel is divided into two periods separated by sixteen years – "the gap of time" that gives the book its title – and has a theatrical construction: it is composed of three parts, subdivided into different sections and separated by two "Intervals." The first is an intensely lyrical and poetic two-page-long section, composed of mini-paragraphs and a string of disjointed sentences, apparently disconnected from the main narrative, except for the initial reference to "stories of lost and found" (127). In it, the narrator steps out of the story and addresses the reader on the themes of separation and loss. The second three-page-long Interval at the beginning focuses on Zel and Perdita, then moves on to Leo, MiMi and Xeno as avatars in the game created by the latter. These two scenes contrast an image of fusion and love embodied by the young couple with one of separation and death in the videogame.

Though self-contained and complete in itself, *The Gap of Time* constantly summons up and produces its doppelgänger: its *double* as its *Other.* Shakespeare's play is evoked in the list of Contents as "The Original," and the novel starts with a synopsis of the plot, followed by the rewriting. This "remnant" of the past text houses the traces of what is absent, working much as an archeological fragment does, i.e., a testimony of what is no longer there, at least not in its original form, and yet a witness of its existence in the past and persistence in the present. Thus *The Gap of Time* forcibly does not stand alone: it is preceded by the absent text to which it harks back even in the title of some sections. This lingering ghostly presence returns as a rupture bringing about difference and may encourage one to consider *The Gap of Time* as a "fragment," the *part* of a distant *whole* to which it is related while being irreversibly separated from it, an act of (re)creation that follows the destruction of its *other.* Thus, by its nature, Winterson's novel bears in its body the marks of a fragmentary mode that is articulated on the threshold between obedience to, and disruption of, the authority of Shakespeare's play. It is a text that oscillates between convention and tradition, on the one hand, and creative manipulation and reinterpretation of a canonical work, on the other.

The sense of fragmentation in *The Gap of Time* is partly caused by the constant use of intertextuality, of palimpsestic quotations or echoes of other writers and artists, as well as lines or phrases from Shakespeare's play. Intertextuality acquires the quality of the fragmentary, because quotes from a variety of sources and dissimilar units are often juxtaposed with no transitions or explicit relations, resulting in a collage-like effect. Besides, Winterson's rearticulation of *The Winter's Tale* transforms the Shakespearean text, itself already an exploration of the limits of traditional genres, into a labyrinthine, polyphonic narrative, in which there are multiple border-crossings of time, space and gender.

The reader thus witnesses the metamorphosis of *The Winter's Tale* into a multiple, shape-shifting body marked by a conflation of different genres, an unbounded dialogism of texts and a polyphony of voices – a postmodernist text that produces sites where, as Umberto Eco maintains, "fragments of a large number of possible orders glitter separately" (246). In terms of genders, *The Gap of Time* presents a trenchant cultural critique of hypermasculinity and misogyny in the figure of Leo, celebrates Xeno's gender fluidity, and refers to the coupling of Shep's son with a transgender receptionist. As regards class and power, the novel offers a scathing attack on the arrogance and greed fueled by money, and the ruthless urge to command and dominate the weak and powerless, which is embodied by Leo.

Multiple layers and interrelatedness

Structurally, *The Gap of Time* is a multilayered narrative set in different spatial and temporal dimensions, which escapes linearity and continuity. The novel's structure is probably best described by the words Xeno uses to illustrate the video game that should have "layers, levels, poetry as well as plot," where "each level ... will be a time frame – specific but porous," so that "you can operate simultaneously on different levels" (61–62). This structure brings to mind what Frank Kermode, in *The Sense of an Ending*, wrote about plots as being the purging of "mere successiveness" (qtd. in Frank 246). Glossing Kermode, Joseph Frank argues that plots "seem to work *against* the flow of time, and to keep alive, or to create, an indigenous kind of unity which overarches and reshapes the constraints of pure temporal linearity" (Frank 246). *The Gap of Time* seems to include such plots that create relations of meaning detached from pure chronological succession. The novel, scattered across genres, alternating between the real and the fantastic, with a significant incursion in the world of video games, tells a story of jealousy, loss, repentance, and forgiveness by weaving together, and continually moving between, three story-worlds.

The first level is the story Winterson tells through her own lens, interspersed with references both to herself and her work, frequently echoed or quoted,[1] and to other contemporary artists and writers. The second layer is the rewriting of Shakespeare's play, itself a reworking of Robert Greene's *Pandosto* (1588). The third is the story created by Xeno, in the online video game called "The Gap of Time," which is based, in turn, on a dream of the French poet Gérard de Nerval. The video game contains, in a nutshell, the story of Perdita, which in the main narrative is to be told later.

The three layers resonate with motifs, images, refrains and metaphors that arise and fade into the text at precise intervals through the various sections, a choice that hints at a careful narrative design and adds a lyrical rhythm. They also permeate one another and are interconnected by the mirroring of events and discourses in the different narratives, as well as by the reiteration of some of her familiar concerns, such as the themes of love, loss, abandonment at birth and adoption, which establish an analogy between the writer and Perdita, the abandoned child of Leontes and Hermione in Shakespeare's play. The loose and often disjointed episodes are conjoined by the main narrative thread, which, weaving its way along, ties together the different storylines and events. In the end, the overall structure of the novel, by dint of its careful patterns of images and tropes, achieves a formal aesthetic unity that transcends the fragmented perspective while, at the referential level, it describes discordance, fragmentation and disharmony.

Thus Winterson's novel shows an intense internal animation manifested through inner correspondences, embedded in the various strata of symbolic references scattered in the whole text – a device that collapses the space between different discursive universes and achieves a form of coherence *in* and *through* language. This dialogical style, in which "each part supports the others to create the semblance of a perfectly meaningful and coherent world" (Brand 40), originates a form of interrelatedness independent of the time-sequence of the narrative.

---

[1] For instance, the novel includes a fictional Wikipedia entry which claims that "MiMi made her acting debut in a [theatrical] adaptation of *The PowerBook* – a novel by the British writer Jeanette Winterson" (42).

An instance of this interrelatedness can be found in one of the central images of the book, that of the Dark Angel and its fall. It is an entry in Wikipedia with reference to Gérard de Nerval's dream; the title of a song by MiMi; a protagonist in Xeno's video game; and part of a dream MiMi has while in hospital, besides being echoed continuously by Leo's behavior and psychological makeup. This symbolic image is also recalled by a tattoo that covers Xeno's torso to disguise the scars left by a traumatic accident when, as an adolescent, he fell off a cliff, pushed by Leo. Later on, Xeno transforms this episode into a source of artistic creation in his video game narrative.

The figure of the fallen angel – hinting at a fallen world inside the novel – is not a simple rhetorical technique to interweave the different story layers. It is, above all, an image that connects the characters at a deeper psychological level and provides personal histories and motivations for their apparently obscure behavior, suggesting that there are motives hidden somewhere in the gaps of their psyche. Therefore, this image, together with other recurrent motifs and tropes, allows Winterson to approach the complexity of the protagonists by going beyond the tradition of psychological realism. Indeed, the subject that Winterson is portraying in her novel is no longer a unified being but a fragile self in crisis, splintered by several opposing drives and desires, constantly questing after an object that has been lost.

At the structural level, fragmentation sometimes aims to evoke the polymorphous and chaotic essence of modern life, which, in its complexity, resists full comprehension and does not yield to a conventional narrative. That is why the ruptures between sentences, the spatial blanks on the page, formally and visually simulate the fracture and disorder of reality, as well as the splintered and dissociated psyche of the modern man. Such features can be observed when Perdita mistakenly suspects that Zel, with whom she is in love, might be her brother and reveals her doubts to the boy, who, fearing that his emotional world is disintegrating, runs away from her:

Perdita said, "I think you might be my brother."

Zel was on his feet. He was running. He wasn't breathing. He was sweating. His chest hurt as if someone was throwing a brick at him. She was his new world. She was sight of land. She was the stretch and chance of time. And he had kissed her. And he wanted to go on kissing her. He hated his father. (200)

The halting staccato rhythm of the passage, composed of juxtaposed short sentences with no links, reflects Zel's sense of disintegration. He appears to be "a wounded being [whose] speech wells up out of an aching for love" (Kristeva, *Tales* 372), a voice captured in the scrambled tumult of interior experience. Perdita's words, which sound as a threat of death, push the boy violently towards a place where meaning collapses; he must repudiate the desire that is the foundation of his new self, and this denial pulverizes his identity.

A polymorphic world of words: structural fragmentation

In *The Gap of Time*, structural fragmentation is achieved through the disruption of narrative linearity and continuity, cutting back and forth between the various levels of action through the frequent use of sudden analepses, both internal and external to the story. These narrative shifts are occasionally signaled by different typefaces, sometimes embracing distant periods and episodes in very few pages.

Right from the beginning, Winterson inverts the structure of Shakespeare's play by opening with a dramatic sequence similar to a thriller. Shep's first words – "I saw the strangest sight tonight" (5) – are an attempt to start a tale which is aborted at once and picked up again after two pages. The "strangest sight" is that of a baby – Perdita – being deposited in a hospital baby hatch and rescued by Shep who will adopt and love her as his own child, a scene that in Shakespeare's play only comes at the end of the third act. Before this discovery, the opening section of *The Gap of Time* zooms in on the violent death of Tony (beaten up by two hoods in the street), the man who should have abandoned the baby on Leo's orders, but is moved to compassion and saves her life by leaving her in the baby hatch. The episode of Perdita's abandonment is first told proleptically by Shep as a first-person narrator who was a witness to the scene, and then, after a hundred pages, by a third-person narrator; it also keeps resurfacing at different points in the novel, being a pivotal event with far-reaching implications.

The first-person account of this crucial episode is a four-page fragment followed by a blank, after which narration resumes on the next page, when Winterson rewinds time with the story of Shep's life. The choice of moving the incident of Perdita's abandonment to the very first pages, leaving it suspended, as it were, is very interesting when considered in view of the opening narrative shift. Winterson seems indeed to indicate that abandonment and death belong to a past that cannot be hidden or erased but must provide a heuristic key to interpret the present and consequently offer hope for change. The author therefore immediately leaves the episode behind, affirms the view of the present as a site of uncharted life possibilities, and moves forward to the future, because, she argues, in *The*

Winter's Tale, "the past depends on the future" ("On Writing" 2). By repositioning the desire for (re)unification in a future dimension, the opening fragment can be viewed as a *project*, what Friedrich Schlegel defined as a "fragment ... of the future" (21), and therefore as progressive rather than as a signifier of ruin – a tragic form of melancholic nostalgia for past wholeness.

Winterson thus re-orients the story away from the narrative of loss towards "a world of possible futures" (*Gap* 284), and the as-yet-uncharted territories of a life which contemplates forgiveness and "a second chance" (285), in a poetic blend of realism and fantasy that allows for the possibility of redemption. In the same vein, Winterson entrusts the closure of the novel to Perdita's final speech, because "if the future exists, the new generation will have to discover it, like a territory not subject to the violent destructiveness of the past" ("On Writing" 2). The writer thus reconfigures patriarchal power relations and assigns to a woman of the new generation the vital function of treading a different territory from that of their fathers. Driven by the idealism of youth and by a headstrong quest for her origins, Perdita will succeed in healing the wounds of the past. As in Shakespeare's play, Winterson affirms the positive role exerted by the female principle against male rage and vindictiveness.

The opening fragment in *The Gap of Time* is followed by a brief flashback into a dire phase of Shep's past life, which closes the first section. This second fragment oscillates between two distinct past episodes buried in Shep's mind, a well inhabited by memories still unprocessed by "the elaborate machinery of linguistic constructions and representations" (Donato 576). These events are the death of his wife, terminally ill in hospital, whom he smothered out of pity to end her suffering; and the moment when, one year later, he found Perdita in the same hospital's baby hatch. These pages feature a cluster of themes that reverberate with traces of traumatic losses and destruction, exemplified first by Shep's killing of his wife followed by his psychological disintegration, and second by Perdita's abandonment and the murder of Tony. Both events happened in or around the hospital – a space where place and trauma converge, haunted by absence and a sense of void, and as such recollected only in splintered images. Over time, the hospital becomes symbolically imbued with the texture of a site of loss and mourning for Shep, who muses, "You think you are living in the present but the past is right behind you like a shadow" (6).

On Perdita's arrival in his life, Shep falls into "a gap of time where one time and another become the same time" (12). Here traumatic memory provokes the displacement of the traumatized subject who juxtaposes two different time dimensions connected, in his mind, by the image of himself holding in his arms his baby son Clo and Perdita just lifted out of the baby hatch. He experiences the disappearance of a spatio-temporal ground to support his identity when he witnesses, with disbelief, the transformation of a site of trauma and ruin (the hospital) into the source of an embryonic promise of life and rebirth. Perdita is thus seen as a compensatory and redeeming presence who balances his loss, as he acknowledges, "I've been given a life for the one I took" (15). She dislocates his trauma and guilt and paves the way for his reconfiguration of the hospital: from being a spectral trace of what has ceased to exist it is transformed into the promise of a future life, thus welding together his two broken selves, the past and the present one. So the fragment no longer relates to a sense of rupture or loss but signals towards connection and reunion.

Breaking apart and contesting norms: formal fragmentation

The complex architecture of *The Gap of Time* is underpinned by Winterson's formal choices dependent on the poetics of juxtaposition, fragmentation and collage, which are central artistic features of modernism and postmodernism. Textuality pursues dislocation and disjunction of the narrative by means of polyvalence and bifurcation, where grammar resists norms and syntactical sequence is frequently renounced, the text being composed on the principle of interval and tension between parts, in a constant conversation between unity and disunity. A close analysis of the rhetoric of the text shows heavy, cumulative use of stylistic fragmentation – sentence and paragraph breaks, abnormally emphatic style of punctuation, irregular page layout – used at crucial plot moments as foregrounding devices.

Fragmentation at this level has different purposes and makes use of many techniques, one of which is the mechanics of juxtaposition and organization of disparate shots as in filmic montage:

> *Where are you?*
> Engine roar of a motorcycle. Cars with their windows down and the radio on. Kids on skateboards. A dog barking. The delivery truck unloading. Two women arguing on the sidewalk. Everybody on their cellphone. A guy on a box shouting, EVERYTHING MUST GO. (13)

As noted by Joseph Frank, who is paraphrasing Sergei Eisenstein, "the juxtaposition of disparate images in a cinematic *montage* automatically creates a synthesis of meaning between them; and this supersedes any sense of temporal discontinuity" (Frank 237). In such cases, the synchronic relations within the text take priority over the diachronic referentiality and create a meaningful pattern.

Another technique consists in textual fracture, observable in those cases where, in a string of sentence fragments, the writer omits transitions and thus violates the conventions of syntax and narrative. It is sometimes used to create the sense of clear perceptual impression, of human conscious-ness used as a camera eye, unfiltered by the presence of the narrator:

> One o'clock in the morning.
> The streets fuzzy with light rain. The plastic peel-off shine of the pavements. The shimmer under the sodium street lamps. Cars queuing at the red light, wipers in rhythm, drivers with the windows down against the heat. Big guy in a van, his right arm resting on the rolled-down window, elbow out, letting the rain run in, scrubbing his forearm in relief across his face. Sudden summer rain. (73)

Occasionally, this formal choice offers a direct gaze into the characters' complex thought processes or signals an unpredictably changing distance in the point of view – a technique similar to the cinematic alternation between different types of shot. This happens when Leo follows Xeno, who is driving out of a garage, determined to provoke a car accident and kill him:

> Leo watched Xeno putting Pauline in a cab. Then Xeno went towards the underground car park ...
> Leo followed him. His own car was down there.
> Lower level. Neon-lit. Concrete pillars. Painted bays. Same the world over. Hot like a dry-cleaner's down there, the ventilation shafts whirring to clear the heat. (73)

In some sections, grammar is discarded, and Winterson employs un-structured and truncated sentences, syntactic dislocation, as well as whole sentences in different typefaces. This frequently happens in connection with Leo, especially when he is prey to jealousy. Sometimes Winterson uses sentence fragments or italics to reproduce a character's dramatic dialog with herself/himself or to dissolve barriers between the inside and the outside, between speech and thought. This happens to Leo during the hectic minutes following MiMi's sudden, traumatic childbirth at home, when he refuses to acknowledge Perdita as his own child. He absent-mindedly follows a film that his son Milo is watching on the iPad, in which Superman reverses time, and he wishes this might happen also in real life, hoping to be taken *"back to a time where none of this has happened"* (89). His silent wish and shift in thought is visually signaled by the italics. An-other use of italicized font can be observed when Xeno is in Paris, sent by Leo to convince MiMi to accept his marriage proposal:

Do you always leave your top button undone like that? Just one button? So that I can imagine your chest from the animal paw of hair that I can see? She is not blonde. No. I think her hair is naturally dark but I like the way she colours it in sections and the way she slips off her shoes under the table. Disconcerting, the way you look at me when we talk. *What were we talking about?* (67)

In this case, different character types are used to voice and echo Xeno's and MiMi's inner turmoil of unspoken and unspeakable thoughts and intense feelings of attraction to each other. This device is associated with a constant oscillation from the first to the third personal pronoun, and the fragmentation of a single monolithic voice into a multiplicity of voices. These sentences, characterized by the use of parataxis, appear to answer a question that introduces this section: "What would it be like if ... we communicated as spirits do?" (66) – a form of silent communication of twin spirits.

At one point, the writer combines regular typefaces, italics and sentences all in capital letters, with abnormally emphatic punctuation. The objective is, first, to convey Leo's fluctuation between two levels of consciousness (the imaginary in italics and the real in regular character types), and, secondly, to reproduce a sort of multivoiced internal dialog between the two rigidly opposed fragments of a splintered self-fighting for control in Leo. One of them feels pain and spies unseen on MiMi's and Xeno's banal actions with growing suspicion and irrational, blind jealousy, whereas the other mocks it and imagines scenes of sexual intercourse between MiMi and Xeno, lashing out in vulgar language. Here fragmentation intimates a deep sense of pain and fear of loss, conveying a strong undertone of psychological damage that provokes a form of interpretive hallucination and a schizophrenic misreading of the world around him. Language becomes unruly, the sort of "borderline" discourse typical of Kristeva's "abjection," when the boundaries that structure the subject collapse, a condition that "disturbs identity, system, order" (*Powers* 4), under the recognition of a *want* or a desire. It is almost a psychotic utterance that mirrors an uncontrollable, heightened emotional state of distress. The rhythm and pattern of the fragments reproduce the accelerated or disrupted stream of consciousness:

He would kill them.
NOW WHAT?
MiMi was naked. Underwear off. Naked. Pauline sat on the bed chatting to Xeno. What was this? *The Killing of Sister George?* Pauline was a lesbian! That explained it! She couldn't get a man so she had to pimp women. She was a drunk, ugly lesbian. Well, OK, Pauline doesn't drink. Call me a liar over a bottle of whisky. She is a sober, ugly lesbian.
IT'S A THREESOME! (52)

This mode of writing renders the turmoil of the character's interior experience and his fragmented consciousness – a mental state that makes the violation of grammatical conventions inevitable. Some characters, as Shep at the beginning or Leo throughout the novel, are troubled by pieces of images or memories that erupt unbidden into consciousness. These moments of mental dissonance interfere with logical narration and subvert norms of coherence and unity, but they are also a distressing feature of traumatic memories.

In other moments, the heightening of musical effects, with the use of alliteration, rhythmic phrasing and persistent repetition of words or phrases, reaches the incantatory intensity of poetry:

> We set off in boats. The stars were lights on top of the masts. We didn't know that stars are like fossils, imprints of the past, sending light like a message, like a dying wish.
> We set off in boats, though we'd sail to the rim of the world and slip over the edge like a raft on a waterfall, spinning to the place we knew existed, if we dared to find it.
> It must be somewhere.
> The missingness of the missing. (127–28)

In this brief extract from the first Interval, Winterson refers to the theme of the quest for a lost loved one. She uses the personal pronoun "we" to refer to Perdita and her future search for her "missing" mother's love, as well as her own story of abandonment and loss, both "first wounds" that hurt and need to be healed.

The formal characteristics of this passage signal that the speaking subject, under the impact of unconscious desires and affects, is no longer in control of signification. It is an intensely emotional language that, driven by a lyrical impulse, withdraws into a less controlled space, as frequently happens also when Perdita and Zel are together. Similar features can be observed in the second Interval when, in the video game, both Xeno and Leo try to wake MiMi up from her death-like sleep. In all such moments, language erupts in "a flight of metaphors [and] the precision of reference and meaning becomes blurred" (Kristeva, *Tales* 1–2). It is Kristeva's "amorous dialogue" that is "tension and jouissance, repetition and infinity; not as communication but as *incantation*" (93). Semantic content is less important than the emotionally charged patterns created by the word itself through its rhythms and sounds.

The different sections thus present rupture and discontinuity, "multiple perspectives and narrative threads [that] branch out from the source events ... and supplement one another" (Kaul 2), as well as changes in the prose style, including the lyrical, the poetical, the everyday and the language of the new technologies. Indeed, the novel draws on digital forms, thus reflecting the social and technological reality of the contemporary world. It creates a collage that mimics the postmodern aesthetics of the mash-up, which dominates online media, including social networks like Twitter and Facebook.

However, the seeming abandonment of stable form in *The Gap of Time* is misleading, because Winterson is adopting a typical postmodernist strategy of foregrounding formal devices against narrative events. In fact, behind the novel's apparent irreducibility to unity and harmony, its acceptance of gaps and fragmentation, the reader gradually perceives a hidden framework; inside it a possible *other* writing emerges which does not yield to the lure of the system and embraces the fragment as a different form of artistic accomplishment and Winterson's authentic expression. This choice reflects her aesthetics voiced in *Art Objects*, demonstrating that "it is possible to have done with the bricks and mortars of conventional narrative ... by building a structure that is bounded by language" (190).

Conclusion

The Gap of Time epitomizes various forms of fragmentation, starting from the elaborate, labyrinthine architecture of the novel, to include the structural and formal levels of the text. Breaking up her narrative and playing with Shakespeare's genders and genres, Winterson subverts the original framework of Shakespeare's story to make room for a counter-narrative that refuses the logic of dualisms and, while celebrating plurality, becomes her site of denunciation of, and resistance to, the culturally constructed oppositions of gender and hierarchical power relations. Her act of retelling generates new complex characters who act within reversed systems of power relations and inscribes modern forms of gender-fluid identities, as exemplified by Xeno, or a different way of decoding male gender identity, as Zel does – a character who, in his shyness and gentle nature, may remind Winterson's readers of Henri in *The Passion* (1987).

Winterson deconstructs Shakespeare's play and reinvents it as a postmodernist novel whose very structure becomes an instrument of her artistic intention. She multiplies and juxtaposes worlds in a creative process that manifests her freedom of invention as well as her free use of a variety of literary sources and texts. The necessary destruction and fragmentation of the already given is an artistic choice necessary to affirm her novel's original, autonomous life.

Winterson's choice of fragmentary writing is strategic and mimetic, and has different motivations and objectives. First, she deconstructs the linear fabric of the plot and refuses monologic narratives. By doing so, she foregrounds the shifting and multifaceted essence of both social and individual experience, which can find its best fictional representation by embracing its fragmentary nature. Second, the fragmentary work shows its responsiveness to thought itself; therefore, in order to portray the protagonists' fragmented mind, Winterson needs to lay bare their mental lives. Finally, fragmentary writing in *The Gap of Time* answers an inner quasi-ethical imperative: to be responsive to what remains hidden or tacit in the mainline narratives in which we live, and what these narratives, by themselves, cannot contain.

Works Cited

Brand, Roy. "Schlegel's Fragmentary Project." *Epoché* 9.1 (2004): 37–52.

Donato, Eugenio. "The Ruins of Memory: Archeological Fragments and Textual Artifacts." *Modern Language Notes* 93.4 (1978). 575–96.

Eco, Umberto. "Lector in Fabula: Pragmatic Strategy in a Metanarrative Text." *The Role of the Reader: Exploration in the Semiotics of Texts*. Bloomington: Indiana UP, 1979. 200–60.

Frank, Joseph. "Spatial Form: An Answer to Critics." *Critical Inquiry* 4.2 (1977): 231–52.

Kaul, Aashish. "Mapping Space in Fiction: Joseph Frank and the Idea of Spatial Form." *3:AM Magazine*, 11 Sept. 2014, https://www.3ammagazine.com/3am/mapping-space-in-fiction-joseph-frank-and-the-idea-of-spatial-form/. Accessed 29 July 2017.

Kristeva, Julia. *Powers of Horror: An Essay on Abjection*. 1980. Trans. Leon S. Roudiez. New York: Columbia UP, 1982.

---. *Tales of Love*. 1983. Trans. Leon S. Roudiez. New York: Columbia UP, 1987.

Schlegel, Friedrich. "Athenaeum Fragments." 1798. *Philosophical Fragments*. Trans. Peter Firchow. Minneapolis: U of Minnesota P, 1991.

Winterson, Jeanette. *Art Objects: Essays on Ecstasy and Effrontery*. London: Jonathan Cape, 1995.

---. *The Gap of Time*. London: Hogarth, 2015.

---. "On Writing a Cover Version of Shakespeare." *The Guardian*, 26 Sept. 2015, https://www.theguardian.com/books/2015/sep/26/jeanette-winterson-rewriting-shakespeare-winter-s-tale. Accessed 13 Jan. 2016.

---. *The Passion*. London: Bloomsbury, 1987.

---. *Weight*. Edinburgh: Canongate, 2005.

Part Three

Fragmentation in the age of crisis

Chapter 9

Collage manifestos:

fragmentation and appropriation in

David Markson's *This is Not a Novel*

and David Shields's *Reality Hunger*

Wojciech Drąg,
University of Wrocław

In *Twenty-First-Century Fiction: A Critical Introduction* (2013), Peter Boxall traces in much of postmillennial literature a "fin de siècle mood," which springs from the sense of a "passage from one epoch to the next" and of a "collision between the old and the new" (4). That "sense of an ending" accompanies critical discussions of contemporary literature and can be located in recent assessments of the condition of the novel by Will Self, Lars Iyer and Pieter Vermeulen. In this article, I wish to examine two books published in the first decade of the twenty-first century which forcefully assert the exhaustion of the novel and the need for a new literature, unrestrained by the dictates of plot and character. I shall examine their criticism of the conventional novel as well as their postulates of fragmentariness, free appropriation and the obliteration of the fiction/non-fiction divide. I will argue that the form most suited to accommodating those propositions is collage and that both David Markson's *This Is Not a Novel* and David Shields's *Reality Hunger* are formally works of collage. In that respect, they follow the politics of manifestos, which is to enact what they propose.

Although about a hundred times longer than the classic examples of the genre, both texts can be regarded as manifestos in that they formulate a creed of new art in radical opposition to the art of the present. Whereas in the case of *Reality Hunger*, which is subtitled "A Manifesto," that category is applicable for a number of reasons, Markson's *This Is Not a Novel* – which, despite its title, is still regarded by the author as a novel – can be called a manifesto only in a limited sense. The recipe offered by the father of the avant-garde manifesto, Tommaso Filippo Marinetti, specifies two key ingredients: violence and precision in formulating both the accusation and the insult (Perloff, *Futurist* 81–82). Those qualities are far more conspicuous in Shields as his case against the novel is, after all, the driving force of the book. Contrarily, in Markson, the theory of the new novel emerges parenthetically, in passing, as its consecutive bullet-point-like characteristics are interspersed with numerous unrelated passages. As regards form, both authors avoid blocks of continuous text and favor a compilation of short, often elliptical, statements set apart by empty spaces, which forges a strong link with the poetics of the manifesto. As Laura Winkiel argues in "Manifestos and *Ars Poetica*," the connection between the genre and fragmentation is "striking and apposite" (255). In adopting the form of the fragment with its inherent incompletion, the manifesto fashions itself as a project – a "fragment of the future" – to be realized, or completed, when the advocated ideas are implemented and the utopia is achieved (Winkiel 255–56).

This Is Not a Novel – structure, collage, fragmentation

This Is Not a Novel (2001) comes second in a series of four works which – against Markson's wish – tend to be seen as part of a tetralogy, often named after the opening *Reader's Block* (1996). It is, however, the only work in the series which can be regarded as a manifesto and the one most indebted to the structure of a collage. The remaining two works are *Vanishing Point* (2004) and *The Last Novel* (2007), which did turn out to be Markson's last and was published at the age of 80, three years before his death. The similarities between the four books are so evident that it is difficult not to consider them as part of a single project. Each work is a 150- to a 200-page-long collection of fragments, whose bulk conveys facts and anecdotes about the lives of well-known artists, philosophers, scientists and historical figures. Those erudite trivia are in each case interspersed with metafictional snippets commenting on the properties of the book in hand and on its narrator, who is called differently in every consecutive book: Reader, Writer, Author and Novelist, respectively. The length of a single passage ranges from one word (such as "*Wanhope*") to six lines. Each chunk of text is separated by a space, which makes the layout reminiscent of a collection of aphorisms.[1]

---

[1] That analogy is strengthened by the fact that many featured quotations are followed by the phrase "said X" or "wrote X," in the example above.

This Is Not a Novel is composed out of approximately two thousand passages, which can be formally classified into several categories exemplified by the snippets below:

(1) Dizzy Dean died of a heart attack. (190)

(2) Writer is weary unto death of making up stories. (1)

(3) What is Hamlet reading, in Act II Scene ii, when Polonius inquires and Hamlet says Words, words, words? (27)

(4) The greatest lesbian poet since Sappho, Auden called Rilke. (29)

(5) *Tell all the Truth but tell it slant* – (11)

(6) Ludwig Geyer. (17)

(7) *Timor mortis conturbat me.* (148, 163)

The first passage is an example of the most numerous category constituted by curiosities about famous people. It is also one of close to five hundred nuggets contained in *This Is Not a Novel* which concentrate on the cause and circumstances of the deaths of public figures – in this case, an American baseball player. The recurrence of anecdotes focusing on certain aspects of the lives of renowned individuals as well as the choice of those characters enables the reader to notice emerging themes. Alongside the dominant theme of dying are anti-Semitism,[2] madness, the creative process and the lack of recognition by contemporaries. Markson's concern with death, aging and crisis is introduced on the first page, which contains the second passage above – an example of a metafictional comment on the process of writing. It is the vehicle through which Markson formulates the charges against the novel and the postulates for its resuscitation. The narrator's confession of his weariness "unto death" of story-telling is directly followed by snippets on the deaths of fellow writers Lord Byron and Stephen Crane. In that way, by association, the ensuing discussion of the condition of the novel is infused with a sense of imminent demise. The third passage represents one of many questions which apparently nag the nameless narrator and which are likely to arouse the curiosity of Markson's reader as well.

The fourth example – W. H. Auden's humorous assessment of Rainer Maria Rilke – represents one of several hundred quotations, which despite not being enclosed in quotation marks are accurate and whose attribution is signaled, albeit laconically. The sources of those snippets are multiple and include mostly biographies and encyclopedias. The fifth passage exemplifies one of several hundred unacknowledged quotations – in this case, a line from a poem by Emily Dickinson. Their provenance ranges from high-

---

[2] That theme is even more prominent in *Reader's Block*, which contains as many as 86 snippets following the format, "X was an anti-Semite."

ly recognizable texts such as the Bible or *The Illiad* to rather obscure sources, which readers can identify with the help of a search engine. The last two passages stand for rarer categories. "Ludwig Geyer"[3] is an example of a short cryptic nugget – usually containing a name, a title or a phrase – whose significance is not articulated. It appeals either to the reader's erudition or to their diligence, which – as with the previous category – consists in consulting this element in works of reference or, most conveniently, in typing it into a search engine. The last example represents one of several recurrent lines, or refrains, to be found across the novel. The Latin passage from a Catholic prayer, meaning "fear of death distresses me," appears three times, twice accompanied by its English translation. Another such recurrent nugget is the earlier mentioned "*Wanhope*" (19, 75, 165) – the Anglo-Saxon predecessor of the Norman word "despair." Both refrains accentuate the theme of terminal crisis and invite comparison with the structure of the fugue, as noted by Laura Sims (65). The analogy with the fugue indicates the possibility of seeing Markson's text as less fragmentary than it may at first appear and as endowed with greater coherence once its multiple subtle links have been detected. Both Sims and Joseph Tabbi stress the need for reader's attentiveness and involvement in Markson's "interactive" fiction: "for a narrative to develop at all," Tabbi argues, "significant connections need to form in a reader's mind" (766–67).

The last four passages can be regarded as the quintessential components of collage – readymades, understood as any external material – two- or three-dimensional, verbal or visual – which the artist chooses to incorporate in their work. What in the visual collages of Pablo Picasso and Georges Braque is exemplified by "real objects, such as bits of newspaper or other mass-produced images" (Kostelanetz 124), in literary texts – by T. S. Eliot, William S. Burroughs and Kathy Acker – usually takes the form of unintegrated and often unacknowledged quotations.[4] In Markson no passages are seamlessly integrated with the rest of the texts as they are all spatially set apart from the preceding and succeeding ones. However, one may determine different levels of semantic integration. Whereas the Auden quotation is followed by a three-word commentary indicating its context and therefore has its readymade quality diminished, the last three exam-

---

[3] German artist and stepfather of Richard Wagner.

[4] Agnieszka Karpowicz specifies that, in order to function as a readymade, the quotation needs to be distinctly separated from the rest of the text rather than submerged in it (61). In multimodal literary collages – such as Steve Tomasula's *VAS: An Opera in Flatland* (2002) and *The Book of Portraiture* (2006) – photographs and other kinds of images also function as readymades.

ples offer no interpretive hint – either within the passage itself or in the immediate surroundings.

The lack of a semantic (or narrative) coherence resulting from the incongruity of constitutive elements is, besides the inclusion of appropriated content, another crucial characteristic of collage. Budd Hopkins defines the "collage aesthetic" as "the presence of several contradictory systems in a work of art, and the absence of a single controlling system" (7), whereas David Antin argues that the absence of "explicit syntactical relations" between the work's "disparate materials" is what constitutes a literary collage (169). In a similar vein, Marjorie Perloff sees the principle of collage as based on the replacement of "subordination" by "coordination" and of "logic [and] sequence" by "likeness and difference" ("Collage" 386). In more general terms, she maintains that collage renounces any structural "hierarchy" of its parts and organizes them according to the logic of parataxis – a rhetorical strategy of placing phrases, clauses or sentences alongside one another without the use of any conjunctions (Perloff, *Futurist* 75). The principle of juxtaposition in place of synthesis can be illustrated by the following excerpt from *This Is Not a Novel*:

> *Gammer Guiton's Needle.*
> Goldengrove unleaving.
> It took Eliot forty years to allow that the word Jew in *Gerontion* might be capitalized.
> Then Abraham fell upon his face and laughed.
> June 16, 1904.
> Stephen Dedalus has not had a bath since October 1903. (65)

In the six consecutive passages, Markson juxtaposes the title of a sixteenth-century English comedy, a fragment of the second line of Gerard Manley Hopkins's poem "Spring and Fall," a fact about T. S. Eliot, the beginning of a line from the Book of Genesis (17: 17), the date on which James Joyce's *Ulysses* is set, and a commentary on its protagonist. None of those elements is connected by a conjunction which would account for the logic of this sequence. Instead, the reader may only observe the looser relation of thematic analogy, the common denominators being the child (the addressee of Hopkins's poem and the prophesied heir to Abraham, whose birth is announced in the previous line of Genesis), Jewish origins (of the character in Eliot's poem, Abraham and Leopold Bloom) and *Ulysses*.

The above excerpt also illustrates the radical fragmentariness of the constituent passages in *This Is Not a Novel*. The only self-contained snippets are the comments on Eliot and Dedalus. The opening title and the date in line five, while not technically fragments of any larger whole, are devoid of any explanatory note, which may render them incomprehensible to many non-scholarly readers. The passage on Abraham begins with the word "then," which emphasizes the elimination of the earlier part – a sentence offering the reason for Abraham's surprised reaction.[5] Markson also cuts the rest of the Biblical line, which continues, "and said in his heart, Shall a child be born unto him who is one hundred years old?" ("Genesis"). Perhaps the most fragmentary element in the above excerpt is the minuscule passage from "Spring and Fall," consisting of only the last two words of the poem's opening question: "Márgarét, áre you grieving/ Over Goldengrove unleaving?"

The fragmentariness of Markson's work, alongside its other collage-like characteristics – the use of appropriated material and the programmatic absence of clear relations between successive components – prompts the attentive reader to become a virtual co-author of its meaning. In that respect, it belongs to the Barthesian category of "writerly" (*scriptible*), rather than "readerly" (*lisible*), works (*S/Z* 4) and conforms to Thomas P. Brockelman's argument that in every collage "sense is something to be *made* rather than secured" (37, emphasis original). It is for all those reasons that Markson's "Writer" acknowledges the structural indebtedness to collage in the following self-reflexive snippet, which appears in each volume of the tetralogy: "Nonlinear. Discontinuous. Collage-like. An assemblage" (112).

This Is Not a Novel as a manifesto

Despite the apparent rejection of the novel as an apt generic category for Markson's composition expressed in the ironic title of *This Is Not a Novel*, the author ensured that each book in the series contains the contentious word "novel" either in the title (as is the case with *This Is Not a Novel* and *The Last Novel*) or the subtitle (both *Reader's Block* and *Vanishing Point* are subtitled *A Novel*). Furthermore, the numerous manifesto-like passages in the book under consideration formulate postulates regarding "the novel" even if most attributes of the genre that the narrator wishes to conceive may be called anti-novelistic. The term "anti-novel," however, is curiously absent from the entire tetralogy.[6] What Markson proposes, both in the

---

[5] Alternatively, "then" may be interpreted as signaling an action subsequent to the one described in the Eliot passage, although the chronological relation between the two events is evidently disturbed.

[6] The multiple links between Markson's tetralogy and the poetics of the anti-novel are the subject of my article "'A Novel Against the Novel': David Markson's Antinov-

programmatic strand of snippets and through the construction of the book, is the novel stretched beyond recognition – the novel composed through a consistent elimination of devices traditionally associated with the genre.

The earlier cited expression of weariness of "writing" and "making up stories," which opens the book, is followed by an admission of tiredness of "inventing characters" (1). Those statements prepare the ground for a series of snippets scattered across the ensuing seven pages. It begins with the passage "A novel with no intimation of story whatsoever, Writer would like to contrive./ And with no characters. None" (2). The consecutive snippets prescribe the following characteristics: "Plotless. Characterless" (2); "Actionless ... with no *sequence of events* ... with no indicated *passage of time*" (3); "with no *setting*" (5); "with no social themes" (6); "with no politics" (7); "entirely without symbols"; and "without even a subject" (8).[7] The last passages echo the book's epigraph from Jonathan Swift's *A Tale of a Tub* (1704): "I am now trying an Experiment very frequent among Modern Authors, which is, to write upon Nothing."[8]

The passage announcing the renunciation of "subject" is directly followed by the three consecutive snippets:

> There is no work of art without a subject, said Ortega.
> A novel tells a story, said E. M. Forster.
> If you can do it, it ain't bragging, said Dizzy Dean. (8–9)

Besides being another example of the collage technique of juxtaposing appropriated material, the sequence is the culmination of Markson's manifesto. Ironically, it is a remark by a baseball player, rather than one of the ubiquitously cited artists, that affords the most direct insight into Markson's strategy in *This Is Not a Novel* – to formulate a manifesto for a new novel and to embody its radical claims in the selfsame book.[9] Despite the opening expression of exhaustion by the novel and the recurrent references to death, Markson's work is not defeatist. The author – or Writer, as

---

elistic Tetralogy," which attempts to situate Markson's ideas about literature in the tradition of the *nouveau roman*.

[7] All italics in the original.

[8] It also ties in with Gustave Flaubert's famous declaration about wanting to "create a book about nothing" (qtd. in Brown 289).

[9] Dizzy Dean's words – this time without any attribution – reappear on the last page of the book, confirming their importance (167). The juxtaposition of figures associated with high art with a sport celebrity, and thus a representative of popular culture, may be seen as a highly postmodernist strategy. Baseball, incidentally, constitutes a frequent reference point throughout the tetralogy.

he prefers to call himself – professes faith in his project by comparing it to the works of Joyce and Picasso.[10]

One of the nine references to the Spanish painter is the following exchange:

> You can actually draw so beautifully. Why do you spend your time making all these queer things?
> Picasso: That's why. (137)

Several pages later, a parallel passage appears:

> Writer has actually written some relatively traditional novels. Why is he spending his time doing this sort of thing?
> That's why. (144)

It is difficult not to interpret Writer's statement without considering the obvious autobiographical analogy with Markson's own career as an author of several formally conventional novels such as *The Ballad of Dingus Magee* (1965), who, during the last two decades of his life, dedicated himself to experimental fiction. Markson's gesture of discarding "traditional novels" in favor of "this sort of thing" arises from his earlier professed weariness of the standard safety nets of plot and character. Once the art of constructing intricate fictions, or the art of realist painting in Picasso's case, has been mastered, a new direction needs to be pointed out. The direction is forward, as suggested by the words of the hockey player Wayne Gretzky quoted in *The Last Novel*: "I skate to where the puck is going to be, not where it's been" (155).

On the last page of *This Is Not a Novel* Writer wonders if he has managed to escape genre in accordance with his earlier professed ambition. The closing snippet appropriated from the end of Richard Burton's *The Anatomy of Melancholy* – "Farewell and be kind" (167) – is, admittedly, far from the manifesto-like call to action culminating in a lively exclamation mark. Rather, it ends on a note of ambivalence resulting from the lack of a clear logic to the juxtaposed elements – a note familiar in collage but barely welcome in the message-oriented manifesto. The farewell passage ties in with the recurrent theme of death, which is also at odds with the youthful enthusiasm conventionally associated with the poetics of the manifesto. That tone, absent from Markson's book, can be found in *Reality Hunger* – a work of a much younger author, to which I shall now turn.

---

[10] Among numerous labels (some of them ironic) that Writer considers for his book is that of a "synthetic personal *Finnegans Wake*" (185).

Reality Hunger – structure, collage, fragmentation

David Shields's book is composed of 618 numbered passages, which have been arranged into 26 sections titled from "a" to "z." Although its length (close to two hundred pages) is unusual for a manifesto, the layout – snippets surrounded by a lot of space – and the use of numbering are common in the genre. In her study of the poetics of avant-garde manifestos, Marjorie Perloff notes that enumeration is practiced in order to hold the reader's attention and endow the text with a sense of practicality – each consecutive passage serves as another goal to be attained (96). The length of passages varies from two words ("I exaggerate" [80])[11] to two pages, which makes the average nugget considerably longer than in Markson's book. Over two-thirds of Shields's passages are either direct or slightly modified quotations from multiple sources. Among the most commonly cited authors are Ralph Waldo Emerson, W. G. Sebald, John D'Agata, Jonathan Raban, Vivian Gornick, Ross McElwee and Geoff Dyer. Shields, like Markson, never uses quotation marks to set off original from appropriated content. Unlike Markson, Shields never credits the author in the text, only in the endnotes contained in an appendix at the back of the book, which – as he admits – he was forced to attach by the lawyers of his publisher. In order to dissuade the reader from looking up the origin of each passage, he advises them to cut the section off along the indicated dotted line (p. 209).

The composition of *Reality Hunger* is very much indebted to Jonathan Lethem's essay "The Ecstasy of Influence: A Plagiarism" (2007). Published in *Harper's Magazine*, the piece is woven out of numerous quotations by, among others, Roland Barthes, Michel de Certeau and David Foster Wallace. What is more, Lethem has also included at the end – in this case voluntarily – the key to his text, where he explains the origins of all the plagiarized passages. Both authors admit to having edited certain passages in the appropriated parts in order to grant their texts a greater coherence in terms of style as well as content. Such practices are common in collage literature and were implemented quite frequently by, among others, the founder of the cut-up technique – William S. Burroughs. To hide the seams between consecutive appropriated passages, Lethem integrates all of them into a continuous, fluid text divided into standard paragraphs. As a result, "The Anxiety of Influence" reads like a sustained argument in favor of plagiarism as an artistic strategy. According to Zara Dinnen, Lethem "fully

---

[11] When referring to *Reality Hunger*, I shall offer the number of the passage rather than that of the page, as it is a more precise indicator of location (also applicable in the electronic version of the text). For quotations from the appendix, I shall give the page number (preceded by "p.").

reconfigures others' words within his own framework" and "stifles the differences between the discrete materials" while Shields presents them as "distinct fragments" (219–20, 226).

Besides the use of numbering and blank space between consecutive passages and the incorporation of a variety of sources, Shields enhances the fragmentariness of the text by occasionally employing snippets which do not constitute self-contained semantic elements. An example of that is passage 345: "—the singular obsessions endlessly revised," which, as the appendix explains, is taken from Thomas Lux's "Triptych, Middle Panel Burning." Even when the passage takes the form of a sentence, as is the case with the earlier cited "I exaggerate" from Lauren Slater's *Lying* (2000), the eradication of the original context heightens the sense of its incompletion. The resulting disorientation is a common feature of fragmentary writing and collage texts alike.

As far as its composition is concerned, *Reality Hunger* meets all the earlier outlined criteria of collage literature. It is fragmentary, heterogeneous, non-linear and appropriates multiple external elements as readymades. It is also an essentially hybrid text, interspersing the genres of critical essay, autobiography and manifesto. Its formal structure can be exemplified by the following excerpt:

121
These are the facts, my friend, and I must have faith in them.

122
What is a fact? What's a lie, for that matter? What, exactly, constitutes an essay or a story or a poem or even an experience? What happens when we can no longer freeze the shifting phantasmagoria which is our actual experience?

123
During the middle of a gig, Sonny Rollins sometimes used to wander outside and add the sound of his horn to the cacophony of passing cabs.

124
Have you ever heard a song that makes you feel as good as Stevie Wonder's "Fingertips – Part 2"? I haven't. It's so *real*. When you listen to the song, you can hear a guy in the band yelling, "What key? What key?" He's lost. But then he finds the key, and *boom*. Every time I hear that guy yelling, "What key?" I get excited.

In the passages 121 and 122 Shields juxtaposes a quotation from Cicero with that of John D'Agata's *The Next American Essay*. Although both are concerned with the notion of fact, they are contradictory in their assessment of the accessibility of facts. Passage 123 is an original text, whereas the last snippet is by John Mellencamp; both regard music. As soon becomes evident, the excerpt is not marked by what David Antin calls "explicit syntactical relations." Instead of logic and sequence, one can observe relations of likeness and difference.

The common denominator for all the passages is their interest in authenticity, but there is little sense of a coherent arrangement of parts that would unify the multiple voices. On the contrary, the distinctness of the passages is emphasized – both by their physical distance from one another and by the lack of logical consistency between them.

Reality Hunger as a manifesto

Shields's ambition to create an artistic program for a literature of the present and future is articulated in the opening passage. He begins by arguing that the prime motivation of each new artistic movement is to "smuggle more of what the artist thinks is reality into the work of art" (1). Each movement, he adds, also needs a formulated set of beliefs and principles. Shields's ensuing enumeration of classic manifestos – from Horace's to the Dogme 95 filmmakers' – is interpreted by Lara Winkiel as a manifestation of self-consciousness about the history of the genre which is characteristic of contemporary (or postmodern) manifestos (264). The author then goes on to state his aim, which is to "write the *ars poetica* for a burgeoning group of interrelated but unconnected artists in a multitude of forms and media ... who are breaking larger and larger chunks of 'reality' into their work" (1). Although the exact make-up of that group is never specified, from the recurrent references to their works it may be inferred that Shields has in mind such authors as, among others, Renata Adler, Lydia Davis, David Foster Wallace, Jonathan Lethem, Jonathan Raban, Dave Eggers, Douglas Coupland and David Markson.

Shields devotes a lot more attention than Markson to asserting the inadequacy of the novel form. He sees the traditional tools of the novel – plot, character, genre – as long expired conventions which are incapable of conveying the experience of being alive in the twenty-first century. For Shields, the "apparatus of the novel" is a "huge, elaborate, overbuilt stage set" which makes the reader plough through "seven hundred pages to get the handful of insights that were the reason the book was written" (379). Why not strip it from all the unnecessary machinery and convey only the gist, Shields is asking. His is the principle of divestment, which he formulates using the words of David Mamet: "How much can one remove and still have the composition be intelligible? This understanding, or its lack, divides those who can write from those who can really write. Chekhov removed the plot. Pinter, elaborating, removed the history, the narration;

Beckett, the characterization. We hear it anyway. Omission is a form of creation" (357). The elimination of successive elements of the novel is precisely what Markson proposes in the metafictional passages at the beginning of *This Is Not a Novel*. While Markson's Writer admits to being tired of the novel, Shields goes so far as to pronounce it defunct: "The novel is dead. Long live the antinovel, built from scraps" (327).

In one autobiographical passage, Shields describes his artistic epiphany when, having written "two linear, realistic novels and dozens of conventionally plotted stories," he was struck by an alternative: "I could take various fragments of things – aborted stories, outtakes from novels, journal entries, lit crit – and build a story out of them. I really had no idea what the story would be about; I just knew I needed to see what it would look like to set certain shards in juxtaposition to other shards" (514). "Scraps" and "shards" are the building blocks of the literature which Shields postulates and celebrates – fragmentary, appropriative and hybrid. His rationale for advocating these three properties is that they allow for "smuggling" more of reality into the work. Fragmentation, Shields suggests, results from candor and the rejection of the idea of life as "prepackaged along narrative lines." "Reality-based art" cannot bear the straitjacket of narrative and inevitably "splinters and explodes" (70). Appropriation and plagiarism, in turn, are discussed in *Reality Hunger* as woven into the fabric of all creativity and art. One of the epigraphs to the book is Picasso's statement that "art is theft," on which Shields later elaborates and notes that "all of culture is an appropriation game" (261, 289).[12] His advice for contemporary artists echoes William S. Burroughs's manifesto for the cut-up published five decades earlier: "Take a source, extract what appeals to you, discard the rest. Such an act of editorship is bound to reflect something of the individual doing the editing" (Shields 350).

Shields's postulate of a hybrid literature springs from his distrust of genre, described as a "minimum-security prison" (210), and his aversion to the terms "fiction" and "non-fiction," which he calls an "utterly useless distinction" (184). His skepticism about literature that complies with neat classifications is highlighted in the epigraph by Walter Benjamin: "All great works of literature either dissolve a genre or invent one" (590). In the course of the book, Shields quotes various authors – from Emerson to Terry Gilliam – asserting the need for art that combines multiple sources,

---

[12] Like Lethem in "The Ecstasy of Influence," Shields condemns those who attempt to staunch appropriation through the appeal to copyright laws. In the appendix, when he urges the reader to cut off the ensuing bibliography, he argues that "reality cannot be copyrighted" (p. 209).

disciplines and genre conventions. Another combination which Shields considers unavoidable is that of fiction and non-fiction. Both of them are tinged with the other: all that is ostensibly fiction is in some way anchored in reality and all apparent non-fiction (of which the memoir is Shields's favorite example) resorts, deliberately or not, to fictional tools.

Shields's literary forms of choice, which accommodate fragmentariness, appropriation and hybridity, are the lyric essay and collage. The former is a recent notion used to refer to writing which draws on the conventions of poetry, autobiography and criticism. He embraces it as a novel conflation of "art and fact ... imagination and observation, rumination and argumentation, human faith and human perception" (72). Among the authors most often associated with the lyric essay are writers frequently cited in *Reality Hunger:* John D'Agata, Anne Carson and Annie Dillard. The second form which he celebrates is collage, to which he devotes an entire 63-passage-long section. In it, he juxtaposes statements about its poetics and politics by authors such as Walter Benjamin, James Joyce, Ronald Sukenick, W.G. Sebald and Lance Olsen.[13] What Shields appreciates most about collage is the renunciation of plot and its teleology – the sense that "everything happens for a reason" (321). As such, it constitutes an "evolution beyond narrative" (328). "Everything I write," he declares, "is to some extent collage" (330).

Collage and the future of literature

As I have attempted to demonstrate, *This Is Not a Novel* and *Reality Hunger* give a similar diagnosis of the ailments of contemporary fiction and suggest a similar antidote. What they see as its greatest burden is the excessive reliance on what Shields calls the "apparatus of the novel" – the demands of plot, character and genre. In place of meticulously crafted narratives, they advocate heterogeneous structures that incorporate "shards" of seemingly incompatible materials and flaunt their borrowings from multiple sources. In other words, they point to collage as the most accommodating form for literary experimentation in the twenty-first century. It may appear paradoxical that collage, invented by the Cubists just over a hundred years ago, has retained its avant-garde status and can still be advocated as the form to which contemporary writers should aspire.

I want to offer two main reasons for its continued productivity, neither of which is suggested by Markson or Shields. Firstly, collage – of all literary

---

[13] One of the passages in this section is a direct quotation from Markson: "Nonlinear. Discontinuous. Collage-like. An assemblage. As is already more than self-evident" (359).

forms – is best suited to represent the experience of crisis, inaugurated – in the first year of the century – by the fall of the Twin Towers and followed by the collapse of Lehman Brothers and the election of Donald Trump, to speak only of the American context. Each collage, after all, enacts a clash of distinct, often opposing voices and incompatible elements, which results in their uneasy coexistence and tension. Because of its structural reliance on an inner contradiction, Thomas P. Brockelman calls it "an art of crisis – an art *in* perpetual crisis" (35, emphasis original). Among the crisis-inducing collisions which contemporary collage has been used to represent are those between liberalism and fundamentalism (in Lance Olsen's *Head in Flames*, 2009) and between the human and the posthuman (in Steve Tomasula's *VAS: An Opera in Flatland*, 2002).

The second reason for the artistic validity of collage today has been indicated by David Banash in his book *Collage Culture* (2013), in which he deems it a very apt and popular metaphor for the "phenomenal experience of everyday life," marked by fragmentation, overproduction and media saturation (14). Banash argues that collage remains relevant because it requires the same kind of attention as the twenty-first-century world, with its proliferation of media stimuli that need to be integrated by the individual for any meaning to emerge (200). Budd Hopkins notices that, because of their immersion in the mediascape, the contemporary recipients of collage have been better trained to "grasp a sequence that has missing parts" and "make connections between seemingly disjunctive units" than the audience of the first collagists – Picasso and Braque (12). What is more, the availability of affordable planes has made traveling, previously a laborious and time-consuming process, into an experience resembling "an immediate juxtaposition of locations" – a "collage of places" (12). Paradoxically, those recent developments have increased rather than decreased the timeliness of collage. Among the most recent and most successful works to take advantage of that phenomenon are Maggie Nelson's *Bluets* (2009), Jenny Offill's *Dept. of Speculation* (2014), Will Eaves's *The Absent Therapist* (2014) – examined in Mariano D'Ambrosio's article in this volume – and Olsen's *Dreamlives of Debris* (2017) – all of which embrace the main postulates formulated by Markson and Shields, and substantiate Luc Sante's prediction made in the *New York Times* that *Reality Hunger* "probably heralds what will be the dominant modes in years and decades to come."

Works Cited

Antin, David. *Radical Coherency: Selected Essays on Art and Literature, 1966 to 2005*. Chicago: U of Chicago P. 2011.

Banash, David. *Collage Culture: Readymades, Meaning, and the Age of Consumption.* Amsterdam: Rodopi, 2013.

Barthes, Roland. *S/Z.* 1970. Trans. Richard Miller. New York City: Hill and Wang, 1974.

Boxall, Peter. *Twenty-First-Century Fiction: A Critical Introduction.* Cambridge: Cambridge UP, 2013.

Brockelman, Thomas P. *The Frame and the Mirror: On Collage and the Postmodern.* Evanston: Northwestern UP, 2001.

Brown, Frederick. *Flaubert: A Biography.* Cambridge: Harvard UP, 2007.

Dinnen, Zara. "In the Mix: The Potential Convergence of Literature and New Media in Jonathan Lethem's 'The Ecstasy of Influence.'" *Journal of Narrative Theory* 42.2 (2012): 212–30.

Drąg, Wojciech. "'A Novel Against the Novel': David Markson's Antinovelistic Tetralogy." *Polish Journal of English Studies* 1 (2015): 11–25.

Dussel, Ines. "Foucault and Education." *The Routledge International Handbook of the Sociology of Education.* Eds. Michael W. Apple, Stephen J. Ball and Luis Armando Gandin. Abingdon: Routledge, 2010. 27–36.

"Genesis 17:15." *Bible Hub*, http://biblehub.com/genesis/17-15.htm. Accessed 1 Jan. 2018.

Gibbons, Alison. *Multimodality, Cognition, and Experimental Literature.* Abingdon: Routledge, 2012.

Hassan, Robert. *The Age of Distraction: Reading, Writing, and Politics in a High-Speed Networked Economy.* New Brunswick: Translation, 2012.

Hopkins, Budd. "Modernism and the Collage Aesthetic." *New England Review* 18.2 (1997): 5–12.

Karpowicz, Agnieszka. *Kolaż: Awangardowy gest kreacji: Themerson, Buczkowski, Białoszewski.* Wydawnictwa Uniwersytetu Warszawskiego, 2007.

Kostelanetz, Richard. *A Dictionary of the Avant-Gardes.* Abingdon: Routledge, 2001.

Markson, David. *The Last Novel.* Berkeley: Counterpoint, 2007.

---. *Reader's Block.* Normal: Dalkey Archive, 1996.

---. *This Is Not a Novel.* London: CB Editions, 2010.

Perloff, Marjorie. "Collage and Poetry." *Encyclopedia of Aesthetics.* Ed. Michael Kelly. Vol. 1. Oxford: Oxford UP, 1998. 384–87.

---. *The Futurist Moment: Avant-Garde, Avant Guerre, and the Language of Rupture.* U of Chicago P, 2003.

Sante, Luc. "The Fiction of Memory." *New York Times*, 12 Mar. 2010, http://www.nytimes.com/2010/03/14/books/review/Sante-t.html. Accessed 12 Nov. 2017.

Shields, David. *Reality Hunger: A Manifesto.* New York: Vintage, 2011.

Sims, Laura. "David Markson and the Problem of the Novel." *New England Review* 29.3 (2008): 58–70.

Tabbi, Joseph. "Solitary Inventions: David Markson at the End of the Line." *Modern Fiction Studies* 43.3 (1997): 745–72.

Winkiel, Laura. "Manifestos and *Ars Poetica*." *The Routledge Companion to Experimental Literature.* Eds. Joe Bray, Alison Gibbons and Brian McHale. Abingdon: Routledge, 2012: 253–66.

Chapter 10

Fragmentation in David Foster Wallace's fiction

Jarosław Hetman,
Nicolaus Copernicus University, Toruń

A strange kind of patricide

There are many reasons why David Foster Wallace is considered one of the leading figures, if not the most significant representative, of his generation. The towering, bandana-clad, soft-voiced approachable and unpretentious presence in American letters – with thousands of devoted fans drawn to his scruffy exterior and the legends of his kindness – also happens to have won acclaim by publishing an experimental novel of encyclopedic length in a country where the average literacy is below eighth grade level (Kirsch, Jungeblut, Jenkins and Kolstad 25). By all principles of the American publishing market, Wallace, with his fragmented and at times outright frustrating narrative style, should have stayed in his narrow academic niche along with all those post-war experimentalists that have preceded and, to a considerable degree, shaped him; yet he has not. Although the reasons for this peculiar state of affairs are undoubtedly many, I would like to argue that the prevalent one has to do with the shift in the literary tradition *Infinite Jest* (1996) has caused. One can make a valid claim that it is impossible to attribute a significant change in thinking about literature to one particular work by one particular author, yet I would like to put forward that Wallace has made that shift occur in the minds of hundreds of thousands, in spite of the formal challenges that his literature puts before his readers. Moreover, I would like to argue that formal fragmentation plays a crucial role in the author's reception: on the one hand, it poses a rewarding challenge that the literary audience appreciated after being exposed to a tradition of writing that left them intellectually and spiritually undernourished; on the other, it helps to depict an aesthetically shattered reality of popular culture in which the audience were raised.

We should not look for the reasons of *Infinite Jest*'s spectacular commercial success (for an experimental piece of fiction, that is) in the novel itself, but rather in the general *geist* of postcapitalist, and perhaps, more importantly, postmodern America. A ruthless, honest and acute critique of the world's last superpower at the turn of the centuries pronounced the fears, anxieties, and frustrations of a generation raised in the opulent shallowness of the Reagan Era. With many of the most prominent literary voices closed off in the ivory towers of the country's best universities, the former subscribers of the now withered magazines were left to the mercy of a televised culture, whose fragmented poetics, the aesthetics of MTV music videos and the cynical discourse of advertising have taken their toll. The comforts of the campuses and the security of tenure proved hardly the conditions for literary innovation, and soon its exhaustion was announced.[1]

The young Dave Wallace (the middle name was added later, on a suggestion from one of the publishers) found himself in the unlikely position of being on both sides of the fence: a campus child of James D. Wallace, a moral philosopher, and Sally Jean Wallace, an English professor, he grew up both reading extensively and watching, in his own words, "grotesque amounts of television" (McCaffery). A college overachiever with a double *summa cum laude* in philosophy and English, Wallace understood well the perilous situation that American postmodernist fiction found itself in. His ties with such authors as John Barth, Robert Coover, Donald Barthelme and William Gaddis were strong and complex, which is most clearly visible in his early fiction, *The Broom of the System* (1987) and "Westwards the Course of Empire Takes Its Way" (1989). Wallace relied on his old postmodernist masters in terms of style but simultaneously expressed his reservations concerning the moral implications of postmodernist experimentation. With its roots deep in poststructuralist theory, postmodernist literature not only lacks but dismisses the possibility of ever possessing a center, any center, also a moral center, which is a danger that Wallace, the son of a moral philosopher, was quick to notice. The writer's position from early on in his career was difficult because he grew up as a successor to a generation of literary rebels that have brought the rebellion to the point of anarchy and then left it there. Deprived of his natural right to overturn his literary forefathers, in his famous essay "E Unibus Pluram" Wallace observed that the rebels of the new era would have to be a peculiar group of anti-rebels: unhip, boring literary conservatives, who he himself, surprising at it may seem, has grown to represent (192–93). It is surprising because Wal-

---

[1] I am referring here of course to the famous essay by John Barth, "The Literature of Exhaustion" (1967).

lace's public image screams rebellion against the very institutions that have educated, employed and published him over the years.

Upon reflection, we will soon discover that the writer's entire *oeuvre* rests on contradiction, on a sense of friction between the compelling and the repelling, the pleasant and the painful, the entertaining and the challenging, the mainstream and the niche. Such is his relationship with his predecessors, a strange kind of patricide, as Boswell puts it: "both an act of murder and an act of homage" (168–69). In his "crime," Wallace employs tools that are characteristic of American experimental literature of the 1960s and 70s, but he uses them to completely different ends. One of the chief stylistic features the author shares with the likes of Coover and Barth is fragmentation, but whilst postmodernist fiction's fractured narratives conveyed the deconstructivist model of a disconnected world without a center, Wallace, as I shall argue, uses the very same sense of brokenness to bring together, a venture beyond the poststructuralist façade of textuality and towards a neo-Platonic sense of possible transcendence. His aim, and the aim of all literature is to "alleviate loneliness and give comfort, to break through what he characterized in *Infinite Jest* as each person's 'excluded engagement in the self'" (Max 149),[2] to oppose solipsism, which, according to Boswell, his great philosophical mentor Ludwig Wittgenstein saw as "the ultimate threat to modern people" (19). Depicting a fragmented world through the means of formal fragmentation, as is the case in the works of the leading American postmodernists, is not only not enough, it would seem; the real consequence of not taking a step further to counter this brokenness, is a way of affirming it, and as such, it is harmful. Identifying a quality of the surrounding reality without moving on to forming an axiological judgment carries the danger of complacency that Wallace was quick to identify.

In Wallace's writing I have been able to identify three types of fragmentation, and though they by no means form a closed set, I believe these categories help to understand the complexity, originality, and depth behind this unique stylistic feat. It would be easy to show that in Wallace's fiction each fracture deserves more than one label, but for the sake of clarity, I have decided to discuss the different types separately using different literary examples. Firstly, I would like to discuss brokenness as a mimetic technique, an epistemological function of a strange kind of realism that Wallace mentioned when speaking about his fiction. I will focus on *Infinite Jest* and expose the "unifying" quality of fragmentation, mainly as part of

---

[2] D. T. Max is referring here to a conversation Wallace had with fellow novelist and close friend, Jonathan Franzen.

Wallace's project aiming to "liberate" American fiction from the impasse brought about by poststructuralist thought. Secondly, I will turn to his famous collection *Brief Interviews with Hideous Men* (1999) to study fragmentation as a formal strategy and a reflection on the solipsistic disconnection haunting postcapitalist societies as a result of postmodernism entering the mainstream of culture. Thirdly, I will reflect on Wallace's premature death in relation to his unfinished novel *The Pale King* (2011) and examine the fascinating relationship the author managed to forge with his readers as a counterbalance to the unintended fragmentation of the published version of the novel.

Lower-case reality

In 1993 Wallace gave an interview which is perhaps the most important one in his life, because aside from the book-length *Although of Course You End Up Becoming Yourself: A Road Trip with David Foster Wallace* (2010) by David Lipsky, it is the most often-quoted piece of conversation in critical accounts of his fiction. It is especially valuable to scholars of Wallace because Larry McCaffery, himself a scholar, managed to incite the author to formulate many comprehensive yet compact statements about his fiction. The question of "formal tendencies" in Wallace's early fiction led the writer to make a distinction between Realism and realism, the former being associated with "stuff in the Howells/Wharton/Updike school," which was "absorbed and suborned by commercial entertainment" (McCaffery), the latter, an essentially recognizable way of depicting a chaotic, fragmented world. The lower-case realism becomes the narrative mode for much of Wallace's fiction, best exemplified by *Infinite Jest*.

Formal complexity is an integral part of Wallace's project, and fragmentation is one of its many features. In a way, one can perceive its role like that of conceptual art: the audience must experience the thing itself, rather than its representation; in the case of this novel, the experience is that of hardship. First encounters with *Infinite Jest* are often intimidating. A great many of the novel's reviews and critical accounts give the volume's exact page count (1079), some also mention the extensive footnotes (388). Bell and Dowling open their introduction to *A Reader's Companion to* Infinite Jest with a mention of a reviewer who gave up on the novel after the first page (9). The seemingly chaotic façade that the reader is initially confronted with stands against the commercially appropriated approachability of Realist narratives. Underneath we discover an overarching narrative structure that testifies to Wallace's fascination with mathematics, a fascination that finds numerous occasions to sneak into the plot of the novel, its metaphorical and metaphysical strata. *Infinite Jest* is organized around a geometrical figure known as the Sierpiński gasket, a fractal that illustrates the triangular organization of the text's plotlines as it also facilitates a reflection on the everlasting re-iteration in the poststructuralist reality. The figure suggests a compulsive repetition, which ties in well with addiction, the main theme of the novel. Additionally, being a fractal, it emphasizes the sense of brokenness, and in this sense, is consistent with the poetics Wallace employs. Thus fragmentation becomes the poetics of addiction, an affliction that defines *Infinite Jest*'s two protagonists, Don Gately and Hal Incandenza.

Coming from completely different social spheres, the two live in proximity without ever actually meeting each other (at least on the realist level of the plot, for in one of Gately's trauma-induced hallucinations, there is a hint that the two might know each other in the not-too-distant future, which is not depicted in the novel itself). The fact that their paths never intersect in the novel's "reality" is consistent with the theme of fragmentation reflected in the plot, on the level of mores, in other words. Hal's family, at first glance, could be classified as "privileged." His father, James Incandenza, a significant physicist with numerous patents in optics, established the elite tennis academy where Hal lives and trains, and in his spare time, James developed a career as an independent filmmaker. Underneath, however, he is a lonely alcoholic, whose disconnection leads him to a gruesome suicide. The inability to penetrate the walls that separate him from his family is perhaps best displayed by Wallace in the scene in which Hal is asked to meet with a "professional conversationalist," who, as it turns out, is James in disguise. The determination that the father shows in his efforts to communicate with his son clashes with the artificiality of the encounter: the two meet in a rented office that resembles the study of a psychotherapist. James's grotesque makeup and costume emphasize his desperation, as they also render his attempt a tragic failure. The scene's primary function is to help us understand the motivation behind the creation of the novel's eponymous film: the protagonist's father makes *Infinite Jest* in a final attempt to establish a relationship with his son, but in this too he fails spectacularly. The picture becomes a perversion of its creator's intention; it proves so compelling to the viewers that, unable to stop watching it, they slowly starve: the connection with the inanimate object becomes an embodiment of mortal alienation that defines postcapitalist life.

The second protagonist, Don Gately, comes from a dysfunctional family with a long history of physical abuse and alcohol addiction. The promising young man with an impressive stature has virtually no chance of living up to his athletic potential before he is consumed by a world of violence and drugs. Having committed manslaughter during one of the burglaries in which he specializes, Don hits rock bottom before he finally manages to enter rehab. His freedom from substance-dependency is dearly-bought, but his resolve is firm beyond belief. Gately, one of Wallace's most likable characters, becomes our guide in the world of AA and NA recovery programs; he introduces us to the smoky rooms where therapeutic sessions are held, and where the most terrifying and heartbreaking stories are told by those who amass enough courage to stand up and speak. These broken narratives take us through a broken world, but as they do, they also build an air of trust, truthfulness, and sincerity, an empathy indispensable to genuine human contact. Somewhat paradoxically, the fact that we are deliberately allowed only glimpses from lives of pain and humiliation produces a unifying effect. The fragmentation brought out by the language of those who have suffered so immensely, the separateness of each individual tragedy and the fracturing traumas that have defined the lives of those in the therapeutic sessions is mediated and made whole in the compassionate eyes of Don Gately.

By introducing a myriad of characters loosely organized around two protagonists, antithetical in many ways, Wallace produces an interesting effect: a world that is clearly falling apart, where people live lonely, detached lives, also gives hope. It is apparent that the brokenness is caused by the desire for pleasure that dominates the culture of the postcapitalist West. However, where there is fragmentation, there must also be a sense of unity, and in the case of Wallace's novel, this transcendent feeling can only be achieved by opposing pleasure with hardship. Reading *Infinite Jest* is a toil, from flipping through its many pages to finding the appropriate endnote – and then having to consult encyclopedias, chemistry textbooks, mathematical treatises, etc. – to the pain that comes from empathizing with the victims of violence and sexual abuse of the worst kind. But the work has an integrating quality: by venturing beyond individual comfort, one can escape the rushing solipsism of fragmentation.

Talk to me

Boswell explains Wallace's fascination with the thought of Wittgenstein by showing that in the philosopher's model of communication language itself becomes the greatest weapon against solipsism, for "language can *mean* only when the rules are agreed upon by more than one person" (Boswell 26). This, in itself, does not render communication either simple or efficient, for, to paraphrase Wittgenstein, once the rules are set, the game begins (Wittgenstein #31).

Brief Interviews with Hideous Men follows *Infinite Jest* by three years and is the first volume-length piece of fiction Wallace published after his great novel. Although the book is most often classified as a collection of short stories, there are significant reasons to see it instead as a cycle of separate yet connected pieces of short fiction (Boswell 182). Just as in *Infinite Jest*, the stylistic fragmentation is in touch with the cycle's metaphorical and thematic layers: sex and loneliness. According to Boswell, "Wallace has repeatedly said that the book is his attempt to address the subject of sex, which his work has hitherto shied away from addressing" (183). Having in mind *Infinite Jest*'s aforementioned accounts of rape, sexual obsession, and anxiety, it is difficult to agree with the author fully. It is clear, however, that human sexuality not only stands at the center of the volume's thematic scope, it also becomes a kind of catalyst for a discussion of all other interpersonal relationships, and as such, can be seen as an extension of Wallace's reflection on loneliness, so apparent in his *opus magnum*.

The entire book takes its title from a sequence of mock-interview transcripts that feature the eponymous men. Distinguished from each other only by an identification number that reveals that we are reading only a selection from a longer collection of "documents" in a seemingly random order, the men talk about their various problems with sex. They have little in common with one another; from their virtuously stylized words, it is easy to infer that they represent a variety of social classes with different educations, in at least one case also a different racial background, and yet their problems, also different, apparently have the same source. The plurality of voices, the separateness of the speakers emerging from the lack of narrative connections between the stories they tell and the way in which the interviews are dispersed around a volume that contains short stories governed by a different set of poetic principles enforces a sense of fragmentation, but as is the case with *Infinite Jest*, here too brokenness is counterbalanced by a "togetherness." In the case of *Brief Interviews*, the degree of belonging comes from a thematic consistency that binds the entire volume.

The format – cold, matter-of-fact and scientific – guarantees a guise of truthfulness, but as we read we soon discover that the seeming sincerity with which the men talk about the most intimate of their problems is simply another mask, and to our enormous readerly frustration, we are forced to conclude that perhaps to those men, and the many more like them, there is no hope for genuine communication. They are sentenced to lonely superficial lives because they are not willing to acknowledge the fact that they have transformed their capacity for being sincere into a peculiar, cynical form of anti-sincerity, which in the long term undermines anyone's credibility, but in the short term, gives them sexual privileges. The deep, destructive influence of poststructuralist thought on the everyday lives of the clueless inhabitants of a post-capitalist world cannot be overstated in the case of Wallace's fiction. In the words of Boswell, "Over and over again Wallace demonstrates how self-professed 'openness' can become an even more sinister form of deception. All the characters are in a sense metafictionists of their own feelings, with the result that their openness leaves them even more lonely and despairing than they would have been, had they simply remained dishonest" (183). The harboring of narcissistic disconnection, self-conscious anxiety and alienating irony has produced a generation entirely incapable of dealing with its own loneliness.

Finally, *Brief Interviews with Hideous Men* emphasizes this unbridgeable gap between people by removing the questions from the transcripts. The only voices that we have access to belong to the mischievously self-indulgent men. But this one-sidedness, typically for Wallace, also has a paradoxical consequence. The significant difference between the author and those who directly preceded him is that for the postmodernists it was enough to object. Echoing Linda Hutcheon, we may conclude that to a postmodernist author, to show and ridicule is enough, and irony in its subversiveness is an adequate tool for the job. For Wallace, identifying the problem without suggesting a solution falls desperately short of the writer's task, as I argued before. And indeed, in *Brief Interviews with Hideous Men*, in the absence of questions, we as readers are forced to guess what was asked. Thus, in our efforts, we summon our empathy, trying to reach out to the one to whom we have no ultimate access. The hideous men might be a lost cause; they will probably never find in themselves the capacity to venture beyond their narcissistic fantasies, but we, Wallace's audience, are shown not only the consequences of disconnection but also the means with which that solipsism can be overcome. Interestingly enough, it is not solely the language that enables us to transcend our individuality, for as we learn from the collection, language can be used masterfully to take us precisely nowhere. Thus, in the last "Brief Interview," it is something else, something unidentifiable and almost spiritual behind the way in which we use language that allows us to make contact with another human being.

This conclusion might come as a surprise to those aware of Wallace's obsession with language, which he most openly gave vent to in his famous sixty-page essay called "Authority and the American Usage" of 1999,[3] but it

---

[3] A reprinted version of this essay is available in his collection of essays *Consider the Lobster and Other Essays* from 2005.

can convincingly be explained with the author's strictly neo-Platonic convictions, the very same ones that made him question the poststructuralist assumptions of American postmodernist fiction. Perhaps it is his sincere belief in language combined with an acute understanding of its limitations that gives Wallace the authority to talk about such an elusive issue as the truth behind language, a distant recognition that emerges from behind broken sentences and unfinished thoughts.

Always already absent

I have borrowed the heading for my reflections on *The Pale King* from the French pragmatist philosopher, Jean-Jacques Lecercle, who used this formulation to describe the way in which the author functions in a relationship with their reader (62). In many ways the posthumously published novel is a fragmented text *par excellence* – the unfinished manuscript was assembled with much difficulty into a sequence by Wallace's longtime editor, Michael Pietsch, whose lengthy introduction to the book points out that the various fragments of the text were found at different stages of completion: "[t]he novel's central story does not have a clear ending, and the question inevitably arises: How unfinished is this novel? ... Some notes among David's manuscript pages suggest that he did not intend for the novel to have a plot substantially beyond the chapters here." A possible conclusion here is that, according to the editor, "the novel's apparent incompleteness is in fact intentional" (Pietsch).

This in itself would not be anything new to Wallace's readers; after all, his debut novel, *The Broom of the System*, ends mid-sentence. However, *The Pale King* arrives in the hands of readers well-familiar with at least a significant part of Wallace's previous fiction. I would even argue that the book was published *for* Wallace's devoted audience, as I can hardly imagine someone starting to discover an author's *oeuvre* with their unfinished work. Such a knowledgeable reader is likely to appreciate both the connections with the writer's remaining fiction and the elaborations and developments on his previous accomplishments. The Wallace-connoisseur, as one might call the reader of *The Pale King*, is able to find satisfaction in reading the novel because of an understanding of Wallace formed prior to its publication, and therefore, yet again somewhat paradoxically, despite his apparent absence, the author is more present here than ever before. It is the figure of the author that allowed both Pietsch and all other readers of the novel to put together all its existing fragments.

The publication of *The Pale King* was long-anticipated, which put a lot of pressure on Wallace, especially since after *Infinite Jest* the expectations were high. "It just made him crazy to think that he had been working on it for so long," reveals D. T. Max quoting his wife (Green qtd. in Max 261) before he moves on to discuss the terrible medical conditions that eventually led to the writer's suicide (261). The connection made by the biographer renders them quite meaningful: switching from Nardil[4] to a newer type of antidepressant would help Wallace not only avoid dietary restrictions but, much more importantly, it would help him achieve the kind of concentration levels that he felt were necessary to finish *The Pale King*. Sadly Wallace never did finish the novel in a form that would satisfy him, yet from Max's account of the writer's last evening, we can infer that he wanted the book published after his passing: "Green returned home at 9:30 and found her husband. In the garage, bathed in light from many lamps, sat a pile of nearly two hundred pages.... In his final hours, he tidied up the manuscript so that his wife could find it ... This was his effort to show the world what it was to be 'a fucking human being'" (265). The last quote from the paragraph concluding Max's biography of David Foster Wallace comes from the aforementioned McCaffery interview and is a fundamental statement on the function of fiction, on its capacity to bring people together with the skillful use of language. In the case of *The Pale King*, the distance between Wallace and his readers has never been smaller.

In one of the novel's most memorable scenes, we witness an unlikely barroom conversation between Drinion, possibly the most boring IRS officer working in the Peoria compound of the agency, and Meredith Rand, the office's most sexually desirable employee. As opposed to the lusty men of the *Brief Interviews*, Drinion is asexual and potentially also semi-autistic. While the interviewees in the short story cycle are hideously narcissistic and aiming for sexual conquest, the federal accountant is capable of paying his undivided attention to his interlocutor. His disinterested focus allows him to achieve a nirvana-like state, which, shockingly in an otherwise realistic narrative, manifests itself physically as Drinion begins to levitate. On the surface, *The Pale King*, a novel about the Internal Revenue Service, is a reflection on boredom and the significance of this elusive condition, yet much deeper, it becomes a study of transcendence. D. T. Max, who had access to Wallace's notebooks deposited at the Harry Ransom Center in Austin, shares the following comment the author meant for himself: "Bliss – a second by second joy and gratitude at the gift of being alive conscious [*sic*] – lies on the other side of crushing, crushing boredom. Pay close attention to the most tedious thing you can find ... and in waves,

---

[4] An antidepressant that Wallace had been taking for many years, with much reservation: "Wallace had never been certain that being on Nardil was the right thing, and whenever he was not writing well, he wondered if it played a role" (Max 261).

a boredom like you've never known before will wash over you and just about kill you. Ride these out, and it's like stepping from black and white into color" (Wallace qtd. in Max 229).

In many ways, the state that Drinion can achieve by his deep, empathetic concentration on the words of a fellow human being is the opposite of what the postcapitalist culture preaches: we are told to avoid boredom at any cost. The fullness in which Drinion can pay attention distances him from himself and brings him close to Rand, so close in fact that we are often tempted to presuppose some form of eroticism, which then Wallace quite persistently continues to rule out. Rand is telling Drinion the story of how she met her husband while being confined to a mental ward, a story that is both profoundly intimate and deprived of a sexual agenda. Thus Wallace ushers in another seeming contradiction, a Kantian disinterested interest, but focused not on art, but on another human being.

Falling into place

In Wallace's fiction ethics and aesthetics exist in a state of convergence. The aesthetics of fragmentation is counterbalanced by the ethics of harmonious transcendence. In *Infinite Jest*, this is expressed by the dichotomy between fractured narratives brought together by a mathematical organizing principle, the metaphorical dimension of which is exposed by the careful reader, whose effort, an extension of Wallace's ethical beliefs, functions as the link between the author and his audience. Literature is a communal enterprise, wherein separateness and togetherness jointly propel it towards infinity.

Communication is flawed, and perhaps nowhere within Wallace's *oeuvre* is this more visible than in *Brief Interviews with Hideous Men*, but it is precisely this imperfection that necessitates its unbreakable continuity. We shall never know, for instance, whether the subject in Brief Interview #20 indeed fell in love with the formerly despised granola-crunching sexy posthippie that he initially just wanted to take advantage of, or if he is merely fooling the interviewer, but this uncertainty fuels our efforts to understand him, Wallace, and each other. It is no accident that in the climax of Drinion's conversation with Rand in *The Pale King* the man begins to levitate. The supernatural quality of his attentiveness testifies to the inaccessibility of the ideal, but at the same time, it does not fail to point us in a direction.

In light of what I have been arguing, it should not be surprising that Wallace's fiction has won him an extensive following. His readers were strongly affected by the type of prose with which they were able to identify. In his narratives, they were able to identify their own disconnection, and the challenges put before them enabled them to alleviate the pain of leading fractured lives surrounded by a fragmented reality. This created a connection between Wallace and his readers, which proves that his efforts in kindling the spirit of community in an increasingly solipsistic world were successful.

Works Cited

Bell, Robert, and William Dowling. *A Reader's Companion to* Infinite Jest. Xlibris: Bloomington, 2005.

Boswell, Marshall. *Understanding David Foster Wallace.* Columbia: U of South Carolina P, 2003.

Kirsch, Irvin S., Ann Jungeblut, Lynn Jenkins and Andrew Kolstad. *Adult Literacy in America: A First Look at the Findings of the National Adult Literacy Survey,* 3rd ed., U.S. Department of Education, 2002, https://nces.ed.gov/pubs93/93275.pdf. Accessed 23 Feb. 2018.

Lecercle, Jean-Jacques. *Interpretation as Pragmatics.* New York: Palgrave Macmillan, 1999.

Max, D. T. *Every Love Story Is a Ghost Story: A Life of David Foster Wallace.* New York: Viking, 2012.

McCaffery, Larry. "A Conversation with David Foster Wallace." Dalkey Archive, 1993, https://www.dalkeyarchive.com/a-conversation-with-david-foster-wallace-by-larry-mccaffery/1993. Accessed 24 Dec. 2017.

Pietsch, Michael. Editor's Note. *The Pale King.* By David Foster Wallace. Boston: Little, Brown, 2011. Kindle edition.

Wallace, David Foster. *Brief Interviews with Hideous Men.* Little, Brown, 2009. Kindle edition.

---. "E Unibus Pluram: Television and U.S. Fiction." *Review of Contemporary Fiction* 13.2 (1993): 151–94.

---. *Infinite Jest.* Boston: Little, Brown, 2009. Kindle edition.

---. *The Pale King.* Boston: Little, Brown, 2011. Kindle edition.

Wittgenstein, Ludwig. *Philosophical Investigations.* 1953. Trans. G.E.M. Basil Anscombe. Oxford: Blackwell, 2011.

Chapter 11

Trauma and the mechanics of fragmentation in *Extremely Loud and Incredibly Close* by Jonathan Safran Foer

Caroline Magnin,
Sorbonne Université

In the aftermath of 9/11, writers have struggled to come to terms with the event, some resorting to new or at least unusual devices as a means to communicate differently, thereby standing against the normalization or domestication of an event exceeding available categories of representation. In his 2005 novel *Extremely Loud and Incredibly Close*, Jonathan Safran Foer opts for a form of visual writing which surprises the reader because of its unconventionality. The reading process is often interrupted by facsimiles representing images collected in a scrapbook by Oskar Schell, a nine-year-old boy who has just lost his father in the 9/11 terrorist attacks, or by pages from the notebook that his mute grandfather uses to communicate. His grandmother struggles with silence and erasure, and the chapters that she narrates display sentences separated by large blank spaces, as if disconnected from each other, when her words do not simply turn into blank pages. These visual devices make for a particularly fragmented narrative which challenges the reader's expectations.

In this paper, I contend that the fragmentary nature of the novel pertains to a traumatic narration, in which the text itself bears the marks of trauma. To that end, I would like to establish a specific theoretical psychoanalytical framework.[1] The term "trauma" tends to be used rather loosely, often erro-

---

[1] I am going to rely on the works of Sigmund Freud, who first formulated the concept and offers the most comprehensive approach to trauma. Recent trauma theorists (Caruth and LaCapra, to name but a few) base their arguments on his works, but often tend to focus on a single aspect of his theory, at the risk of oversimplifying it.

neously assimilated to shock. For instance, when Matthew Mullins suggests that Oskar suffers from "the traumatic loss of his father" (298), that
the "'us versus them' mentality" can result in "more violence and trauma"
(299), and even that one can "inflict" trauma (304), it seems that the word
conveys very different realities from one occurrence to another. Similarly,
Philippe Codde refers to Oskar's inability to answer the phone to listen to
his father's last words as a "traumatizing 'betrayal'" (244), as if the term
was self-explanatory.[2]

According to Freud, three conditions need to be met in order to diagnose
psychological trauma. The first one is to be found in the etymology of the
word itself, which comes from the Greek for "wound," and whose Indo-
European roots evoke the idea of a breach or a penetration: trauma is a
brutal irruption into the psyche. It is so violent and unexpected that the
brain cannot properly assimilate the event, as Freud explains in his *Introductory Lectures on Psycho-Analysis*:

> [T]he term "traumatic" has no other sense than an economic one. We apply
> it to an experience which within a short period of time presents the mind
> with an increase of stimulus too powerful to be dealt with or worked off in
> the normal way, and this must result in permanent disturbances of the
> manner in which the energy operates. (275)

The second criterion is the notion of latency, which Freud describes in
Moses and Monotheism, using the example of a train accident:

> It may happen that someone gets away, apparently unharmed, from the
> spot where he has suffered a shocking accident, for instance a train colli-
> sion. In the course of the following weeks, however, he develops a series of
> grave psychical and motor symptoms, which can be ascribed only to his
> shock or whatever else happened at the time of the accident. He has devel-
> oped a "traumatic neurosis." (105)

The symptoms only become apparent after a certain period, so that it
does not seem, at first, that the person has suffered any physical or psychological injury. The event that cannot be registered into consciousness is
repressed, and only belatedly may it emerge, in the form of nightmares,
flashbacks, and other haunting images:

> The forgotten material is not extinguished, only "repressed"; its traces are
> extant in the memory in their original freshness, but they are isolated....
> They cannot establish contact with the other intellectual processes; they are

---

[2] Several articles on *Extremely Loud and Incredibly Close* mention the word "trauma"
in their title without defining the notion (Mullins) or use the term "shock" as a synonym for trauma (Pederson, Donn).

unconscious, inaccessible to consciousness. It may happen that certain parts of the repressed material have escaped this process, have remained accessible to memory, and occasionally reappear in consciousness, but even then they are isolated, a foreign body without any connection with the rest of the mind. (Freud, *Moses* 150–51)

The idea of fragmentation appears as symptomatic of the scarring effects of trauma on the psyche: when memory is not entirely suppressed, only disconnected elements remain accessible.

The third and last characteristic of trauma is *Nachträglichkeit*, usually referred to in English as deferred action, which differs from latency insofar as it is not simply about deferral but rather about the reinvestment of a past experience in the light of a new trauma which adds meaning to the first. As devastating and shocking as it may have been for Oskar, it is not a given that the death of his father should have been traumatic in the strictest sense of the term. And should we conclude that he suffers from trauma, it remains problematic to say that he "is traumatized when" he receives the phone messages from his father (Donn 24). A traumatic event occurs precisely because a correspondence is established with an older repressed trauma, which explains why different people have different reactions to the same catastrophe.

Collective trauma therefore cannot be so easily appropriated metaphorically and I will avoid referring to 9/11 as a traumatic experience for survivors and witnesses alike. Rather than trying to assess the potential for psychological trauma in fictional characters, I am going to show that the writing itself in *Extremely Loud and Incredibly Close* borrows from the clinical manifestations of trauma, and especially the two contrasting ways it may adopt, as delineated by Freud:

> The effects of the trauma are twofold, positive and negative. The former are endeavors to revive the trauma, to remember the forgotten experience, or, better still, to make it real – to live through once more a repetition of it.... These endeavors are summed up in the terms "fixations to the trauma" and "repetition-compulsion."
>
> ...
>
> The negative reactions pursue the opposite aim; here nothing is to be remembered or repeated of the forgotten traumata. They may be grouped together as defensive reactions. They express themselves in avoiding issues, a tendency which may culminate in an inhibition or phobia. (Freud, *Moses* 118–19)

The literary translation of the clinical phenomena results in both ellipsis and excess, amnesia and hypermnesia, silence and logorrhea, which makes for an unstable fragmentary narrative, reminiscent of Sandór

Ferenczi's observation that fragmentation is a means to prevent the total collapse of the psyche.[3] In *Extremely Loud and Incredibly Close*, the textual fragmentation effectively echoes the fragmentation of the self, but also that of memory, as Philippe Codde underlines by referring to Pierre Janet's "distinction between this fragmentary and visual 'traumatic memory' on the one hand, and 'narrative memory' on the other" (249). Whereas Codde only chooses to explore the visual dimension of Foer's novel, I suggest that the images inserted into the pages of the novel are fragmenting devices in their own right, which the narration will attempt to stitch back together, by providing the missing links between disconnected elements.

The dissemination of disconnected elements

Foer's novel surrenders to images of multiplicity, often much preferred to singularity. To begin with, instead of having one authoritative narrative voice, the novel follows the perspectives of three different characters, whose intertwined storylines further complicate the plot. Each of them tells in the first person the stories of people they met, especially Oskar, who takes time to introduce and at least briefly characterize each of the Blacks[4] he visits. Furthermore, these narratives remain unconnected; although the three narrators are related and interact with each other on a regular basis, they never seem to broach what is genuinely important to them. At no point is the reader told that Oskar reads the letter his grandmother addressed to him in her chapters; as for the letters written by the grandfather to his son, he never musters the courage to send them and ends up burying them in his son's coffin without anyone reading them first. Consequently, the narrator is offered three different accounts of 9/11 without anyone weighing in on them at any point, and each is given the same importance. The event itself seems to be multiplied in the same way as the images of the attack proliferate on several television screens in the electronics store window which informs the grandfather of what has just occurred (272). The historical event occupies even more space in the fragmented narrative, as if what resisted interpretation needed to be multiplied for the reader even to begin to comprehend it.

---

[3] "Should the quality and quantity of suffering exceed one person's powers of comprehension, then one capitulates; one endures no longer; it is no longer worthwhile to combine these painful things into a unit, and one is split into pieces. I do not suffer any more, indeed I cease to exist, at least as a complete ego" (Ferenczi 170).

[4] After his father's death in the 9/11 attacks on the World Trade Center, Oskar finds an envelope containing a key in his closet; he soon realizes that the word "black" written on the envelope is actually a last name, and sets out to visit every person named "Black" in New York City.

Many other elements in the novel attest to this propensity for the multiple, and none more so than the doubles that haunt its pages. Before Oskar meets his real grandfather, he becomes acquainted with one of the Blacks, an old man who lives in his building. The two develop a close relationship, and the old man accompanies the boy on his outings across New York. A substitute grandfather, he becomes entirely superfluous once Oskar meets the man to whom his grandmother refers as "the renter," and disappears from the narrative altogether, to such an extent that both characters were merged in Stephen Daldry's 2001 movie adaptation. Similarly, Oskar's father, Thomas Schell junior, was named after his own father, thereby creating a constant confusion, so that when he reads the names of the dead in the newspaper after 9/11, Thomas Schell senior is at first shocked to read his own name: "I saw it, Thomas Schell, my first thought was that I had died" (273). The grandmother, who after all is the one who chose to name her son after the husband who abandoned her, is later amazed at their resemblance and remarks, "He wanted to be his own father" (277). She herself suffers from a certain lack of individuality; indeed, before Thomas married her, he was in love with her sister Anna who died in the Dresden bombing. Her sister's name itself, a palindrome, evokes the image of a mirror. The confusion between the two women is emphasized by the fact that the grandmother is never named and always referred to in relation to somebody else (Anna's sister, Thomas's wife, Oskar's grandmother). Against Thomas's will, the substitute wife ends up carrying a substitute child who symbolically replaces the one who died with his pregnant mother in Dresden. When the grandfather later addresses the child he has never known in his letters, the addressee is twofold: he reaches out to both the one he lost and the one he abandoned. It seems that, symbolically, each character is fragmented into two separate entities so as to alleviate their pain. This is precisely what Marc Amfreville suggests may happen in the literary translations of trauma, in reference to the characters of Edgar and Clithero in Charles Brockden Brown's *Edgar Huntly* (1799): "The fragmentation of a single being [has] to do with ambivalence, the explosion of a unified ego into several atoms which, according to Ferenczi, aims to divide the intolerable suffering of the person" (78, my translation).

The motif of the double also echoes the iconography of the twin towers. Jean Baudrillard remarks on the fascination they exert because of their duplication effect, of their architecture which evokes "cloning," or "a changeless genetic code." He dwells on the beauty and architectural perfection of these parallelepipeds, although he remarks they can also be interpreted as "a kind of perfect crime against form, a tautology of form which can give rise ... to the temptation to break the symmetry" (Baudrillard 46). This doubling effect results in the cancellation of their symbolic significance: "the fact that there were two of them signifies the end of any original reference" (43); "only the doubling of the sign truly puts an end to what it designates" (43). The multiplying effect could, therefore, result in dissolution, and points to the idea that the fragmentation of the text mimics the fragmentation of the traumatized self. Not only is fragmentation a recurrent theme in the novel, but it is also to be found at the micro level of textual analysis; for instance, the father's messages left on the answering machine become increasingly scrappy, as illustrated by the unconventional use of punctuation: "Sorry if. It's getting a bit. Smoky. I was hoping you would. Be. Home" (69). The poor quality of the phone call is rendered graphically, but one cannot help but think that this degradation of the sentence's coherence symbolically represents the father's impending death, and the dissolution of his very self looming over the text.

The prevalence of disconnected elements creates fragmentation, both in the characters' discourses and in the overall structure of the novel, which results in a disconcerting reading experience. The reader is forced to adopt the point of view of slightly unreliable narrators whose narratives often lack coherence, except for the connective tissue of the page. I argue that the fragmenting devices at play in the novel confront the reader with the effects of trauma, forcing them to set out on a quest for both meaning and direction.

Experiencing the clinical effects of trauma

Not only is *Extremely Loud and Incredibly Close* narrated from the perspectives of three different characters, but they also have very distinct preoccupations. While Oskar is obsessed with making sense of his father's death in the 9/11 attacks, his grandparents are haunted by the memory of the Dresden bombing, in which they literally lost everything, since they were both the sole survivors in their families. Therefore, the chapters alternate between one centered on 9/11 and one dealing with Dresden and its consequences. On the narrative level, it seems that, for the grandparents, the two events create a phenomenon of *Nachträglichkeit*: 9/11 reactivates the past trauma of the Dresden bombing. I would argue that the grandfather is not "retraumatized" (Uytterschout 66), but rather that the two events are in themselves constitutive of his trauma. Amfreville uses the image of the rhyme to illustrate the mechanisms of trauma: the occurrence of the second line retrospectively brings the reader back to the first one, thereby enabling the poetic device; it is not simply about the second line echoing the first, but rather the very idea of the rhyme implies a correspondence, a dialog between the two (Amfreville 125). Similarly, what happens on 9/11 seems to taint what happened in Dresden. The characters reference this previous traumatic event when they describe the images of the attacks they witnessed on television. For instance, the grandmother summons images of an ice rink, used to store the dead in Dresden: "Bodies falling. Planes going into buildings... They thought there would be thousands of bodies. They were going to put them in an ice rink" (231). On the macro level too, numerous clues are disseminated in the text, bringing the reader to establish a connection between the two events and the inner workings of trauma. It is no coincidence that the grandfather should find out about the terrorist attacks in the very city of Dresden. Likewise, while all television sets seem to be broadcasting images of the planes, a lone screen continues to display a nature program ("a lion was eating a flamingo" [272]), which does not make it "odd" (Pederson 348) but, on the contrary, directly connects the events of 9/11 with the Dresden bombing, when the grandfather was tasked with shooting all the carnivores escaped from the nearby zoo.

The second characteristic of trauma that the reader is made to experience is that of a sudden breach. Indeed, what adds to the specificity of trauma and partly explains its scarring effects is the unpredictability of the traumatic event for which the victim can never be prepared. The images inserted into the pages of the book tend to mimic such a disruptive effect, barging into the novel and interrupting our reading experience. According to Sien Uytterschout, "the composition of [the] novel ... seriously founders any reader's expectation of a smooth, straightforward narrative" (68). To begin with, such illustrations are unexpected in a book primarily intended for adults. In addition, some of them force their way into the book even before the reader reaches the title page, as if words could only come second to image. Most of them are found in the chapters narrated by Oskar, who collects images for his scrapbook entitled "Stuff That Happened to Me," although some also appear in the chapters narrated by the grandfather. While most are illustrative, like the one on page 92, which displays a view of Abby Black's house on Bedford Street, as evoked two pages earlier, others immediately seem to call for interpretation on a deeper level. For instance, the grandfather takes pictures of everything in his apartment for insurance purposes; yet most show doorknobs and keyholes, which have no material value whatsoever, and appear before any explanation for them is suggested. Therefore, they cannot be understood as mere illustrations and must be attributed a symbolic value, be it the need to "unlock" one's trauma (Uytterschout 69) or merely the idea of a threshold that needs to be crossed. Symbolically too, the numerous photographs of keys, doorknobs and keyholes, as well as the grandfather's obsession with protecting the contents of the apartment, allude to this very possibility of a break-in.

Lastly, the reader is often confronted with a phenomenon of latency, which accentuates the impression of a disjointed narrative. The answers to some of the reader's questions are often deferred, to the point that it might seem that Oskar's telling of his story is only meant to postpone the moment when he finally has to face his guilt. Indeed, if the father's messages left on the answering machine are evoked in the very first chapter, they are literally repressed,[5] only to emerge again in Oskar's second to last chapter, when he meets William Black. Similarly, the reader is forced to go back to previous passages that only become comprehensible in retrospect, so that their first reading is necessarily incomplete. For instance, in the same chapter, Oskar understands that his mother has known of his wanderings all along and that she has even been calling his visitors ahead. He then proceeds to draw the reader's attention to certain coincidences, while leaving other situations to be reexamined during the second reading of the novel.

The fragmentary nature of the novel thereby appears to echo the shattering effects of trauma: the text often falls apart, and the reader is forced to make sense of the disconnected elements as best they can. And yet, I argue that the result is not so much destruction as a mere breaking down of the narrative to be able to build it anew on a stronger basis.

Creative uses of fragmentation

Faced with an event which exceeds traditional categories of representation, the characters often resort to breaking reality into smaller, more manageable units. Much in the same way that Oskar carefully scrutinizes the findings of his treasure hunt in the Park "one piece at a time" (9) in the hope of finding a connection between them, the grandfather and the grandson share the habit of photographing everything around them as a way to grasp reality more gradually and understand it better. In her essay *On Photography*, Susan Sontag suggests,

> Anything can be separated, can be made discontinuous, from anything else: all that is necessary is to frame the subject differently.... Photography reinforces a nominalist view of social reality as consisting of small units of an apparently infinite number.... Through photographs, the world becomes a

---

[5] Oskar explains his stratagem in the third chapter: "I bought the exact same phone and ran home and recorded our greetings from the first phone onto it. I wrapped up the old phone in the scarf that Grandma was never able to finish because of my privacy, and I put that in a grocery bag, and I put that in a box, and I put that in another box, and I put that under a bunch of stuff in my closet" (68).

series of unrelated, freestanding particles.... The camera makes reality atomic, manageable and opaque. (22–23)

Photography therefore appears as a way to extract something from its larger context, to zoom in on it, and examine it more closely. By insisting on the singularity of what it represents, the photograph enables a focus on what might otherwise be overlooked. Oskar regularly flips through the pages of his scrapbook to make himself feel better when he is unable to sleep. Towards the end of the novel he exclaims, "The whole world was in there" (325), as if, divided into small enough parts, the whole world could be made to fit into the small book and be rendered less threatening as a result. The same seems to apply to the grandfather, who appropriates his environment by taking pictures of the tiniest and most insignificant elements in his new apartment:

He took pictures of everything.   Of the undersides of the shelves in the closet. Of the backs of the mirrors.   Even the broken things.... He could have rebuilt the apartment by taping together the pictures. (175)

Rebuilding might indeed be the ultimate aim of this process of deconstruction. This possibility of a link between separation and unification is implied in the very semantics of the verb "to cleave," which possesses two contradictory meanings: to part, divide, or split, but also to stick, cling or adhere tightly (Amfreville 92). Mr. Black's collection of rocks may be interpreted as a solution to the complexity of history. As each pebble is inscribed with a specific date and place (for instance "Normandy, 6/19/44"), they stand for the historical event itself; by putting them one next to another, one can almost piece together History.[6] Similarly, his biographical index is filled with cards bearing a single name and a corresponding qualifier. If the process seems at first overly simplistic ("Just *one* word?" Oskar exclaims [157]), the sheer number of cards[7] in the index suggests the breadth of the old man's undertaking.

The characters often express themselves through the use of what appears to be coded messages. The reader is, for instance, confronted with several pages composed of nothing but numbers, transcribing the grandfather's pitiful attempt to call his ex-wife to let her know that he is back in New York. Having lost the ability – or perhaps the will – to speak in the aftermath of the Dresden catastrophe, he proceeds to press the keys corre-

---

[6] Codde identifies the "failure and inaptness of language for historical reconstruction" as an "important theme of the novel" (244).

[7] "There must be tens of thousands by this point! Maybe hundreds of thousands!" (157).

sponding to the letters that he needs to form the words in his sentences. The numbers are reproduced on the page, separated by commas, and interspersed with a few punctuation marks signaling the end of the sentences. Neither the grandmother nor the reader is able to understand what he means to say, as she does not even realize that the beeps she can hear are an attempt to communicate with her. And yet, this constitutes an extremely creative stratagem on the part of the grandfather who deconstructs his words not as a way of withholding meaning – if this looks like a coded message to the reader, the character does not mean it to be so – but rather in the hope that his interlocutor will be able to recompose the message on the other end of the line. Similarly, when Oskar struggles to express his feelings, he often resorts to decomposing his message. He transforms his father's messages into jewelry for his mother, using different colored beads to represent the different parts of speech:

> As for the bracelet Mom wore to the funeral, what I did was I converted Dad's last voice message into Morse code, and I used sky-blue beads for silence, maroon beads for breaks between letters, violet beads for breaks between words, and long and short pieces of string between the beads for long and short beeps. (35)

The atomized message is nevertheless bound together with string, so that it still finds coherence, only waiting for the mother to crack the code. In much the same way, the concluding flipbook devised by Oskar unites the disparate images of a man falling from one of the Twin Towers, which up to that point would emerge unexpectedly, reminiscent of the haunting images characteristic of Post-Traumatic Stress Disorder. A lively narrative starts to emerge from the series of photographs, which marks "a decided shift to monoglossia" (Saal 471). From the multitude of discourses which prevailed earlier arises a single voice which borrows from several ones: it is at the same time a translation of Oskar's hope for a safer future, of his grandmother's recurrent fantasy of turning back time,[8] and of his grandfather's obsession for apprehending reality through photographs.

Fragmentation therefore appears as a symptom of trauma in the novel, which bears the marks of its shattering effects. The characters suffer from the discontinuity of their very selves, their lack of wholeness and individuality, while the structure of the novel itself is informed by the clinical manifestations of trauma, so that the text sometimes threatens to disintegrate. And yet, the idea of fragmentation can prove to be an effective creative tool. The multiplicity and plurality which results from fragmentation does

---

[8] "In my dreams, the tears went up his cheeks and back into his eyes" (309).

not necessarily equate dissolution; on the contrary, it creates new possibilities for interpretation and testifies to a certain need for renouncing an illusory wish for totality. Several interpretations can coexist, and no fixed meaning is assigned to the text or to the historical event. Indeed, events like 9/11 cannot aptly be represented in a single, authoritative way, so that even though the novel constantly manifests a certain nostalgia for wholeness, it becomes apparent that it cannot be imposed from the outside. Just as Oskar, violently separated from his father, finds some closure in being reunited with his mother in a final embrace, it is up to readers to restore wholeness through their own reading experience, weaving together all the seemingly disparate elements that constitute the novel.

Works Cited

Amfreville, Marc. *Écrits en Souffrance: Figures du Trauma dans la Littérature Nord-Américaine*. Paris: Michel Houdiard, 2010.

Baudrillard, Jean. *The Spirit of Terrorism and Requiem for the Twin Towers*. 2002. Trans. Chris Turner. New York: Verso, 2003.

Codde, Philippe. "Philomela Revisited: Traumatic Iconicity in Jonathan Safran Foer's *Extremely Loud and Incredibly Close*." *Studies in American Fiction* 35.2 (2007): 241–54.

Donn, Katharina. "The Multidirectionality of Memory: Networks of Trauma in Post-9/11 Literature." *Miscelánea* 50 (2014): 15–33.

Ferenczi, Sándor. *The Clinical Diary*. 1932. Trans. Michael Balint and Nicola Zarday Jackson. Cambridge: Harvard UP, 1988.

Foer, Jonathan Safran. *Extremely Loud and Incredibly Close*. 2005. London: Penguin, 2006.

Freud, Sigmund. *Introductory Lectures on Psycho-Analysis*. 1917. *The Standard Edition of the Complete Psychological Works of Sigmund Freud*. Vol. xvi. Trans. James Strachey. London: Hogarth Press, 1991.

---. *Moses and Monotheism*. 1939. Trans. Katherine Jones. New York: Knopf, 1947.

Mullins, Matthew. "Boroughs and Neighbors: Traumatic Solidarity in Jonathan Safran Foer's *Extremely Loud and Incredibly Close*." *Papers on Language and Literature* 45.3 (2009): 298–324.

Pederson, Joshua. "Speak, Trauma: Toward a Revised Understanding of Literary Trauma Theory." *Narrative* 22.3 (2014): 333–53.

Saal, Ilka. "Regarding the Pain of Self and Other: Trauma Transfer and Narrative Framing in Jonathan Safran Foer's *Extremely Loud and Incredibly Close*." *Modern Fiction Stories* 57.3 (2011): 451–76.

Sontag, Susan. *On Photography*. New York: Farrar, Straus and Giroux, 1978.

Uytterschout, Sien. "Visualised Incomprehensibility of Trauma in Jonathan Safran Foer's *Extremely Loud and Incredibly Close*." *Zeitschrift für Anglistik und Amerikanistik* 56.1 (2008): 61–74

Part Four

Multimodal and multimedial fragments

Chapter 12

Singularity, multimodality, transmediality: fragmentary future(s) of the novel?

Grzegorz Maziarczyk,
John Paul II Catholic University of Lublin

Singularity, multimodality and transmediality are crucial aspects of the transformation that the material form of the novel is currently undergoing in response to the impact of electronic means of information storage and dissemination. On the one hand, contemporary fiction mobilizes medial singularity and multimodal potential of both print and digital formats; on the other, it transgresses media boundaries. Significantly, such creative departures from the default medium of the supposedly transparent printed codex more often than not involve fragmentation of the novelistic discourse. The present essay discusses selected instances of this process, focusing in particular on the recent developments in electronic literature, which remain a largely uncharted territory in comparison to book-bound experiments. By doing so, it seeks to extrapolate the directions in which the novel is likely to develop and to assess the extent to which fragmentation can be expected to become the inherent quality of its medial form.

In his classic study *The Rise of the Novel*, Ian Watt goes so far as to suggest that the novel is perhaps "the only literary genre which is essentially connected with the medium of print" (196), and the fate of the latter appears to have been sealed, as the hyperbolic title of Jeff Gomez's study *Print is Dead: Books in Our Digital Age* (2007) makes abundantly clear. The impact of the digital revolution on the form of the novel has been construed by new media theorists in two opposite, if equally extreme, ways. Early enthusiasts of electronic textuality predicted that it would involve a radical alteration in the form of literary fiction: in 1992 Robert Coover famously declared that "the novel ..., as we know it, has come to its end" and will soon be replaced by various forms of digital hypertext fiction. The other camp, by contrast, has argued that even if electronic media replace print, this change will not influence the novel as genre. In "Narrative Literature in the Turing Universe," an essay closing the monumental history of the novel edited by Franco Moretti, Espen Aarseth provocatively questions the need to ponder on the digital future of the novel: "Instead of asking how the novel will change, perhaps we should ask why the novel should change. The novel is a verbal system that channels words from a creator to a reader and could exist happily on most readable surfaces or audio formats" (866).

As might be expected, neither the hypertextual revolution happened nor the novel remained unchanged, not least because it is an inherently mutable literary form. The editors of the collection of essays, appropriately entitled *Reinventions of the Novel: Histories and Aesthetics of a Protean Genre*, point out the inherent generic instability of the novel as genre, if a genre it is at all:

> The Novel seems to be an inveterate bastard genre, and as such it may incorporate all other genres in itself. It overflows with drama, lyrics and non-literary documentary fragments, anecdotes, journalism, diary notes, essayistic digressions and so forth. Thus, the initial question – "what is a Novel?" – may be rephrased as "what can a Novel be?" or rather "what can be a Novel?" (Simonsen et al. 3)

This description of the novel suggests that all novels are in a sense fragmentary, though – to paraphrase George Orwell – some novels are more fragmentary than others. Significantly, whether or not we perceive a particular novel as highly fragmentary depends on the devices through which fragmentation is signaled. These devices are usually, if not always, non-verbal as they materially or visually indicate some form of partition and range from such basic strategies as division into paragraphs or chapters to the radical format of the unbound book.

The very concept of fragmentary writing thus demonstrates that contrary to what Aarseth and the authors of the passage quoted above assume, the novel should not be understood as a purely verbal form, which develops solely through cross-pollination with other speech genres. What the novel can be depends not only on the verbal genres it incorporates but also on the ways in which it uses the semiotic potential of its particular medium and appropriates the affordances of other media. This is not to deny the importance of language, which remains the key component of the novel and which allows distinguishing its more prototypical incarnations from such borderline cases as the photo-novel or the graphic novel.

In contemporary culture, the book has become merely one available medium – along with ebook and audiobook formats – even for novels which rely primarily on purely verbal narration. The question as to what the novel can be thus inevitably involves its position in the media ecology. As Jay David Bolter and Richard Grusin suggest in *Remediation: Understanding New Media* (2000), all media compete with each other and in this "media war" each medium refashions other media and simultaneously insists on its own medial singularity and representational supremacy (44–50).

One response to the threat of obsolescence posed by digital formats is thus to resort to what Jessica Pressman has called the aesthetic of bookishness and "[to] exploit the power of the print page in ways that draw attention to the book as a multimedia format." (465) This trend is represented by a growing number of contemporary writers – suffice it to mention Mark Z. Danielewski, Jonathan Safran Foer, Graham Rawle, Salvador Plascencia, Steve Tomasula, Marisha Pessl, Zenon Fajfer and Katarzyna Bazarnik. Naturally, the foregrounding of the bookhood of the novel is not a uniquely contemporary phenomenon. Laurence Sterne laid bare the textual materiality of the newly-born genre in *Tristram Shandy* and in the 1960s and 1970s B. S. Johnson and Raymond Federman, to mention two most famous names, exploited "the technological fact of the book" (Johnson 11). However, as N. Katherine Hayles points out, the recent engagement with textual materiality involves, on the one hand, the intensification of print tradition and, on the other, the imitation of electronic textuality (162). Furthermore, while postmodernist typographic experiments were a niche trend within high-brow literary fiction, the aesthetic of bookishness has gone mainstream in contemporary culture: one fairly recent example of ostentatious bookishness – *S.* – has been conceived and promoted by the filmmaker J. J. Abrams, best known for his genre-bending TV series *Lost*.

As many books foreground their bookhood, creators of digital fiction respond to the readers' familiarity if not fatigue with ebooks which merely recreate the format of the print book in the electronic environment by foregrounding the medial singularity of the digital. The recently launched digital publishing platform, Editions At Play, thus describes its mission:

> The goal of Editions At Play is to allow writers to create books which change dynamically on a reader's phone or tablet using the internet, and to engage the next generation of readers on their phones as well as in print.... People sometimes say that physical books have qualities that do not transfer well to digital. We want to show that digital has narrative qualities that cannot transfer to print. ("About Us")

Significantly, in the passage quoted above the book appears to be treated simultaneously as a synonym for a novel and a medium in its own right. At another point Editions At Play admit that "there have been several iPad Apps published recently as 'books' that explore the potential of using uniquely 'digital' qualities in novels" ("About Us") and then go on to describe their own publications as "digital books," even though digital novels would be a more precise term, highlighting the singularity of the digital medium. This terminological oscillation between books, novels and digital books can be interpreted as a paradoxical attempt to emphasize simultaneously the continuity and divergence between print books and digital books: the latter are exactly like the former in that they provide "delightful and surprising reading experiences" ("About Us"), but they do so in their own unique way.

Written for promotional purposes, this mission statement willfully ignores the history of digital fiction, going far beyond a few recently published iPad apps, which – as a matter of fact – are as innovative as those produced by Editions at Play. Suffice it to mention Eastgate Systems, which published Michael Joyce's groundbreaking hypertext *afternoon: a story* (1987). What makes Editions at Play different from earlier publishers of digital fiction is their exclusive focus on such devices as smartphones and tablets. In her overview of electronic literature, Astrid Ensslin points out that mobile media represent the latest stage of its development and argues that "a sea change from static to mobile media ... has given rise to a multitude of new narrative forms" (188), which can be subsumed under a general category of app fiction.

Both the aesthetic of bookishness and digital singularity go beyond the purely verbal understanding of the novel, typical of classical, word-centered poetics of narrative fiction, and turn it into a multimodal work, in which verbal and non-verbal means of expression are co-deployed within a particular interface, understood as "a boundary space ... that constitutes reading as an activity" (Drucker 216) and that mediates the reader's interaction with a particular semiotic object: it prompts but also determines and limits his/her tasks and behaviors. The material organization of the text in the print novel can thus be described as an interface provoking a particular type of haptic engagement, which may well go beyond the mere turning over of pages, just as digital novels rely for their effect on the peculiarities of a touchscreen interface.

Visual fragmentation appears to be one of the primary strategies of the aesthetic of bookishness as it subverts the conventional transparency of print, which – as Jay David Bolter writes – "has often been regarded as a medium that should disappear from the reader's conscious consideration"

(43). The medial singularity of the book and its semiotic potential are somewhat paradoxically emphasized via the technique of defamiliarization: books which foreground their own materiality do not allow the reader to forget that he/she is reading a book, because they do not look like typical books, in which each page contains a familiar rectangle of text.

Graham Rawle's *Woman's World* (2005), for instance, employs fragmentation on the level of typeface: it resembles a ransom note, as it has literally been created from fragments cut out from women's magazines published in the early 1960s. Far from being a mere gimmick, the peculiar form of the novel functions as the material embodiment of the constructed identity of its transvestite protagonist. Danielewski's *House of Leaves* (2000), in turn, combines the visual heterogeneity of multiple typefaces with the fragmentation of paginal space reflecting the multiplication of narrative strands. The reader is forced to choose his/her own path through the novel, as the material organization of the text functions as an iconic representation of the crucial aspect of the storyworld, namely the maze-like nature of the eponymous house. Furthermore, in the aesthetic of bookishness textual fragmentation often ties in with the incorporation of various other forms of visual representation. The most spectacular example of such verbovisual merger is Steve Tomasula's *VAS* (2004), in which textual chunks are combined with black-and-white illustrations, pedigree trees, Internet advertisements, Mendelian diagrams and many other visual elements. By turning his novel into a dense verbo-visual collage, Tomasula probes the limits of the novel as genre, as the standard narrative components of the plot, characters and setting give way to a plethora of fragments of non-fictional discourses and numerous images. *VAS* thus becomes a "total book" in which the interplay between the verbal and the visual, the narrative and the discursive reflects, refracts and reveals its central theme – the transition from the human to the posthuman, from being our bodies to having bodies.

Heterogeneous as Danielewski's and Tomasula's works are, they – just like other examples of the contemporary aesthetic of bookishness – retain the integrity of the book as a physical object and refrain from disintegrating the book itself in the manner exemplified by twentieth-century novels in a box: Marc Saporta's *Composition No. 1* (1962) and B. S. Johnson's *The Unfortunates* (1969). If contemporary novels are published in box-like slipcovers, it is so because they are accompanied by additional materials. The most striking instance of this publishing practice is Abrams and Dorst's earlier mentioned *S.*, which pushes the aesthetic of bookishness to the extreme by fetishizing the bookhood of the book as a material object and exploiting what David Shields has called the "reality hunger" of contemporary culture. The novel takes the form of a fictional writer V.M. Straka's equally fictional book *The Ship of Theseus*, whose material form has all the trappings of an old library book. More importantly, its margins are full of notes in different colors and two different handwritings. Inserted in-between its pages are newspaper clippings, postcards, a map drawn on a napkin and many other textual documents – all these elements drawing the reader's attention to the artifact he/she is holding in his/her hands.

In the manner familiar from *House of Leaves*, *S.* employs fragmentation and multimodality to create multiple narrative strands: one of them is told in *Ship of Theseus* and the other in the handwritten notes of two readers – Eric and Jennifer – who use the book as a medium of communication through which they can discuss the novel and its author. In *S.* multimodality and fragmentation are primarily employed to achieve the Barthesian reality effect on the level of textual materiality. The yellowish pages of *Ship of Theseus*, the handwritten and therefore supposedly authentic notes, the inserts – all these elements create a perfect simulacrum of the book the reader could have come across in a library or a second-hand bookshop and provoke his/her forensic desire by providing him/her with all the clues that the characters have investigated.

As can be seen, fragmentation and multimodality are employed in many contemporary novels to defamiliarize the book and thus foreground its medial singularity. Contemporary digital novels, designed for mobile media, appear to rely on the inversion of this semiotic mechanism. As they are exploring a new territory, they expect the reader to rely on the gestures and patterns of data access he/she knows from his/her everyday use of mobile phones or tablets in the context of literary reading or, speaking in broader terms, aesthetic experience. In her discussion of the phenomenology of contemporary, screen-based, reading, Jennifer Rowsell observes that "the embodied cognitive acts of engaging with digital content calls on [*sic*] different kinds of practices that demand different methods of analysis" (117) and argues that "touch and haptics have replaced or at least will replace visuals as modes of interaction" (118). Indeed, haptic engagement constitutes one of the medium-specific properties that are exploited in the recently released digital works which have been championed as representing the future of the novel (cf. Lea) – *The Pickle Index* (2015) by Eli Horowitz and Russell Quinn, *Entrances & Exits* (2016) by Reif Larsen, and *Pry* (2015) by Danny Cannizzaro and Samantha Gorman – though it must be noted that it augments rather than replaces sight, which remains the primary sensory channel through which the reader gains access to textual data.

Significantly, all these works attenuate or simply reject radical hypertextual fragmentation and the multiplication of reading paths represented by such classics of electronic literature as Joyce's *afternoon* and Shelley Jackson's *The Patchwork Girl* (1995) in favor of a more linear organization. It is the multimodal co-deployment of various semiotic resources that makes them fragmentary on the level of the interface. *The Pickle Index* combines the verbally rendered pseudo-recipes with an animated map and drawings; *Entrances & Exits* fluctuates between verbal sections and geovisual images coming from Google Street View; while *Pry* consists of high-resolution video clips, static images and dynamic, animated texts.

Paradoxically, *The Pickle Index* resembles, on the one hand, a traditionally understood novel as the word remains its primary vehicle for meaning and, on the other, a non-literary app, which on the surface level of its textual organization is much closer to a database than a narrative in that it gives the reader a freedom of choice vis-à-vis a limited set of textual segments. It purports to be an app through which the reader can gain access to the news and recipes coming from a grotesque dystopian land, whose citizens are obliged, among other things, to keep creating and exchanging recipes for pickles through a fictional device called the scroller. In order to reconstruct the storyworld, the reader has to assume the role of one of the citizens and dutifully read the news and the recipes. While the former represent official propaganda, the latter hide a counter-narrative of resistance delivered by the narrator-protagonist, Flora Bialy, via the recipe-exchanging network. Admittedly, textual fragmentation of this kind could be achieved in print; what makes *The Pickle Index* unique and foregrounds its medial singularity is a temporal fragmentation of the act of reading. Each day the reader is given one newspaper article and a set of ten recipes, only one of which comes from Flora Bialy. If he/she stops reading or rather interacting with *The Pickle Index* for a few days, he/she will still only get one news article and one set of recipes and will have to wait until the following day for the story to develop. This fragmentation of the act of reading creates suspense, as it happens in other forms of serialization, as well as contributes to the reality effect: the fictional story unfolds for ten days, and the story-time is supposed to coincide with the time of reading.

While *The Pickle Index* enforces temporal discontinuity, Larsen's *Entrances & Exits* relies on fragmentation of space for its effect. The unnamed narrator-protagonist of Larsen's digital novel travels across the globe through mysterious doorways and other passages, which always take him to a new place, often thousands of kilometers away from the previous one: in a split second he moves, for instance, from a Siberian village to an island in the middle of the Pacific. With one exception, the interface of *Entranc *es & Exits* is constructed according to the same pattern. Each section opens with a screen presenting a Google Street View of some location. A short introductory verbal passage is superimposed on the image together with two arrows, which can be used to explore the geovisual representation of space, though only to a limited degree, as at some point one of the arrows disappears, making it impossible to move any further. An equally important element of the opening screen is a compass-rose-like circle, which can sometimes be immediately seen and sometimes has to be found by exploring a particular location. When the reader touches it, the Google Street View fades into a purely textual screen.

The primary function of geovisual images in the multimodal set-up of *Entrances & Exits* is obviously to depict the spatial dimension of its fictional storyworld and ground it in a rather uncanny manner in what is often assumed to be a truthful visual representation of a particular location. As Sarah Pink observes, Google Street View "affords viewers possibilities to use their existing experiences of environments to sense what it might be or how it might feel to move through the 'real' locality represented on screen" (11). The narrative aspect of *Entrances & Exits* is developed, as might be expected, by verbal means as well as the sequential organization of images and words. Significantly, the subjectivity of the narrator-protagonist emerges from the combination of these two modes of representation. The navigable image opening a particular section puts the reader in the deictic center and allows him/her to explore the storyworld by rotating the view and/or moving along a street. His/her haptic engagement with Google Street View enhances his/her immersion as the position he/she is invited to occupy within the fictional space coincides with that of the narrator-protagonist.

The interplay between fragmentary representation and the medium-specific haptic engagement of the reader is pushed even further in Cannizzaro and Gorman's *Pry*, in which the typical iPad gestures of spreading and pinching become the primary means whereby the reader interacts with the interface in order to access the consciousness of the protagonist, a Gulf War veteran James, and reconstruct his past. In major parts of the novel, his thoughts are represented by means of fragmentary, disjointed sentences, typical of the stream of consciousness. When the reader spreads and holds open the text, he/she can see the visual stimuli that enter James' mind. Finally, when he/she pinches his eyes or the text representing his thoughts closed, he/she sees images, short video clips and disjointed phrases flashing quickly across a white square and representing James' subconscious mental processes in all their elusiveness. In *Pry* the reader is thus confronted with "raw," fragmented and indeterminate cognitive data, which he/she has to process on his/her own. The three streams of the data the reader receives are interrelated, though they do not coalesce into a completely clear, coherent whole. It is precisely the interplay between fragmentation and the reader's tactile and ocular engagement with *Pry* that allows Cannizzaro and Gorman to represent multiple layers of the human mind in a manner peculiar to touchscreen devices.

As can be seen, the inherent multimodality of digital novels can be combined with many other semiotic mechanisms, including serialization, the use of online resources and the exploitation of the reader's haptic engagement, which usually involve various types of fragmentation. These digital forms of segmentation go beyond the fragmenting techniques observable in the aesthetic of bookishness and foreground the unique semiotic potential of literary apps. This tendency towards medial singularity is counterbalanced in contemporary culture by a twin process of media convergence, in which "multiple media systems coexist and where media content flows fluidly across them" (Jenkins 282). In *Convergence Culture* Henry Jenkins argues that the media saturation of contemporary culture is conducive to transmedia storytelling, which he describes in the following way:

> A transmedia story unfolds across multiple media platforms, with each new text making a distinctive and valuable contribution to the whole. In the ideal form of transmedia storytelling, each medium does what it does best – so that a story might be introduced in a film, expanded through television, novels and comics; its world might be explored through game play or experienced as an amusement park attraction. (96)

In the perfect transmedia story, the novel becomes only an element of a larger project designed to create a fragmentary, multi-faceted and multimedia representation of a particular fictional universe. Transmediality can, however, be also understood in less expansive terms as the use of other media to extend the novel, which remains in the center. This is precisely what happens in the case of Abrams and Dorst's *S.* and a number of other recently published books, including Steven Hall's *The Raw Shark Texts* (2007) and Marisha Pessl's *Night Film* (2013). All these works display medial self-awareness and are conspicuously multimodal in their incorporation of multiple fragments of documents and media texts. Transmedial novelistic projects thus aim at the synergic integration of different media platforms that Jenkins envisions in his description of a transmedia story. In the case of *S.* the reader is, for instance, provided with further clues to Straka's identity through *Eotvos Wheel*, the "official" website dedicated to the novel; *Radio Straka*, a series of iTunes podcasts throwing additional light on the mysterious figure of the author of *Ship of Theseus* as well as a number of fan sites. Furthermore, the conspicuous presence of *S.*-related content on the social media reinforces the reality effect: both Eric and Jennifer have Twitter accounts, though they appear to have stopped tweeting in 2014; the latter also has a tumblr blog, which includes, among other things, a pseudo-facsimile of an alternative ending for *Ship of Theseus*. It is only by collecting and juxtaposing all these fragmentary representations that the reader can hope to gain a more comprehensive understanding of the storyworld and central characters, though obviously he/she will never achieve a complete picture, for these additional data create further mysteries, the hermeneutic code of enigma structuring the reader's interpretive engagement with *S*.

With the book no longer being the default material form for the novel, the three interrelated categories of singularity, multimodality and transmediality appear to constitute the key parameters of the tendency towards fragmentation observable in its current medial transformation. Time can only tell whether transmedial and multimodal projects will co-exist with books whose tactile materiality will comprise a significant part of their appeal and more traditional, word-centered (e)books or whether they will ultimately effect a metamorphosis of the novelistic discourse into a new, digital form of artistic expression which will bear little resemblance to the book, which we nowadays still associate with the novel. What remains certain is that "this most fluid of genres" (11), as Mikhail Bakhtin has it, will continue to evolve.

Works Cited

Aarseth, Espen J. "Narrative Literature in the Turing Universe." *The Novel. Vol. 2: Forms and Themes*. Ed. Franco Moretti. Princeton: Princeton UP, 2006. 839–67.

"About Us." *Editions At Play*, https://editionsatplay.withgoogle.com/#/about. Accessed 11 Dec. 2017.

Bakhtin, Mikhail. "Epic and Novel: Toward a Methodology for the Study of the Novel." *The Dialogic Imagination*. Ed. Michael Holquist. Trans. Caryl Emerson and Michael Holquist. Austin: U of Texas P, 1998. 3–40.

Bolter, Jay David. *Writing Space: The Computer, Hypertext, and the History of Writing*. 2nd ed. Mahwah: Lawrence Erlbaum, 2001.

Bolter, Jay David, and Richard Grusin. *Remediation: Understanding New Media*. Cambridge: MIT Press, 2000.

Drucker, Johanna. "Reading Interface." *PMLA: Publications of the Modern Language Association of America* 128.1 (2013): 213–20.

Ensslin, Astrid. "Electronic Fictions." *The Cambridge Companion to Postmodern American Fiction*. Ed. Paula Geyh. Cambridge: Cambridge UP, 2017. 181–98.

Hayles, N. Katherine. *Electronic Literature: New Horizons for the Literary*. Notre Dame: U of Notre Dame P, 2008.

Jenkins, Henry. *Convergence Culture: Where Old and New Media Collide.* New York: New York UP, 2006.

Johnson, B. S. Introduction. *Aren't You Rather Young to Be Writing Your Memoirs?* London: Hutchinson, 1973. 11–31.

Lea, Richard. "What Apps Next? Publishers and Developers Embrace 'Unprintable' Fiction." *The Guardian*, 3 Feb. 2016, https://www.theguardian.com/books/2016/feb/03/publishers-developers-digital-technology-unprintable-fiction-google-editions-play. Accessed 11 Dec. 2017.

Pink, Sarah. "Sensory Digital Photography: Re-Thinking 'Moving' and the Image." *Visual Studies* 26.1 (2011): 4–13.

Pressman, Jessica. "The Aesthetic of Bookishness in Twenty-First Century Literature." *Michigan Quarterly Review* 48.4 (2009): 465–82.

Rowsell, Jennifer. "Toward a Phenomenology of Contemporary Reading." *Australian Journal of Language and Literacy* 37.2 (2014): 117–27.

Simonsen, Karen-Margrethe, Marianne Ping Huang and Mads Rosendahl Thomsen. Introduction. *Reinventions of the Novel: Histories and Aesthetics of a Protean Genre.* Eds. Karen-Margrethe Simonsen et al. Amsterdam: Rodopi, 2004. 3–12.

Watt, Ian. *The Rise of the Novel: Studies in Defoe, Richardson and Fielding.* Berkeley: U of California P, 1957.

Chapter 13

From Wunderkammer fragmentation to alternative history in *Hexen 2.0* by Suzanne Treister

Zofia Kolbuszewska,
University of Wrocław

Hexen 2.0 (2012), a multimodal project by Suzanne Treister, can be con-strued as a Wunderkammer vision of contemporary history in the vein of Walter Benjamin – an allegorical assemblage created out of fragments, rubbish, and refuse collected by a rag-picker historian. A melancholy alle-gory constructed out of fragments, Treister's history interrogates links between the occult, the scientific research on communication and the workings of the human mind, as well as the military's investment in new technologies. Yet, the project does not fall prey to the entropy inherent in centrifugal tendencies of fragmentation and dispersion, nor does it mourn the fall from grace of the science tarnished by politics. On the contrary, the artist employs the energy arising from the tension between fragments of multifarious origin to critique the status quo and posit a connection be-tween the occult, anachronistic epistemologies, and political resistance.

Suzanne Treister (1958–), is a world-renowned artist active in the field of the digital and new media and web art. Her interest in arcane and unacknowledged bodies of research finds expression in works reinterpret-ing typologies, narratives and histories that uncover the impact of the unseen corporate, military and paranormal forces on the world (Treister, Bio). *Hexen 2.0*, her fourth artistic project, was preceded by *Hexen 2039* (2006). The eponymous term "hexen," which means "witches" in German, signals the author's interest in alternative, arcane, and feminine episte-mologies. While the year 2039 invokes history and commemorates the outbreak of World War Two, the connectivity of social media and the con-nectedness of the world saturated with communications technologies are implied by the "2.0" index. The artist's complex ways of employing the convergence of art, science and technology in her projects are reflected in her note about "Graphites" – the reproductions of graphite-drawn facsimiles of photographs in *Hexen 2039*. The note both functions as a paratext and is part of the artistic text; it belongs to the world of the reader and the world conjured up by the artistic project:

> [This is a] series of graphite drawings of key areas of HEXEN 2039 research. By passing an electric current through the graphite, additional information is extracted and converted into psychic frequency clusters using an Electro-encephalographic Current Converter. These clusters are reproduced to form non-aurally transmittable frequency groups for use in psychological operations equipment. (Treister, *Hexen 2039* 10)

The publication of the album *Hexen 2.0* accompanied by a separate set of working Tarot cards coincided in 2012 with the exhibition *Hexen 2.0* at the "Work" gallery and in the Science Museum in London. The viewer of Treister's project is thus initially confronted with four fragments of a bigger event: an album, a Tarot cards pack and two exhibitions. Lars Bang Larsen's introductory essay constitutes the first part of Treister's album. The second part contains five historical diagrams reminiscent of Kabbalistic drawings of the Tree of Life, alchemical charts and cognitive maps. By artistically rendering the complex webs of social and political control and their fault lines, Treister encourages the viewer to transcend the dichotomy of art and science and helps visualize the non-linearity and multidimensionality of the entanglements of culture, technology and politics. The third section of the album reproduces an artistically and ideologically re-worked Tarot cards deck. To each card, the artist ascribes a particular event, notion, name, tendency, trend or movement. The fourth section contains photos, brief bios and fragments of interviews with Macy Conferences attendees, including fabricated photos presenting them as participants of a "Cybernetic Séance." Macy Conferences, convened by the Josiah Macy, Jr. Foundation in New York in the years 1941–60, promoted communication and interdisciplinary cooperation across scientific disciplines. Treister's fragmentary presentation of the conferences ironically underscores the aim of those meetings to restore unity to science. An image of a large hieroglyphic that depicts an eye within a triangle, often referred to as the Eye of Providence, or the All-Seeing Eye, precedes the fifth part of the book, which presents mirror images of the first edition title pages of twelve selected countercultural, contestatory, revolutionary, and innovative texts published in the years 1854–2003.[1] The strategy of visual reversal corresponds with the revolutionary character of those texts.

---

[1] From Henry David Thoreau's *Walden; or, Life in the Woods* (1854) to H. G. Wells's

By employing different strategies of visualizing fragmentation, the artist invites her audience to a more general reflection on the phenomenology of the fragment. The term derives from the Latin *frangere* – to break (Calabrese 72). The fragment evokes the autonomy of an element ultimately separated from the whole. A broken-off piece "becomes a 'de-archaeologized' material [and] maintains the fractal form required by the situation, but, rather than being reconducted to its hypothetical whole, its by now autonomous form is retained" (86). Although the recontextualization of fragments leads to "the cancellation of a systemic and contextual memory" (87), a fragment keeps evoking the specter of former totality. A new whole composed out of fragments gives, in turn, the impression of "being in pieces," while "its sense of totality stresses irregularity and asystematicness" (87). Indeed, the former wholes insinuate themselves into a new totality as specters, which leads to multiple centrifugal tensions within a work composed of fragments. The resulting polyvocality and heteroglossia of the new composition contribute to the uncertain and fortuitous nature of the emerging work. So does recognizing the spectral presences of the hypothetical former totalities, which enter dialogical relations with one another. "The aesthetic of the fragment ... is a spreading around, an evasion of the center, or order, of discourse" (86–87). A pleasure can also be derived from the study of fragments' provenience and hypothetical reconstruction of the spectral wholes.

Treister's project places the audience precisely at the cusp of all tensions inherent in its fragmentariness, invites them to participate in the adventure of uncovering suppressed knowledge and unacknowledged connections, and teaches how to listen to the multivocality arising from a fragmentary form. In search of the overt and covert technological and political genealogy of contemporary communicational connectivity and connectedness, the artist practices a Foucauldian archeology of knowledge. Composed of fragments of multiple origin and volume as well as artistic, social, and political urgency – all bound to one another by relations of similarity, correspondence, sympathy or repulsion – her project is reminiscent of a theatricized epistemological engine in the vein of the Memory Theater, a mnemonic strategy, familiar since antiquity, employed to retrieve knowledge committed to memory. It may also evoke an electronic search application that playfully performs, in front of an eager and curious spectator, complex relationships between individuals, things and affects which hold true in the world at large.

The New World Order (1940) to Alston Chase's *Harvard and the Unabomber – The Education of an American Terrorist* (2003).

Indeed, Treister's artistic enterprise coincides with a contemporary surge of an epistemological paradigm marked by the revival of interest in early-modern curiosity and the ways it represented the world. The contemporary mind is in particular fascinated by the space which showcases the strategies of knowledge production in the age of curiosity – the Wunderkammer, or the cabinet of curiosities. The artist participates in the current reversal of the process which at the turn of the seventeenth and eighteenth century led to the transformation of "[a] scene of amazing spectacles ... into a scene of knowledge" (Harries 510). Conversely, the late twentieth and early twenty-first century see the scene of knowledge fade back into the scene of the spectacle.

As on a theatre stage, objects at display in a Wunderkammer would be considered a dramatic enactment of synchronic and diachronic relationships between "natural formations, ancient sculptures, works of art and machines" (Bredekamp 78). The curiosity cabinet is inherently "pansemiotic" (Westerhoff 644). Yet, it "[is] far from being a chaotic array of curiosities without order, but its order [is] rather an order which [arranges] things in such a way that they could communicate with one another, thus making their hidden interrelations visible" (Westerhoff 645).

Some contemporary writings on the art of arranging Wunderkammer collections stress the similarity of the container and the contained: "the cabinets for displaying the collection should be made in the form of the marvels of the world, adding to each the name of the planetary deities which dominated them" (Quicchelberg qtd in Westerhoff 645). The relationship between the Wunderkammer and the external world is thus presented as that of a microcosmic model to the macrocosm. Treister's entire artistic project *Hexen 2.0* is based on the concept of the macrocosm finding a reflection in the microcosm, the latter serving as the model of the former. As in a holographic image and in an autopoietic structure, all parts of an emergent whole reflect its entirety, and, conversely, the whole mirrors them all. Consequently, each part or fragment of Treister's project – the book, Tarot cards pack and the two exhibitions – mirrors the whole project.

Treister's artistic activities can be considered part of the tradition that connects knowing with images. This tendency can be traced to the earlier mentioned Memory Theater, which involved the strategy of visualizing the location where the information to be remembered or retrieved was placed in an imagined theater. The early modern preoccupation with the visualization of knowledge was also bound up with the emergence of utopia as a literary genre, and with endeavors to design an ideal city. Making knowledge visible "is an essential component in the modern, yet utopian project" (Bolzoni xix). On the walls of an ideal, utopian city there was supposed to be depicted the compendium of all accumulated knowledge, ranging from mathematical figures through fauna, raw materials, and human inventions, to statues of moral and religious leaders (Yates 298). Frances Yates compares the arrangement of images and sculptures in the ideal city to "an encyclopaedic lay-out of a universal memory system" (298). The public space in ideal cities was conceived of as an occult mnemonic system "through which everything could be quickly learned, using the world 'as a book' and as 'local memory'" (377).

The performance of universal knowledge suggests associations not only with a theater, but also with anatomy. The illustrations used by Robert Fludd in the early seventeenth century to depict theatres of memory and to teach how to build them "have prompted Frances Yates to suggest an association with the Globe Theatre" (Bolzoni 241). Kate Cregan, in turn, points to "significant links which ... exist between the playhouses of early seventeenth-century London and that city's most active site of anatomical pedagogy" (Cregan 45) – anatomical theatres.

Aimed at representing and thus bringing to light the synchronic and diachronic entanglement of subjects and bodies in multiple networks of institutional, commercial and governmental practices, Treister's artistic project employs dynamic and emergent transmedia technologies of knowledge production, whose provenience is pre-modern (occult), early-modern, and ultra-modern. Drawing on the relations and connotations linking Wunderkammer, the occult, theater and early-modern medicine, it can be cogently argued that in the vein of Robert Burton's *Anatomy of Melancholy* (1621–38), Treister enacts in *Hexen 2.0* an alternative, allegorical anatomy of the history of contemporary communication and control systems. Rather than being a linear narrative, her history builds a Wunderkammer out of multiple fragments.

A cherished place in this Wunderkammer is accorded to the Macy Conferences. Indeed, Part Four of Treister's album contains photo-text presentations of the 1946–53 Macy Conferences participants and the ideas they debated. The Josiah Macy, Jr. Conferences on Cybernetics were pivotal in the development of cognitive science and Artificial Intelligence, especially with regard to what has come to be known as "connectionism" (Collins 25). According to the artist's own note which opens part two of *Hexen 2.0*, Treister became interested in the subject in early 2009, when she "first observed a possible connection between the mid-twentieth century theories and applications of cybernetics, which arose out of World War Two, primarily in the USA, where they answered a perceived need for a more controlled society, and our current world of online social media and what is referred to as Web 2.0" (12). The link that she felt best accounted for the affinities she observed was the concept of feedback loops. The artist immediately saw the creative and artistic potential of "connectivity" (12) where the participants of the feedback web – humans and machines – "learn how to learn" (12), but she also realized the connecting systems' capacity for facilitating ever more radical governmental control. Her interest in Macy meetings has contributed to Treister's project of mapping out specific histories whose so far obscure aspects, connections and ramifications have become apparent in her fragmented transmedia presentations.

Aptly, in Part Four of her album Treister offers the reader fragmentary glimpses of the extensive material concerning the Macy conferences – passages from interviews with the most famous participants and their photos. In this way, she foregrounds the role incompleteness and fragmentariness play in communication. Indeed, this is one issue with which the participants of Macy conferences were preoccupied. They pondered over how communication systems are capable of locally turning chaotic fragmentation of the world into islands of order. In other words, they reflected on how signification emerges out of the sea of what is designated in information theory as noise, and discussed the role of observers in communication systems; observers, whose selective, or fragmentary, access to knowledge and environment engenders feedback loops. Treister also emphasizes how fragmentary our knowledge is of all projects debated during those meetings, and draws the reader's attention to the fact that various historical narratives about the Macy meetings are selective and fragmentary as well. Throughout ten Macy Conferences held between 1946 and 1953, many of the notions linked to the study of Artificial Intelligence, such as neural nets, von Neumann architecture, and Shannon's quantitative definition of information, contributed to the hegemony of mechanical models of thinking (Collins 25). Although Macy meetings debates touched on such crucial issues as the question of the observer, and often concerned other anthropological and sociological problems, the anthropology was largely repressed during the Macy Conferences. Yet, it is noteworthy that the conferences anticipated the emergence of multi-agent systems composed of human and non-human agents (Collins 25).

The disputes concerning self-regulating systems with feedback and circular causality, i.e., feedback loops systems, later resulted in the interest in self-organizing and emergent systems, that is, autopoiesis, artificial intelligence, neuron networks as well as research connected with adaptation to ecosystems (Heims 283–84). Treister is mainly concerned with the legacy of the conferences reflected in the subsequent development of research on self-emergent systems and adaptation to ecosystems, and applications of its results in social media as well as military industry. Her artistic projects focus on, among other things, teasing out relationships between value systems, scientific research, and its practical and political uses.

It might be observed that she takes up where the Macy Conferences left off. By devoting an artistic project to the issues of communication and interdisciplinary exchange of knowledge and practices, discussed during the conferences, Treister emphasizes the anthropological and ethical perspectives neglected or repressed in the heat of debates. The artist creates elaborate multi-agent systems by engaging human and non-human agents in a complex network of artistic practice; a practice that, in the process of interdisciplinary dialogue, draws itself on sciences.

It is intriguing to what extent the history of the successful implementation of the ideas associated with cybernetics that were first explored at Macy Conferences, has eclipsed other histories – those tracing the subsequent vicissitudes of issues pertaining to human sciences. Yet, these problems were also subjects of heated debates during Macy meetings. Aptly, the rivalry of the victorious and repressed historical accounts is the subject of historical reflection of Walter Benjamin. In *Hexen 2.0*, Treister assumes the role of Benjamin's rag-picker historian who constructs a history from uncovered, broken fragments.

In Benjamin's theoretical reflection on writing history,[2] the fragment is invested with the power of exploding "the continuity of universalizing conceptions of history" (Hanssen 66). This belief manifests itself in the German thinker's own method of composition evinced in the unfinished monumental work *The Arcades Project*. There, the image of the poet as a rag-picker ("chiffonier" in French) first introduced by Charles Baudelaire, serves as the holographic image of a compositional strategy employed throughout the whole text (Wohlfarth 144). Benjamin conceives of the materialist historian as a rag-man (German: "Lumpensammler"). The rag-man's systematic and persistent search for reclaimable waste materials results in chance findings of different rejected fragments, multitudinous rubbish items, refuse and detritus. Design and chance meld in rag-picker's pursuits.

The rag-picker historian articulates a version of the past susceptible to the requirement of the political urgency of the present, whereas the painstaking reconstruction of history by the historicist stems from the need to eclipse the now: "Part tourist, part archaeologist, [the historicist] seeks to

---

[2] Most of the material on Walter Benjamin's view of history presented here appeared in my article "Forensic Imagination and the Materiality of Experience" (Kolbuszewska).

'relive' the past through an idle act of 'empathy' calculated to blunt the point of the here and now" (Benjamin 256; Wohlfarth 153). Conversely, the materialist historian gives expression to "an authentic experience of historical mourning" (Wohlfarth 153) instead of nostalgically reconstructing the past. For Benjamin, it is crucial to reveal the loyalties of the adherents of historicism. He asserts that they inevitably empathize with the victor, and points out that such a stance invariably avails the powers that be. Therefore, the materialist historian "regards it as his task to brush history against the grain" (Benjamin 256–57). In contrast with a historicist's narrative, Benjamin's conception of history gives voice to the defeated. In order to do so, the rag-picker historian must be ready to deal with the historical anamnesis of violence and trauma (Benjamin 255).

Yet, Benjamin's melancholy history of the defeated told allegorically through the means of a rubble heap of fragments, is refracted in Treister's project by the aleatoricity introduced by the Tarot play and divination practices. After all, even as playing or reading Tarot requires skill and intelligence, "the player [is] still subject to the vagaries of chance introduced by the other participants" (Farley 50–51). However, the game of Tarot also gives expression to a belief in a higher, emergent, harmony of the cosmos. Paradoxically, aleatoricity contributes to revealing this harmony. Carl Gustav Jung's "theory of synchronicity," according to which all occurrences taking place at a certain moment of time manifest the unique properties inherently bound up with that moment, is often adduced to justify the claim about the accuracy of horoscopes and Tarot cards oracle (Douglas 201).

When used in divination, Tarot cards are shuffled, laid out in various spreads, and interpreted by the reader (Douglas 202). The meaning of the cards in the major and minor arcana of the Tarot pack either individually or in combination can be made to cover practically any set of circumstances; for instance, each major arcana card, which illustrates an important stage in the path of life, can be read at several levels. A card "can point to important principles and forces operating in the world; it can unveil significant processes in the expansion of mystical consciousness; it can indicate the emergence of as yet unevolved aspects of personality, and when reversed, it can warn of physical or psychic pitfalls which may be encountered" (Douglas 43). In its combinatorial proliferation of meaning, the Tarot cards divination resembles the workings of an epistemological machine, or a contemporary search engine that operates on the principle of randomization.

By ascribing to the Tarot cards in her deck images associated with the official history of the development of the communications systems, those with connotations of alternative, countercultural practices, and those referring to visionary art and literature, the artist further multiplies the number of card readings. Therefore, Larsen emphasizes, Treister's employment of the Tarot deck is not aimed at making some "quick-fix" effort to re-enchant the world. Rather, by acknowledging that Tarot divination mirrors and performs procedures of mass intelligence gathering, she indicates a homeopathic aspect of occult practices in the history leading up to control society, and points to Tarot's productivity as a knowledge-generating engine "in the service of a new epistemology" (Larsen 7). In this sense, Tarot might be compared to a Turing Machine, "a virtual system capable of simulating the behavior of any other machine or apparatus of knowledge, including itself" (7). In the *Hexen 2.0* project, the diffusion of knowledge "through unofficially connected networks is affirmed by way of the Tarot deck as an encyclopaedic format" (7). Yet, Treister's encyclopedia is dynamic and constantly under self-construction. It is an autopoetic system, "a kind of alchemical hypertext" (7).

Autopoetic systems are self-organized and emergent. They can be conceptualized as "patterns of ongoing events continually under construction" (Livingston 80). The autopoetic system creates its components and – what sounds very counterintuitively – is itself one of its own parts. Ira Livingston explains that "autopoetics," the name he employs instead of the more widely recognized term "autopoiesis," refers to the study of 'self-making' systems. Autopoetics demonstrates and explores reciprocal exchanges between arts, literature and sciences in an interzone defined by affinities among, on the one hand, "self-reference and performativity in literary and cultural theory" and, on the other hand, "notions of autopoiesis and self-organizing systems in biology and other sciences and social sciences" (Livingston 1). Livingston purports to describe self-making processes in the realm of meaning, language and culture. The removal of the "I" from the word "autopoiesis" is intended to make the word sound more vernacular, but mainly to "mark what [he] would like to remove from the concept (its reliance on specific, ideologically bound notions of the self, the I) and, by referencing *poetic* more pointedly" (Livingston 2), to throw into relief the realms of culture and meaning.

Feedback loops regulate a system's emergence. The system is emergent when it monitors both its own behavior and interactions with the environment. Auto-referentiality means that the system is aware of its structure, operations, and growth. However, in order to grow, the system needs to acknowledge the existence of an external world – to be aware of the conditions and to gather information about them so as to be able to adapt to the environment. The system's awareness of itself is inseparably linked to its awareness of the environment. Therefore an autopoetic system is simultaneously open and closed, where "[c]losure is closely related to autonomy ... which can be sustained only along with an equally thorough-going *dependence*" (Livingston 84). The system's self-referentiality and performativity (the stage of the system's development where the system assumes shape without recourse to the outside world) remain in tension with its referentiality (the stage of the system's development where the system negotiates its shape with the outside world). In this way a system is built out of multiple fragments that belong to different facets of the world; an organized yet dynamic entity of higher order thus emerges out of the chaotic fragmentation of entities that belong to a lower order, where the higher order is more than a simple sum of the lower order components.

Treister's project can be considered an autopoetic system. She is open to various notions of the self and, as an artist, particularly susceptible to the original meaning of the word, which can be traced to the Greek *poietikos*, literally meaning "creative, productive" ("Poietikos"). The system involves an album, a Tarot cards pack, two exhibitions, and the activities of audience members. The album's four parts or fragments visualize and connect ideas, people and events, usually not linked together, in order to tell repressed and hidden stories. The Tarot cards spreads provide permutations, corrections and new juxtapositions of images and facts they represent, varying in accordance with the Tarot cards reader. Two institutions (an art gallery and the Museum of Science) provide an external context, an environment via which new information is fed back in loops to the system, of which all members of Treister's audience are also a part.

The external context provided by the gallery and the museum is in itself multifaceted because the two exhibitions vary regarding the kind of entanglement in the cultural politics of presenting information; politics shaped by the processes of technological development and the rise of communications systems which Treister's project scrutinizes. The gallery enables a greater degree of ideological independence because its creatively arranged displays of artistic works manifest an affinity with the premodern and early modern aleatory strategies of knowledge production evinced by the Tarot and the Wunderkammer. By contrast, the museum belongs to institutions that support the official history of the technological progress and, through the systematic arrangement of artifacts at display, represents modern strategies of knowledge production.

The singularity of the fragmentation strategy employed by Treister brings to light the genealogies that have so far remained largely untold (Larsen 8). By juxtaposing the occult practices, Wunderkammer epistemology, and specific microhistories, and showing how these elements interrelate through autopoetic loops, the artist constructs a new, alternative, Benjaminian history of contemporary communications systems, social media and technologies which facilitate connectivity. Her fragmentary, nonlinear alternative narrative unfolds as an allegory, whose melancholy entropy is at each feedback loop countervailed by an injection of energy deriving from the aleatoricity of Tarot practices and the performativity of Wunderkammer epistemology. Aptly, the multimodality and autopoetic potential of the *Hexen 2.0* project encourage the transformation of hypothetical futures, projected by political calculations and scientific research, into alternative possible futures (cf. back cover blurb *Hexen 2.0*). The metamorphosis of the hypothetical into the possible happens in *Hexen 2.0* due to the feedback loops which incorporate early-modern curiosity and the supersensible experience into the construction of history.

Works Cited

Benjamin, Walter. "Theses on the Philosophy of History." 1940. Trans. Harry Zohn. *Illuminations: Essays and Reflections.* New York: Schocken, 1969. 253–64.

Bolzoni, Lina. *The Gallery of Memory: Literary and Iconographic Models in the Age of the Printing Press.* Trans. Jeremy Parzen. Toronto: U of Toronto P, 2001.

Bredekamp, Horst. *The Lure of Antiquity and the Cult of the Machine: The Kunstkammer and the Evolution of Nature, Art and Technology.* Trans. Allison Brown. Princeton: Markus Wiener Publishers, 1995.

Calabrese, Omar. *Neo-Baroque: A Sign of the Times.* 1987. Trans. Charles Lambert. Princeton: Princeton UP, 1992.

Collins, Samuel Gerald. "Do Cyborgs Dream of Electronic Rats? The Macy Conferences and the Emergence of Hybrid Multi-Agent Systems," http://www.aaai.org/Papers/Symposia/Fall/2007/FS-07-04/FS07-04-005.pdf. Accessed 14 Sept. 2017.

Cregan, Kate. *The Theatre of the Body: Staging Death and Embodying Life in Early-Modern London.* Turnhout: Brepols, 2009.

Douglas, Alfred. *The Tarot: The Origins, Meanings and Uses of the Cards.* London: Penguin, 1991.

Farley, Helen. *A Cultural History of Tarot: From Entertainment to Esotericism.* London: I.B. Tauris, 2009.

Hanssen, Beatrice. *Walter Benjamin's Other History: Of Stones, Animals, Human Beings, and Angels.* Berkeley: U of California P, 1998.

Harries, Karsten. "World-Picture and World-Theater: Wonder, Vision, Knowledge." *Collection, Laboratory, Theater: Scenes of Knowledge in the 17th Century.* Eds. Helmar Schramm, Ludger Schwarte and Jan Lazardzig. Berlin: De Gruyter, 2005. 507–25.

Heims, Steve Joshua. *The Cybernetics Group.* Cambridge: MIT Press, 1991.

Kolbuszewska, Zofia. "Forensic Imagination and the Materiality of Experience." *American Experience – The Experience of America.* Eds. Andrzej

Ceynowa and Marek Wilczyński. Frankfurt am Main: Peter Lang, 2013. 37–49.

Larsen, Lars Bang. "The Secret Life of Control: Suzanne Treister's Radical Enlightnment." *Hexen 2.0*. By Suzanne Treister. London: Black Dog, 2012. 6–9.

Livingston, Ira. *Between Science and Literature: An Introduction to Autopoetics*. Urbana: U of Illinois P, 2006.

Quicchelberg, Samuel. *Inscriptiones vel Tituli Theatri amplissimi....* Munich, 1565.

"Poietikos." Def. 2. *Online Etymology Dictionary*, Harper Douglas, www.etymonline.com. Accessed 16 Sept. 2017.

Treister, Suzanne. Bio, Suzanne Treister Net, http://www.suzannetreister.net/info/bio.html. Accessed 14 Sept. 2017.

---. *Hexen 2.0*. London: Black Dog, 2012.

---. *Hexen 2039: New Military-Occult Technologies for Psychological Warfare: A Rosalind Brodsky Programme*. London: Black Dog, 2006.

Westerhoff, Jan C. "A World of Signs: Baroque Pansemioticism, the *Polyhistor* and the Early Modern *Wunderkammer*." *Journal of the History of Ideas* 62.4 (2001): 633–50.

Wohlfarth, Irving. "Et Cetera? The Historian as Chiffonnier." *New German Critique* 39 (1986): 142–68.

Yates, Frances. *The Art of Memory*. London: Ark, 1984.

Chapter 14

Unbox the story: a look at contemporary shuffle narratives

Côme Martin

"Shuffle literature" is perhaps a term unfamiliar to some readers, inasmuch as it has remained a niche genre since its apparition in the 1960s. According to Zuzana Husárová and Nick Montfort, it "formally consist[s] of text segments that may be read in any order" and for which "a reader is still supposed to read every word of text, as with a typical book," which unfortunately does not account for comics. Others, such as Ben Carey, prefer to talk about "reader-assembled narratives," stories that "require[] the reader to physically assemble a fragmented narrative." However, Carey's definition cannot include digital literature: that is why the term "shuffle narratives" seems preferable as it includes both comics and digital productions. According to the few articles devoted to the subject, shuffle narratives "appeared in the 1960s out of a post-war opposition to form" (Carey); for Julia Jordan, the 1960s were associated with "[a]n awareness of the possibilities of new forms and a desire to move away from the conservatism that distinguished the art of the immediate post-war era" (90). Other critics, such as Jan Baetens, posit that the avant-gardes of this period were mostly characterized by "the use of anti-form ... or the use of chance as a compositional tool" (116). Both chance and anti-form are indeed important concepts for shuffle narratives, although, as it shall be shown, they do not codify the genre *per se*.

The present article focuses on eleven shuffle narratives that present a comprehensive spectrum of what such texts can offer their readers. The first two are the grandfathers of the genre, Marc Saporta's *Composition No.1* (1962) and B. S. Johnson's *The Unfortunates* (1969), both "very book-like in their external appearance" (Husárová and Montfort). They are followed by Eric Zimmerman's *Life in the Garden* (2000), also book-like but in a more playful/restrictive way: it is the only shuffle narrative in the corpus that asks its reader to discard some of its fragments before reading. Off-springs of *Composition No. 1*, whose introduction requests the reader to "shuffle [its] page like a deck of cards," include Robert Coover's short story "Heart Suit" (2005), printed on an oversized series of fourteen cards, and Jedediah Berry's *The Family Arcana* (2015), which is both a complete card set and a fragmentary short story. One might include in the same branch the French comics *Thomas & Manon* (2015), by Alex Chauvel and Rémi Farnos, which uses the panel as its unit of reference, and not the page, implying a completely different way of reassembling their narratives. Another shuffle comics, more closely related to *The Unfortunates*, is Chris Ware's *Building Stories* (2012), presented as fourteen chapters of different length, size and appearance, inside a box. Finally, the digital narratives presented in this paper include both digital adaptations of preexisting works (*Composition No. 1* [2011] and Tom Phillips's *A Humument* [2010]) as well as original creations such as *Récits voisins* (1997), a collective work which is both a series of eight autonomous short stories and eight parts of a greater narrative, stitched together *via* common characters and themes. This long list of narratives, composed mostly by chance, excludes works such as Nanni Balestrini's *Tristano* (1966) whose paragraphs were pre-arranged before any possible intervention by the reader, much like the 1972 Hungarian edition of *The Unfortunates*. In short, this paper focuses on works which potential narrative space is infinite, while their material form is limited.

If shuffle narratives appeared in the 1960s, why did they remain a foot-note in the history of experimental fiction for so long? Why is there such a resurgence of shuffle narratives in the twenty-first century? The answer probably lies in their means of production: it is much easier to publish and distribute an unbound text than it was a few decades ago thanks to the global shift to digital text processing and printing. The development of digital literature has also challenged experimental authors to develop more creative works, as Ben Carey writes. There is, as well, a temptation to see the digital as more able to produce narratives out of chance, or more accurately, computer-programmed chance, as well as an ever more embracing definition of the "anti-form" in an era when each new work has the possibility to invent and define as its own form.

This short study of the different forms of shuffle narratives therefore aims to shed new light on the ever-expanding genre, first by looking at the different formats and media they imitate, from the card game to the oracle to the puzzle – thus asking their readers to take another extra role in the process; then by studying the different ways the reader will reconstruct the narrative; finally, by showing how shuffle narratives question several basic notions taken for granted in the structure of a narrative. Shuffle narratives are a very specific kind of fragmentary writing, both book-like and box-like, both games and stories, both analog and digital; they are thus a precious object of study for anyone who is interested in multimodal narratives as a whole.

The games of chance

Shuffle narratives imitate and emulate many different forms, principally the book and the card game. Playing cards are explicitly referenced in "Heart Suit," even though Coover's cards are much larger than a standard playing card and stripped of any familiar illustration, save for their four corners. On the contrary, Jedediah Berry closely imitates the form with *The Family Arcana*: the cards come in a regular cardboard pack and are similar in every way to normal playing cards, except for the paragraphs, up to seventeen lines, printed on them (the two jokers and two "book-ending cards" feature only a drawing).

Furthermore, as Emily Short explains, in *The Family Arcana* "the suits and numbers do matter. Spades cards tell about the siblings who are the first person plural narrators of the story. Clubs tell about the extended family: father and mother, aunts and uncles, cousins, grandmother and grandfather...." Berry has confirmed this in an interview: "There's a system to it – the hearts, for example, are all about Mother and Father, and the diamonds all have to do with the setting – but it's a purposefully imperfect system. I wanted to achieve a certain kind of balance without making the structure too rigid" (Laskowski). Emily Short adds that *The Family Arcana* even goes one step further and transforms itself from fragmentary text to *bona fide* card game: "If you like, you can order from the same press a Supplementary Pack of cards, *The Family Arcana Card Game*, which introduces a ruleset, several more illustrated cards, and a few curious extras."

References to cards abound in other shuffle narratives: the subtitle of *Life in the Garden* is "a *deck* of stories" (emphasis mine); *Composition No. 1*, as mentioned before, asks its readers to shuffle its pages like a deck of cards; *Thomas & Manon*, which uses not the page but the panel as a unit, refers to them as "cards" in its instructions. One may wonder what is so appealing about playing cards as to make them a favorite of shuffle narratives. It might be because they are, like books, ubiquitous objects that can be manipulated in thousands of ways. There are thousands of different rules that govern the manipulation, shuffling and ordering of a deck of cards. Shuffle narratives only retain their basic characteristic as a finite set of values that can appear in any order. Apart from *The Family Arcana Supplementary*

Pack, in which one can win or lose the story, so to speak, shuffle narratives are closer to a strange kind of solitaire: there are instructions on how to shuffle the cards (most prominently in "Heart Suit") but no objective conditions of success, except perhaps judging that the assembled narrative is satisfactory.

In addition, card games are far from the only playful activity referenced by shuffle narratives and its closest cousins: it is no wonder the OuBaPo[1] has explored the possibilities of reading a comic strip like a game of Scrabble (*Scroubabble*) or of dominoes (*DoMiPo*), or that Julio Cortazar's *Hopscotch* (1963) refers to the most stereotypical of recess pastimes. Allusions to games in shuffle narratives are plentiful: card games are the most often mentioned, but puzzles are also closely associated with their reading mechanisms. It is impossible to talk about puzzles without quoting Georges Perec who, in *Life: A User's Manual* (1978) – another non-linear-but-bound book – astutely remarks, "Despite appearances, puzzling is not a solitary game: every move the puzzler makes, the puzzle-maker has made before ... every blunder and every insight, each hope and each discouragement have all been designed, calculated, and decided by the other" (iii). Therefore, to read a shuffle narrative designed like a puzzle is also to move more or less by chance through a maze so that reading becomes its own kind of topography. "The pieces," adds Hugo Ferraz Maio Gomes, "are gathered into a chaotic jumble which must be organized by the puzzler in order for there to be a sense of purpose or compliance with the 'big picture,' and meaning" (40). There is an element of puzzle-solving, riddle-cracking in all shuffle narratives, as the patient reader reconstructs the story, a seemingly insignificant piece by a seemingly insignificant piece until it suddenly falls into place and the pattern of the puzzle begins to appear.

The analogy with the puzzle and its spatial aspects is most explicit in *Thomas & Manon*, in which the reader manipulates panels as if they were cards, but not exactly of the playing kind, as the apostrophe to the reader explains, "The island on which [the two protagonists walk] is ... impossible to map, since everything moves all the time there ... The principle is simple: you must build the roads Thomas and Manon walk on." The task is made a little easier by providing the reader with beginning and end tiles, as well as tiles which are supposed to be assembled to form a larger picture than usual; but apart from those, any association is possible. This

---

[1] Officially created in 1992, the OuBaPo or "Ouvroir de Bande dessinée Potentielle" is the comics equivalent of the OuLiPo ("Ouvroir de Littérature Potentielle") and seeks to use constraints to push the boundaries of the medium.

freedom means there is no definite solution to the puzzle, any logical link between one tile and the next save for the infrequent popping up of a recurring character, but this is, perhaps, the point of this devious puzzle: to imagine an island made of quicksand, where both characters and readers are meant to lose their bearings until they reemerge, somewhat changed, on the other side – which could be the definition of many postmodernist novels. Incidentally, there is also a topographic element to the new edition of Saporta's *Composition No. 1* published by Visual Editions: at the back of each of the 150 pages, a typographic landscape, so to speak, is visible, a computer-generated map from the text of the novel. In the digital edition of *Composition No. 1*, the reader can even move through this apparently infinite landscape instead of browsing the text.

For the readers who prefer more guidance in their explorations, shuffle narratives provide a third and final kind of analogy, that of the oracle. Oracles share some similarities with playing cards: they are dealt randomly, or sometimes according to some arbitrary rules – tarot divination, for instance – although unlike playing cards they are not meant to entertain but to reveal some hidden truth about the dealer, the reader, the world, or all three. Hints of oracle-like qualities can be found in *Composition No. 1*, whose instructions, as mentioned above, ask the reader to "shuffle [its] pages like a deck of cards: to cut, if he likes with his left hand, as at a fortuneteller's," thus leaving the exploration – and perhaps the interpretation – of its narrative to chance. *The Family Arcana*'s title also hints at its possible use for divination, as Emily Short writes, somewhat mysteriously: "The sense of hidden significances – readings of the arcane – is integral to the experience and makes the deck into a sort of puzzle." Therefore, Jedediah Berry's deck of cards is the only narrative of the corpus which is at the same time a card game, a puzzle and an oracle.

The oracle is mostly present in *A Humument*, whose links to the *I Ching* are well-known and often talked about by its author, Tom Phillips, who says he often opens a page of his book at random to see what revelation it has to offer. The digital version of the book goes much further, since one can either read it chronologically or select two pages at random or according to a given date: "These two pages now combine / Your fate and fortune to divine," says the text. Just like the landscapes of *Composition No.1*, chance is left in the hands of the computer program, although there still is a profoundly human element to this divination since one can share it via email or by posting it on Tumblr, Twitter or Facebook, as one would with horoscopes.

A shuffle narrative by any other name

Shuffle narratives also have in common an element of co-authorship between the original author and the reader of each work. This reconstructive role differs depending on the medium, although it always has to do with Gilles Deleuze and Félix Guattari's rhizome: "A book composed of chapters," they write in *A Thousand Plateaus*, "has culmination and termination points. What takes place in a book composed instead of plateaus that communicate with one another across microfissures, as in a brain?" (24). This section will focus on the analogy between the rhizomatic book and the human brain. Shuffle narratives are indeed particularly well-suited to explore themes like "fragmented memory, the reconstruction of the past, and painful and sometimes traumatic experiences," to quote Husárová and Montfort. Shuffle narratives, in these cases, imitate through randomness the cognitive model of remembering and associating thoughts. The process of remembering and memory as a theme are present in several works of the corpus, mainly *The Unfortunates* and *Building Stories*, which seem the concretization of Deleuze and Guattari's rhizome as "short-term memory, or antimemory" (23).

B. S. Johnson's and Chris Ware's boxes are interesting to study side-by-side, since, in spite of their common exploration of memories, they use opposite strategies: *The Unfortunates* provides a fixed beginning and ending whereas the reader can start with any "chapter" s/he finds when opening *Building Stories*. The difference in medium also has its importance: readers of comics have long been used to reconstructing meaning from fragmentary narratives in a much more concrete way than readers of novels. There is an ongoing debate on the cognitive process of linking two separate panels together: Scott McCloud's famous one-liner about closure – "Every act committed to paper by the comics artist is aided and abetted by a silent accomplice" (68) – downplays the complexity of such a device, even though Ware himself has made great use of the fragmentary nature of comics in previous works, *Jimmy Corrigan* (2000) for instance. Therefore, it is not entirely disconcerting when, in *Building Stories*, he goes one step further and provides his reader with physical spaces between chapters instead of blank pages.

This difference in medium carries over in the rest of the corpus. It has already been mentioned that *Thomas & Manon* can replace the page with the panel as its permutable unit; the opposite is true of *Life in the Garden*, which is presented as a deck but contains a book, or more precisely covers and unbound pages. Like many shuffle narratives, it contains instructions but of a unique kind: it asks readers to select the pages blindly, and to select only a tiny selection of them ("five pages," or "three pages for a brief parable," or "seven pages for an epic tale"). For the story to be properly read, the unbound pages must be placed within the covers, whose inside read "Adam, Eve, and the serpent lived in the garden" – on the left – and "The End" – on the right. Both the instructions and the text make clear that, even if *Life in the Garden* shares with *The Unfortunates* a fixed beginning and ending, its content is a parody of the most famous of books, the Bible: the countless pages of the holy book are replaced by a handful, inserted within the parody of a book, down to its minuscule format. Of note is also that the text of *Life in the Garden*, like many other shuffle narratives, is printed only on one side of the pages. Each verso features, like *Composition No. 1*, a unique image; but unlike *Composition No. 1*, whose topographical arrangements used the text's letters, the images of *Life in the Garden* seem to have no relation to the text whatsoever. They are not referred to in the instructions and can be interpreted in several ways: as another kind of divination device; as illustrations inserted within the text to "separate" it and create "additional distance" between the pages (Husárová and Montfort), hinting once more at the topographical nature of such a text; or as some sort of a surrealist rebus, of obscure meaning, if meaning is to be found at all – this might explain why Eric Zimmerman, on his website, lists *Life in the Garden* among his "ludography."

Also of interest is that the pages of *Life in the Garden* are closer in texture and weight to index cards than regular paper, a sign that they are meant to be manipulated quite frequently. This haptic quality is, of course, common to all shuffle narratives, even the digital ones, though they might appear otherwise at first. The computer-generated landscapes at the back of the pages of *Composition No. 1* serve here as a threshold between the analog and the digital, which is perhaps why a journalist of *The Independent* described them as "a swathe of TV static, or drifting sand" (Gibbs), leaving to his readers the decision to rally to either interpretation. In its digital incarnation, *Composition No. 1* presents a flurry of pages flashing randomly on the screen, until the reader touches the iPad's screen: as soon as the contact between finger and screen is broken, the pages flash again, except the one just read. The effect is explicit: the story can be read only if tactile contact is maintained, making for a great bilingual pun on the word "digital." In any case, it is once again interaction that produces meaning, an interaction that comes from the hand, engaging one's body in the same way as physical shuffle narratives. It is no coincidence that Anna Nacher should call the *Humument* app an "embodiment" of Tom Phillips's entire project (1), stressing once again the link between the body of the reader and the body of the work, an incarnation of and by the hand.

Not all digital shuffle narratives are haptic, of course. It is not the case, for instance, with the digital version of *The Family Arcana*, which is available on Bandcamp in two audio versions: one offers 52 tracks, in which 52 different readers each read one of the story's cards. We are asked to "shuffle tracks before listening," which is a natural tendency today for the users of an mp3 player, but certainly not when presented with a story, whether in printed or audio form. There is also a *Family Arcana* soundtrack meant to enhance the experience, making Berry's work a transmedia project in more than one way and offering its readers different approaches to the text, just as it can be rearranged differently before delving into it.

Finally, *Récits voisins* offers a different kind of digital experience, one less related to touch – although its opening screen features a pair of dice as a possible Mallarmean reference, and one of its chapters is a poem entitled "*La Main* [The Hand]." As Yves Eude wrote in 1998, in *Récits voisins* "all the characters are in 'egg-like situations': a cosmonaut in his pod, an alpinist in his shed, a mad scientist in his laboratory...." The different genres of *Récits voisins*' chapters, from the detective story to science-fiction to eroticism, give different "semantic charges" to our reading of the text: "In the detective story, [the reader] 'inspects' the textual substance by activating its links; in the erotic story, s/he 'unveils' hidden textual parts; ... a photographic story plays on apparition and disappearance, the ambiguous materiality of text and image on a digital medium ..." (Saemmer 48). In short, *Récits voisins* perfectly sums up how the medium of a shuffle narrative, but also its genre and the analogies it allows with other formats shapes not only the reader's approach to the text but also the role of this reader in stitching the story together.

Rhizomatic shuffling

As different as they can be, almost all shuffle narratives have in common the refusal of a definite and linear story. They question several notions taken for granted in the structure of a narrative, beginning with the conventional fragmentation of text in chapters and paragraphs (or, in the case of comics, strips and pages). It is revelatory that critics and scholars still tend to call the different fragments of *The Unfortunates* and *Building Stories* "chapters" only because they contain more than one page; similarly, the terms "panel" and "tile" are used interchangeably when talking about *Thomas & Manon*. Shuffle narratives are engaging precisely because they rearrange our preconceptions of what literature is, much like digital literature a few decades ago. But there is another structural element that some of them question: the notion of beginnings and endings. Shuffle narratives are at heart the embodiment of the rhizome, an object which "has neither beginning nor end, but always a middle (*milieu*) from which it grows and which it overspills" (Deleuze and Guattari 23). Even shuffle narratives with fixed beginnings and endings – "Heart Suit," *The Unfortunates, Thomas & Manon* and, in some sense, *Life in the Garden* – are shifting entities, the walls of their mazes always rearranging with each reading.

Interestingly, the rhizomatic aspect of shuffle narratives applies to the "discourse level" only in most cases, as Montfort and Husárová note. For instance, one can read "Heart Suit" three times in a row and find the king condemning three different culprits, but since he always ends up ordering a retrial, the condemnation does not matter. In the same way, one can read the two halves of the protagonist's life in *Building Stories* as a present time followed by a flashback, or as two chronological periods, but like the memories presented in *The Unfortunates*, the order of the fragments does not matter past the discourse level, since several devices in the story allow the reader to either reassemble (some of) it or not be bothered by its fragmentation.

Ben Carey identifies two techniques, in particular, which authors of shuffle narratives should respect for their stories to remain accessible: "ambiguity" and "constants." In the first one, "the writer introduces and finishes each section in a [*sic*] non-specific way that does not draw attention to a specific time or place, meaning that the segment can occur at any point within the narrative." Constants, on the other hand, "are people, events, objects or locations that repeatedly occur throughout the narrative and thus create an anchor point in the mind of the reader." In *Composition No. 1*, for example, these anchor points would be Dagman, Marianne and Helga – three characters who appear on 90 of the story's 150 pages.

Are those techniques enough to prevent the reader's frustration, especially since, because they are devoid of definite endings, shuffle narratives lack closure? Endings, in particular, provide closure in traditionally composed narratives, a notion Jane Yellowlees Douglas defines as "the single entity that confers cohesion and significance on narratives" (92).[2] It is only once a narrative is complete that one can retroactively consider it as a whole entity that can be synchronically apprehended: "The ending [of a narrative]," writes Douglas, "simply removes any 'residual expectations' I may have – I know that the narrative has nothing left to reveal after I have finished my reading" (95).

Closure and ending are not the same thing, however. Were we to read every page of *Composition No. 1* again in a different order, or every frag-

---

[2] Similar ideas can be found in Frank Kermode's *The Sense of an Ending*, Peter Brooks's *Reading for the Plot* and Wolfgang Iser's *The Act of Reading*.

ment of *Building Stories*, would only the surface of the work change, and not its underlying motives, themes and recurring elements? Does the order in which the narrative information is revealed matter, or does it become irrelevant by the end of one's reading? The answers are probably left for each reader to decide, and depend on whether one considers the *construction* of information – during the first reading – or the *finished product* – after closure is achieved. A narrative composed only of middles – or, perhaps, a narrative where there are only potential beginnings, and/or potential endings – can still be satisfying, as long as there is room for the reader to act as coauthor and connect the dots.

Conclusion

Even with closure intact, shuffle narratives still tend to lend themselves to rereading much more than conventional narratives; perhaps because to read only one of their fragments again is already, in a sense, to reread the entire text. The most remarkable aspect of shuffle narratives is their potential infinity, the promise that the text will never be exhausted, no matter the number of rereadings. In a way, to explore a shuffle narrative is to re-read it before we even begin reading it:

> Rereading is ... suggested at the outset, for it alone saves the text from repetition ..., multiplies it in its variety and its plurality: rereading draws the text out of its internal chronology.... If then ... we immediately reread the text, it is in order to obtain, as though under the effect of a drug ... not the real text, but a plural text: the same and new. (Barthes 15–16)

Shuffle narratives are not simply games to play with or oracles to consult nervously: they are at the same time the most open and the most arcane of texts, both labyrinthine and straightforward, shifting and always the same. Jurij Lotman writes that "a work of art is a finite model of an infinite universe" (210): this cannot be more true of shuffle narratives, which are always beginning and always ending, expanding in all directions and never keeping still.

Works Cited

Baetens, Jan. "OuLiPo and Proceduralism." *The Routledge Companion to Experimental Literature*. Eds. Joe Bray, Alison Gibbons and Brian McHale. Abingdon: Routledge, 2012. 115–27.

Barthes, Roland. *S/Z*. 1970. Trans. Richard Miller. New York: Farrar, Straus & Giroux, 1974.

Berry, Jedediah. *The Family Arcana*. Amherst: Ninepin, 2016.

---. *The Family Arcana Supplementary Pack*. Amherst: Ninepin, 2016.

Brooks, Peter. *Reading for the Plot*. New York: Vintage, 1985.

Carey, Ben. "The Reader-Assembled Narrative: Representing the Random in Print Fiction." *TEXT* 19.2 (2015), http://textjournal.com.au/oct15/carey.htm. Accessed 31 Jan. 2018.

Chauvel, Alex, and Rémi Farnos. *Thomas & Manon.* Angoulême: Éditions Polystyrène, 2015.

Coover, Robert. "Heart Suit." *A Child Again.* San Francisco: McSweeney's, 2005.

Deleuze, Gilles, and Félix Guattari. 1980. Trans. Brian Massumi. *A Thousand Plateaus.* London: Continuum, 2004.

Douglas, Jane Yellowlees. *The End of Books – or Books Without End?* Ann Arbor: U of Michigan P, 2001.

Eude, Yves. "Cinq 'récits voisins forment une œuvre collective." *Le Monde,* 9 Oct. 1998, http://hypermedia.univ-paris8.fr/oVosite/nous/LM091098.html. Accessed 31 Jan. 2018.

Gibbs, Jonathan. "The Writers Who Revel in Losing the Plot." *The Independent,* 4 Oct. 2011, http://www.independent.co.uk/arts-entertainment/books/features/the-writers-who-revel-in-losing-the-plot-2365489.html. Accessed 31 Jan. 2018.

Husárová, Zuzana, and Nick Montfort. "Shuffle Literature and the Hand of Fate." *Electronic Book Review,* 5 Aug. 2012, http://www.electronicbookreview.com/thread/electropoetics/shuffled. Accessed 31 Jan. 2018.

Iser, Wolfgang. *The Act of Reading.* Baltimore: John Hopkins UP, 1978.

Johnson, B. S. *The Unfortunates.* London: Panther, 1969.

Jordan, Julia. *Chance and the Modern British Novel: From Henry Green to Iris Murdoch.* New York: Continuum, 2010.

Kermode, Frank. *The Sense of an Ending.* New York: Oxford UP, 1966.

Laskowski, Tara. "The Family Arcana Deals Out a Full House." *Smokelong,* n.d., http://www.smokelong.com/review-and-qa-the-family-arcana-deals-out-a-full-house/. Accessed 31 Jan. 2018.

Lotman, Jurij. *The Structure of the Artistic Text.* 1971. Ann Arbor: U of Michigan P, 1977.

Gomes, Hugo Ferraz Maio. *Of Structural Denial.* Lisbon: Faculdade de Ciências Sociais e Humanas, 2014.

McCloud, Scott. *Understanding Comics.* Northampton: Kitchen Sink, 1993.

Nacher, Anna. "*A Humument* App by Tom Phillips As a Work of Liberature." *ELO* Conference, 30 June 2013, https://conference.eliterature.org/critical-writing/humument-app-tom-phillips-work-liberature-between-text-and-embodiment. Accessed 31 Jan. 2018.

oVosite. *Récits voisins.* Département Hypermédia, 1997, http://hypermedia.univ-paris8.fr/oVosite/recits/navi.htm. Accessed 16 Apr. 2018.

Perec, Georges. *Life: A User's Manual.* 1978. Trans. David Bellos. London: Vintage, 2008.

Phillips, Tom. *A Humument App.* Tom Phillips, 2010. Version 1.06. *Apple App Store*, https://itunes.apple.com/us/app/a-humument-app/id402755491?mt=8. Accessed 16 Apr. 2018.

Saemmer, Alexandra. *Matières textuelles sur support numérique.* Saint-Étienne: Publications de l'Université de Saint-Étienne, 2007.

Saporta, Marc. *Composition No. 1.* 1962. Trans. Richard Howard. London: Visual Editions, 2011.

Short, Emily. "Card-Deck Narratives." *Emily Short's Interactive Storytelling*, 3 May 2016, https://emshort.blog/2016/05/03/card-deck-narratives/. Accessed 31 Jan. 2018.

Ware, Chris. *Building Stories.* New York: Pantheon, 2012.

Zimmerman, Eric. *Life in the Garden.* New York: Razorfish Studios, 2000.

Chapter 15

Fragmentation as building practice: the literary and musical collaboration between Thomas Ligotti and Current 93 for *In a Foreign Town, in a Foreign Land*

Deborah Bridle,
University of Côte d'Azur

Anyone familiar with the work of horror writer Thomas Ligotti knows that fragmentation is a fundamental element of his creative process. His fictional work is exclusively made of collections of short stories, series of fragments depicting nightmarish and fugitive visions of existence. His characters also undergo an array of physical and psychological experiences of fragmentation. *In a Foreign Town, in a Foreign Land* is no exception. It was published in 1997 as a multimedia voyage composed of four short stories accompanied by a musical soundscape in the form of a CD featuring four tracks, one for each story. The music is the work of Current 93, the main musical project of David Tibet, who is the sole permanent member of the band. Current 93 is a representative of various movements in rock music and is variously described as related to the post-industrial, neofolk, or experimental scenes. It is an offspring of the British industrial movement, which appeared in the late 1970s as a reaction to the political scene of the time and the general disillusionment with humanistic ideals of the 1960s. When its spearhead Throbbing Gristle dissolved in 1981, bands like Psychic TV, Coil, Nurse with Wound and Current 93 emerged, forming the post-industrial movement – more musically open and less politically driven than its forefathers, and imbued with a more mystical and philosophical dimension (Burns 103). *In a Foreign Town, in a Foreign Land* is the first collaboration between the American writer and the British band.

My purpose here is to demonstrate how the musical and literary compositions may be seen as a fragmented whole, a set of works which feature fragmentation as a central element of their structure and meaning, and which echo each other in a mode alternating between resonance and dissonance. On the basis of those observations, I will try to show how the diverse stylistic and structural fragments may be interpreted as bricks in a more unified building process.

Thematic and structural fragmentation

Ligotti is used to assembling his short stories in collections that present a certain thematic continuity, with subparts or chapters further classifying the stories in unified subthemes – for instance, the subparts "Dreams for Sleepwalkers," "Dreams for Insomniacs," and "Dreams for the Dead" in the collection *Songs of a Dead Dreamer* (1989); or "Derangements," "Deformations," and "The Damaged and the Diseased" in the collection *Teatro Grottesco* (2008). *In a Foreign Town, in a Foreign Land* is slightly different: conceived as a collaboration with Current 93, the collection is much shorter than his other ones, including only four short stories, and offers no subdivision to classify the stories under a uniting banner. Besides, each of them functions as its own entity, diegetically independent from the others. The musical counterpart follows the same division, with four tracks bearing the same titles as the stories: "His shadow shall rise to a higher house," "The bells will sound forever," "A soft voice whispers nothing," and "When you hear the singing, you will know it is time."

Thematically, fragmentation is at the core of Ligotti's writing: his characters are subjected to strange experiences which threaten their ontological integrity. The fragmentation can be physical, as is the case with the horribly deformed body of Ascrobius in the first story, or the two hands of Mrs Pyk in the second story: one artificial, and one old and palsied. The body becomes further fragmented as it can be literally torn to pieces: a young woman is dismembered and her body is used in an obscure ritual in the first story, while a macabre parade in the third story displays the severed head of a dog mounted on the bars of a cage. Finally, physical fragmentation can also take on dark magical overtones, as in the case of Mr Crumm who, in the second story, dreams that his body is reduced to his sole head, shrunk and placed at the end of a stick, like a fool's scepter, while he is still alive and conscious.

Fragmentation as a physical process is echoed by the artwork of the CD cover, designed by Steven Stapleton, a member of Current 93: a surrealistic collage mixing photographs and drawings, cutting up the body into several pieces and adding bizarre non-human appendages – a composite form that undoubtedly matches Ligotti's weirdest creations.

Figure 15.1. Steven Stapleton. CD cover: "You will know it is time." *In a Foreign Town, In a Foreign Land,* **by Current 93. London: Durtro, 1997.**

However, the element that supports most of the fragmentary effects in the collection is the setting. The four stories are set in the same unnamed town repeatedly referred to as "the town near the northern border."[1] Both its urbanistic and architectural elements and the atmosphere it exudes contribute to staging a scenery of desolation which facilitates the psychological breakdown of its inhabitants. The town is indeed composed of areas that appear to be quite separate from each other, not only geographically but also in terms of their functions. The first story mentions the "hilltop graveyard," "not far beyond the edge of town" (i), and the house of Ascrobius, the dead man who serves as the focus of that first story, is repeatedly referred to as a "high backstreet house" (iv), somehow separating it from the rest of the town's dwellings. In the second story, the two lodging houses are also clearly separated, one on the west side of town, the other on the east side of town. In the fourth story, there is "a specific street *near the edge of town,* a *dead-end street*" [emphasis mine] that the narrator first considers "the absolute limit" (xlv) to the bizarre and grotesque features that the town had to offer. The street is indeed characterized by its highly gothic architecture: "the houses and the buildings seemed to have grown into one another, melding their diverse material into a bizarre and jagged conglomerate of massive architectural proportions, its peaked roofs and soaring chimnied towers visibly swaying and audibly moaning" (xlv). This type of architecture can be found in descriptions of the town in other stories, culminating in the repetition of the phrase "architectural moan" in the third story. In all four stories, a sense of chaos and delirium pervades the town, which is reduced to a state of quasi-abandonment and decay. In the

---

[1] Variations of the formulation occur on pages i, iii, iv, v, vii, viii, ix, xi, xiii, xxiii, xxiv, xxvi, xxvii, xxviii, xxix, xxxiii, xli, xlii, xliv, xlvi, xlviii, xlix, lii, liii, liv, lv. The first edition used here features Roman numerals for page numbers. *In a Foreign Town, in a Foreign Land* was later republished in larger collections which use Arabic numerals.

first story, the inhabitants gather in the "cellar of an abandoned building" (iii), "back rooms of shops long gone out of business," "some out-of-the-way streetcorner" (iv), "a ruined factory on the outskirts of town" (v), or the "shadows of an old warehouse" (viii). The east side of town, where Mrs Pyk has established her lodging house, used to be a wealthy area but is now full of abandoned buildings. The artwork on the book cover, described by a critic as "neo-expressionistic" for the front and "semi-abstract" for the back (Indick 116) materializes the vision of those high twisted buildings, their sharp edges and angles representing their menacing presence, the strong lines an image of separation and division.

Figure 15.2.   Steven Stapleton.   Book front cover: "In a Foreign Land." *In a Foreign Town, In a Foreign Land,* by Thomas Ligotti.   London: Durtro, 1997.

Figure 15.3.   Steven Stapleton.   Book back cover: "In a Foreign Land." *In a Foreign Town, In a Foreign Land,* by Thomas Ligotti.   London: Durtro, 1997.

The stories indeed all seem to express the idea that the town, itself visually fragmented, causes its inhabitants to undergo a process of the fragmentation of their sanity. Rendered unstable by the ominous and dreary atmosphere of the town and its possibly supernatural power, the few people who are left there are continuously described as hysterics or impostors, lost people whose sole purpose seems to be to wander the streets of the town searching for some kind of ever-fleeting truth. David Tibet's music aptly transcribes the presence of those fragmented psyches by using layers of distant voices, faint murmurs, or through the addition of excerpts read from the text in a chanting and monotonous tone of voice evoking the mystical power that the town holds over its inhabitants.

Echoes and dissonance

The association of music and literature is not a recent practice, although it is a relationship that has evolved through time, both in its purpose and in its practical manifestations. Many critics (Calvin S. Brown, Jean-Louis Cupers, etc.) have studied the question of adaptation from literature to music, or vice versa, as well as the specificities that each media is endowed with. Cupers talks about a "middle ground of compromise" (53) where the music starts from abstraction and emotion and tries to reach a representational level (objects and events), while literature starts from concrete events and objects and strives to reach a more abstract dimension. This opposition between the representative and the presentative is also intimated by Stephen Benson, who writes that music based on literature is first and foremost evocative of ambiance; it is mood music. In order for that music to truly interpret a written text, it has to be "translated into something conceptual and given the cognitive capacity to interpret rather than affect." But he adds that in reality, "music is always an intentional object which must be interpreted before it can be experienced as music" (13).

In the case of a rather experimental musical piece like the one created here by Current 93, one can wonder how, if at all, the music can convey the meaning of the words written by Ligotti. As a matter of fact, I contend that the result is quite close to the one observed by Barricelli in his analysis of Claude Debussy's adaptation of Mallarmé's "L'après-midi d'un faune": Debussy's work is neither a synthesis nor a transposition, but "a free rendering of a mood to accompany the text." Successive settings structurally translate the poem's succession of sensations: "Like the poem, the music must suggest without stating" (241–42).

The text and the music of *In a Foreign Town, in a Foreign Land* work as two fragments vibrating and resonating together to create a whole. Critic

William Burns notes that music is generally "not a primary metaphor in Ligotti's work," which is more riddled with ominous silence than it is with sounds and melody (101). However, *In a Foreign Town, in a Foreign Land* is meant to work as a collaborative multimedia experience, which is why sounds feature much more prominently than usual in this collection of short stories. Three of the titles directly mention sounds, and even musical elements for two of them: "The bells will sound forever," "A soft voice whispers nothing," and "When you hear the singing, you will know it is time." For Burns, those titles "implicate sound and tonality as sinister ingredients in the nightmarish landscape" (105). The atmospheres created by Ligotti in the four stories all use sound as a fundamental element, thus helping the cohesion and resonance with Current 93's work. As Indick writes in his analysis of the book and music, the soundtrack is "a remarkably symbiotic companion to the words ... in which atmosphere is all... Nothing is prelude, all is composition and all defers to the essence, the sense of the book" (120).

Current 93's work on this record is somewhat experimental, with no real melodies to speak of, no songs in the traditional sense of the term. The tracks therefore perfectly match Ligotti's eerie and nerve-racking sound-based atmospheres, as in the introduction to the first story: "In the middle of the night I lay awake in bed, listening to the dull black drone of the wind outside my window and the sound of bare branches scraping against the shingles of the roof just above me" (i). Current 93's track reproduces this low droning sound, a recurrent and fundamental element in all four tracks of the record. The droning sound is alternately throbbing or continuous, sometimes accompanied by various elements such as pulsating noises, shrill mechanical sounds, objects clanking and banging, all contributing to the creation of a frightening and disquieting atmosphere to match the stories. In the second story, bells are constantly heard in the background by the character, and consequently, the whole of the second track is also made of various layers of bells and chimes echoing and reverberating together. The third story features a lengthy description of sounds as the narrator hears a parade approaching in the streets:

> I heard the sounds of something that I could not identify, an approaching racket that caused me to take refuge in a narrow passageway between a pair of high buildings. Nestled in this dark hiding place I watched the street and listened as that nameless clattering grew louder. It was a medley of clanging and creaking, of groaning and croaking, a dull jangle of something unknown as it groped its way through the town, a chaotic parade in honor of some special occasion of delirium.... [T]he noise became louder and louder, the parade closing in .... The formless clamor seemed to envelop everything around me...

and later as the wagon of the parade appears:

> its great wooden wheels audibly grinding the pavement of the street be-
> neath them.... Hanging from the bars, and rattling against them, was an ar-
> ray of objects haphazardly tethered by cords and wires and straps of various
> kinds ... all knocking together in a wild percussion. (xxx-xxxi)

The corresponding track features the growing racket getting closer and
closer, the sound of the wheels on the pavement, the clanking of the bars
on the wagon. Tibet also occasionally uses voice as another instrument of
resonance between sound and text. For instance, he reads the whole of the
parade description for almost four minutes, his monotonous and slow
voice reproducing with precision the onomatopoeic and alliterative quality of words such as "clattering," "clanging," "croaking," and "creaking." The
same highly alliterative and, at the same time, drone-like quality of Tibet's
voice is featured at the beginning of the first story as he reads the opening
paragraph. The cohesion between text and music is therefore obtained
through the reading of certain key paragraphs or phrases of the original
text, and through a close rendition of the peculiar atmosphere of dread
and gloom that Ligotti crafts in his stories.

However, much as the two fragments work in resonance with each other,
there are also points of dissonance which separate the voices of the two
artists. Indeed, Tibet surprisingly alters certain elements of structure or
wording in his adaptations. This is the case in the first track, which seems
to open on a short sequence (a little over one minute) introducing the
whole collection rather than the first story only. A female voice reads the
title of the collection, but with an inversion: "in a foreign land, in a foreign
town," instead of "in a foreign town, in a foreign land." The third and
fourth tracks also offer some surprising changes to the structure of the
stories. If we are to believe Tibet, the CD should be played "at low volume,
at dusk, whilst reading *In a Foreign Town, in a Foreign Land*" (CD leaflet),
which confirms the intended cohesion between the two individual works.
How are we to explain, then, the structural discrepancies in tracks three
and four? Indeed, Tibet seems to entirely discard the initial four pages of
the third story and focuses his track on the parade right from the beginning, his reading starting only thirty seconds into the track. The parts of
the text describing the colorless and mute winter landscape have been left
aside to focus almost only on the cacophony of the parade.

In the fourth story, the title "When you hear the singing, you will know it
is time" appears on the sixth page, where the narrator writes that it was a
sort of "special slogan or incantation" that the people in a certain street of
the town would "repeat ... to whomever would listen" (xlvi). Tibet does not

miss the opportunity given by this ominous chanting and his fourth track features his voice reading over and over the title of the story for more than two minutes. But this incantation appears much sooner than it does in the text, an impression confirmed by the fact that thirty seconds after the end of his chanting, Tibet reads a paragraph appearing on the second page of the story, thereby disrupting the initial chronology. The rest of the track then seems to follow the story quite faithfully, the various movements of the text being translated by changes in the layers of sound and quality of the droning, and by the addition of various noises.

Before trying to account for those differences, one more element of dissonance is worth mentioning: the two artists' philosophies and worldviews. Although the themes that Tibet is used to exploring are rather close to Ligotti's interests (death, mysticism, occultism, esotericism, the apocalypse, to name but a few), and although the two men share a taste for horror literature and a certain bleak vision of today's world, their ultimate outlook on humanity is different. Ligotti's stark nihilism places him in the wake of Schopenhauer and makes him see no redeeming quality to life: existence and consciousness are the curse of humanity and it would be better if one ceased existing altogether. Tibet, as a Christian, albeit a rather unorthodox one, is a firm believer in the Apocalypse and in the Antichrist as being the prelude announcing the imminent Second Coming of Christ.[2] He therefore has faith in the human race and in their redemption. As Burns notes, there is thus "hope and joy in bleakness" for Tibet, where there is none to be found in Ligotti: "Tibet's appreciation of Ligotti may be more of an aesthetic and affective rather than a strict philosophical or metaphysical agreement" (103).

Considering those structural and philosophical dissonances between the two works and the two men's worldviews, I argue that the two fragments of the collaboration actually use this dissonance as a form of construction.

Break up, repeat, build up

Scholars of intermediality have highlighted the specificity of literature and music compared to other media: the fact that "they extend and develop in time rather than in space" (Brown 146), thus requiring "memory and anticipation" from the audience. Although they are composed of four independent stories and tracks, the two forms of *In a Foreign Town, in a Foreign Land* similarly expand in time and build a unified whole through the fragments of which they are made. The first obvious manifestation of that

---

[2] See John Eden's article and following online discussion, and David Tibet's interview by Lee Powell.

unity is the setting of the stories. As shown before, the "town near the northern border" is the main vehicle for fragmentation, both spatial and ontological, but it is at the same time the core of the four stories as it offers a common backdrop to the events. Certain inhabitants are also to be found in the four stories, namely the two hotel owners, Mrs Glimm and Mrs Pyk, whose history of feuding is alluded to and gradually revealed through the four works. Other inhabitants are recurrent, with a repeated mention of the town's "hysterics and impostors." Invariably, those hysterics of some sort always congregate at night to share their thoughts on the strange events happening in town, a "twilight talk" that pervades the sonic landscape of the four stories. The unifying effect provided by the town can be heard in Current 93's counterpart through the fact that the four tracks, although being labeled and segmented as separate pieces, actually blend into one another when one listens to the record as a whole, giving the listener the impression of hearing one long rendition of the collection. The erasure of the tracks' beginnings and endings is echoed by the fact that the town does not seem to have any clear borders, as the narrator of the fourth story indicates when he imagines his death happening "within the town itself or in close proximity to its outskirts, where the dense streets and structures of the town started to thin out and eventually dissolved into a desolate and seemingly endless countryside" (xli). This blending and blurring of the limits contributes to soften the sharp edges of the town's buildings and streets. Similarly, the state of the desolation of the town and its progressive abandonment and emptying transform their effect of ontological and psychological fragmentation to one of unification. This can also be seen through the drabness that reigns over all the stories and the recurring presence of the wind, the "bare branches" of the trees and the "gray sky." The third story makes winter a particular point of focus as a process of unification through monotony and coldness: "dull winter days were succeeded by blinding winter nights," "icy transcendence," "cloudy ether of a December afternoon" (xxviii).

This common setting therefore seems to point to the two works' cyclicality. When put together, the musical and textual fragments depict a desolate landscape where the same events seem to be repeated over and over again. The name the inhabitants give to the indefinite parallel town existing alongside their town in the fourth story is of no real import: "old town," "other town," or "demon town" – the words are different but the reality they name is the same. As the four stories progress, the chaos that presides over the town becomes more complete and more absolute, ultimately leaving the town almost empty: "a place that was all but deserted, the only remaining residents being a few hysterics or impostors who muttered *endlessly* about 'other town' or 'demon town', and even of an 'old town'" (lv, emphasis mine). As the town is eventually left in the hands of those few hysterics, the music finally comes to an end with a slow fade-out to silence. But the two works seem to shed light on the concept of eternal recurrence. Whether in this town or in another, the same absurd and inexplicable chaos will occur because this is what humanity ultimately is: an endless carnival of absurdity where people are merely puppets. As the narrator of the third story discovers, we live in

> a world that is essentially composed of shades of gray upon a background of blackness.... To know, to understand in the fullest sense, is to plunge into an enlightenment of inanity, a wintry landscape of memory whose substance is all shadows and a profound awareness of the infinite spaces surrounding us on all sides. (xxxvii)

The inescapability from this truth is highlighted by the cyclicality of the collection, exemplified by the first story, starting and ending with the narrator lying in bed, "listening to the wind and the scraping of bare branches on the roof just above [him]" (xi). As a result, it is unimportant that the voice at the very beginning of Current 93's record switches the order of the words "land" and "town" from the title if one considers the work as a loop, as a cycle. As Ligotti writes at the end of the final story, the chaos has no end:

> even in a northern border town of such intensely chaotic oddity and corruption there was still some greater chaos, some deeper insanity, than one had counted on, or could ever be taken into account – wherever there was anything; there would be chaos and insanity to such a degree that one could never come to terms with it, and it was only a matter of time before your world, whatever you thought it to be, was undermined if not completely overrun, by another world. (liii)

If the fragments of the collection are to be considered as pieces of a chaotic but overpowering whole, one may take the metaphor one step closer and even regard each separate collection of Ligotti's as a piece of the author's unified vision.

Conclusion

In a Foreign Town, in a Foreign Land is a true multimodal artistic experience: the stories were written before the music was composed but with the knowledge that a soundtrack composed by a visionary such as Tibet would accompany the words, thereby making the whole work a perfect example of fragmentary construction. Two artists with similar and peculiar tastes and interests but different philosophical beliefs worked separately to give life to a hybrid work that can only reach its full potential when words and music collide. However different their approach may be at times, Ligotti and Tibet have one important quality in common: they are uncompromising artists for whom art is a highly personal outlet for their own convictions. William Burns summarizes the experience in those words:

> Thomas Ligotti's relationship with the post-Industrial English underground seems to be one of fellow artistic explorers deviating from mainstream conceptions of literature and music ... The reciprocal nature of the projects creates a network of influence that asks the reader and listener to not accept the world as it is, to see our existence as askew, and to appropriate a mindset that might not be as comforting, secure, or simple as we have been taught. (108)

In that sense, the two artists are using fragmentation as a poetics of creation, one that allows them to deconstruct common and reassuring views of the world, and to tread the same offbeat paths in the lands of art and philosophy. Those paths may be seldom frequented, but those who do explore them instantly recognize their fellow travelers as companions on a quest to a dark enlightenment.

Works Cited

Barricelli, Jean-Pierre. *Melopoiesis*. New York: New York UP, 1988.

Benson, Stephen. *Literary Music*. Aldershot: Ashgate, 2006.

Brown, Calvin S. "The Poetic Use of Musical Forms." *Musico-Poetics in Perspective: Calvin S. Brown in Memoriam*. Eds. Jean-Louis Cupers and Ulrich Weisstein. Amsterdam: Rodopi, 2000. 145–60.

Burns, William. "Twilight Twilight Nihil Nihil: Thomas Ligotti and the Post-Industrial English Underground." *The Thomas Ligotti Reader*. Ed. Darrell Schweitzer. Holicong: Wildside, 2003. 101–10.

Cupers, Jean-Louis. *Euterpe et Harpocrate, ou, Le défi littéraire de la musique : aspects méthodologiques de l'approche musico-littéraire*. Brussels: Publications des Facultés Universitaires Saint-Louis, 1988.

Current 93. *In a Foreign Town, In a Foreign Land*. Durtro, 1997. CD.

Eden, John. "What Ends When the Symbols Shatter? My Time as a Death In June Fan." *Who Makes the Nazis?*, 7 Nov. 2010, http://www.whomakesthenazis.com/2010/11/what-ends-when-symbols-shatter-my-time.html. Accessed 15 July 2017.

Indick, Ben P. "The Dream Quest of Thomas Ligotti: A Study of *In a Foreign Town, In a Foreign Land*." *The Thomas Ligotti Reader*. Ed. Darrell Schweitzer. Holicong: Wildside, 2003. 116–26.

Ligotti, Thomas. *In a Foreign Town, In a Foreign Land*. London: Durtro, 1997.

Powell, Lee. "This Charming Man... An Interview with David Tibet of Current 93." *Heathen Harvest*, 21 May 2014, https://heathenharvest.org/2014/05/21/this-charming-man-an-interview-with-david-tibet-of-current-93/. Accessed 15 July 2017.

Stapleton, Steven. *In a Foreign Town, In a Foreign Land*, by Thomas Ligotti. London: Durtro, 1997. Collage and Drawings. CD and book covers.

Chapter 16

Fragments   a

of   postscript

Alison Gibbons,
Sheffield Hallam University

The ideal of academic writing, be it a postscript or otherwise, is to craft the smooth line of an argument; that is, to write in a manner, and to fashion a finished piece, that is decidedly *un*fragmentary – both in conceptual and textual terms. Fragmentary writing, in this sense, is cast as the negative other of writing that presents an ideal, unified whole. However, as many of the chapters in *The Poetics of Fragmentation in Contemporary British and American Fiction* demonstrate, fragmentation has a multifarious, perhaps contradictory, character. On the one hand, the fragment is a ruin, a snippet, a shard, a scrap; it evokes and induces disintegration, deterioration, discordance, disharmony. On the other hand, "fragmentary writing also serves to illustrate connectivity and community" (Rouverol) and can be used "as a poetics of creation" (Bridle). The fragment, then, is an oxymoron: it enables, in Marcin Tereszewski's words, "creative destruction," or in Jarosław Hetman's phrasing, the "aesthetics of fragmentation is counterbalanced by the ethics of harmonious transcendence." Embracing the playful, paradoxical, and heterogeneous poetics of fragmentation, this postscript is, itself, organized in fragments. As with the fragments of a shuffle narrative (discussed by Kolbuszewska and by Martin), a collage manifesto (explicated by Drąg), or a transtextual or transmedial assemblage (studied by Bayer and by Maziarczyk), you should – dear reader – navigate the pieces of this postscript in the order of your choosing and, in doing so, find links and relations of your own. In the nineteen fragments that follow, I offer my own critical reflections on the themes of *The Poetics of Fragmentation in Contemporary British and American Fiction* as a volume as well as a case study in the practice of scholarly fragmentary writing. Piece them together, dear reader, as you please.

❖   ❖   ❖

❖ Merritt Moseley's fine chapter adds to the literature on fragmentary writing which seeks to classify and identify its varying forms, paradoxically reading order into the disorder of fragmentation. Moseley's three categories – the braid, the bricolage, and the mosaic – resonate across the volume: David Malcolm, for instance, shows that "mosaic" is a term that has been used (by Mary Louise Pratt) to describe the short story whilst Marcin Tereszewski calls J. G. Ballard's *Atrocity Exhibition* "a collection of scenes and tidbits painting a mosaic picture of modern culture." Even David Shields appears to like the metaphor when, in *Reality Hunger,* he proposes (or appropriates) that the lyric essay "often accretes by fragments, taking shape mosaically" (384).[1] Moseley's categories, though, are not absolute; as he himself acknowledges, "an overlap among them is possible." Indeed, Alicia J. Rouverol argues that Ali Smith's *Hotel World* possesses a "*braided* structure, in non-linear narrative excerpts juxtaposed in *mosaic* form, and in individual sentence and word *fragments*" (my emphasis). The mosaic in *Hotel World* is, according to Rouverol, utilized in a single chapter. Perhaps, then, opportunities for this leakage or intermixing of different kinds of fragmentary fiction are presented more readily in longer forms – such as the novel or a collection of short stories.

❖ In form, this postscript most closely resembles a collage manifesto. As Wojciech Drąg convincingly demonstrates in his analysis of David Markson's *This is Not a Novel* and David Shields's *Reality Hunger,* collage – as a form of fragmentary writing – "enacts a clash of distinct, often opposing voices and incompatible elements, which results in their uneasy coexistence and tension." Lance Olsen's *[[there.]]* (2014) features a similar design and could consequently also fit Drąg's category of the collage manifesto. It is, however, described alternatively in its back cover blurb as "part critifictional meditation and part trash diary." Inside the book, in one of its unnumbered fragments (by my count, there are 633 fragments of varying lengths),[2] the author offers another descriptor (43):

:::: This book: a waste aesthetics.

---

[1] For consistency with Drąg's practice in his chapter of the present volume, my citations of material from David Shields's *Reality Hunger* provide passage numbers (instead of page number). Similarly, because this rule does not apply to Shield's' appendix, quotations from the appendix are preceded by "p." to indicate the page number.

[2] Each fragment in *[[there.]]* is opened by "::::" Olsen explains the symbol as a new or "special punctuation" that signifies "what cannot be articulated accurately" (28).

This description might perhaps feed into and inform the poetics of fragmentation. In which case, what is "waste"? Viewed negatively, it is material that is unusable, unwanted, undesirable; "to waste" something is to destroy it. "Waste" is also, though, the excess matter. Can fragmentary writing thus be seen as marked by an aesthetic of excess? Certainly, this applies to *[[there.]]*. There are passages (or fragments) that echo themes and expressions from Olsen's novel *Theories of Forgetting* (2014), written simultaneously with *[[there.]]* whilst the author was undertaking a fellowship at the American Academy in Berlin. The chapters in *The Poetics of Fragmentation in Contemporary British and American Fiction* appear to offer support for such an aesthetic of excess since they repeatedly demonstrate that fragmentation is a form of writing that exceeds and is not contained within the norms of standard grammatical constructions or traditional publishing formats.

❖ Twentieth-century land artist Robert Smithson believed that the disruptive, defamiliarizing effect of fragmentation is fundamental to understanding humanity's place in the world, and the shape of the future: "Only when art is fragmented, discontinuous and incomplete can we know about that vacant eternity that excludes *objects* and determined meanings" (333).

❖ Many of the chapters in this volume pass comment on the effect of fragmentation on readers and the reading experience. For example, Drąg notes that recurrent patterns in Markson's *This Is Not A Novel* "enable the reader to notice emerging themes," Hetman claims that "fragmentation plays a crucial role in [David Foster Wallace's] reception" and Caroline Magnin believes that "it is up to readers to restore wholeness through their own reading experiences, weaving together all the seemingly disparate elements that constitute the novel." Evidence from psychological approaches to text comprehension demonstrates that fragmentation does have an impact on reading. Catherine Emmott and Anthony Sanford have tested how readers respond to "sentence fragments," which they define as "words, phrases or dependent clauses which are punctuated as if they were full sentences, even though they are in fact only fragments of sentences" (118). Such fragments result in "deeper processing" of information for readers. Emmott and Sanford, therefore, provide evidence that literary linguistic fragmentation has a foregrounding effect in reading: that is, fragments attract readers' attention. Moreover, in his empirical studies of difficult poetry, Castiglione has shown that texts which exhibit linguistic narrativity (e.g., at clause level) are processed with greater speed and ease by readers. As such, what he calls "lack of narrativity" is a key indicator of literary difficulty. Thus, the non-linearity that many of the chapters in this

volume discuss as a feature of fragmentation makes reading a more difficult process.

❖ In *Reality Hunger*, Shields argues that it is "the artist's job to mix (edit)
the fragments together and, if needed, generate original fragments to fill
the gaps" (281). As the parenthetical "(edit)" implies, this is also the job of
academic editors: to arrange chapters – as fragments – in coherent combination. Often unseen on the page, the work undertaken by editors also
entails finding gaps in chapters, gaps that need to be filled, and mixing
fragments within and across chapters together through co-references that
"braid" the volume together through critical interconnections.

❖ In this volume, David Malcolm upholds the defining property of the
short story as "shortness" and, in a second theoretical step, interprets the
short story itself as a fragment because "brevity inevitably carries with it
associations of fragmentariness." This leads to his proposal for a "typology" of short story collections based on the relationship between "component texts" – short stories as said fragments – of and within larger collections. Côme Martin suggests that the cards of shuffle narratives – also a
short form – can be interpreted as fragments, yet he notes the tendency in
academic discourse to refer to these cards instead as "chapters." Contrarily, then, chapters – whether fictional or critical – are likewise fragments.
Viewed in this way, *The Poetics of Fragmentation in Contemporary British
and American Fiction* is itself a fragmented whole, a book-bound augmentation of the fragment that fits Malcolm's second category: "Edited collection organized around homogeneity of subject matter."

❖ In their introduction to this volume, Vanessa Guignery and Wojciech
Drąg historicize the literary fragment. In doing so, they demonstrate that
the meaning, function, and value of the fragment metamorphoses under
the penmanship of different writers, in different periods, and within the
context of successive literary movements. Moreover, Guignery and Drąg
argue:

> ...the resurgence of fragmentation at the turn of the twentieth and twenty-
> first centuries deserves to be examined in order to ascertain whether con-
> temporary forms of fragmentary writing constitute a return to the modern-
> ist episteme or the fragmented literature of exhaustion of the 1960s, wheth-
> er they mark a continuity with some aspects of the postmodernist aesthetics
> or signal a major deviation from previous structures.

This line of questioning chimes with critical characterizations of the early
twenty-first century as "metamodern" (Vermeulen and van den Akker
2010; van den Akker and Vermeulen 2017) – a new period in which cultural
forms have moved beyond the dominant tendencies of postmodernism.

Indeed, Vermeulen and van den Akker suggest that the metamodern sensibility "oscillates between a modern enthusiasm and a postmodern irony, between hope and melancholy, between naiveté and knowingness, empathy and apathy, unity and plurality, totality and fragmentation, purity and ambiguity" (5–6). The chapters in this book often position the goals and effects of late twentieth and early twenty-first century literary fragmentation in contrast or successive to those of postmodernist fiction: David Foster Wallace is, for Hetman and many other scholars (cf. Timmer 2010; Konstaninou 2016), a pivotal figure in this sense. Furthermore, Rouverol's reading of the fragmentation in Ali Smith's *Hotel World* in light of globalization explicitly connects fragmented literary form to the larger sociocultural frame of the twenty-first century world and late capitalism.

❖ Any understanding of fragmentation necessarily entails a cognitive conception of a unified whole. In her chapter of this book, Zofia Kolbuszewska poignantly notes that "a fragment keeps evoking the specter of former totality."

❖ Readers seek out ways to create meaning from fragments, whether such fragments take the form of visual collages, textual cut-ups, or nonlinear narrative. As Lance Olsen says of his own collage novel *Head in Flames* (in an interview with John Madera):

> …there's a visual element to the text …. That is, the presentation looks odd on the page because the novel is intent on turning page into collage. And the reader's role is activated in such a way that she or he is invited to create narratives out of the collaged fragments. Different readers will create different narratives, collage my collages together in different ways.

❖ Multimodal literature is by nature a visually fragmented form. Indeed, in his contribution to this volume, Grzegorz Maziarczyk reflects, "[v]isual fragmentation appears to be one of the primary strategies of the aesthetics of bookishness," while Magnin even goes so far as to refer to images in novels as "fragmenting devices in their own right." Fragmentation is taken even further in what I have elsewhere termed "tactile fictions" (Gibbons, "Multimodal Literature" 428–29) which includes the card shuffle or model kit narrative, as discussed by Martin and Kolbuszewska in this volume. In shuffle narratives, both fragmentation and coherence are the result of readers' creativity, whose physical interaction with the cards creates the arc of the story. Another tactile and fragmentary dimension of multimodal texts arises from the use of coded passages. In her chapter in this volume, Magnin considers an episode from Jonathan Safran Foer's *Extremely Loud & Incredibly Close*, in which, during a telephone call and in an attempt to communicate, the mute grandfather character dials numbers, which are reproduced in the text. In my own analysis of Foer's novel, I argued that this code "directs the reader towards enactive participation" (Gibbons, *Multimodality* 155). Certainly, I tried to decode the passage, as did some of the novel's reviewers (Updike). Coded passages appear in other multimodal novels such as Mark Z. Danielewski's *House of Leaves* (2000; see Gibbons, *Multimodality* 81–84) and Joe Meno's *The Boy Detective Fails* (2006; see Gibbons, "Literature and Multimodality" 303–04). While codes do fragment the visual form of such novels, if readers attempt to decode them, such codes also disrupt immersion into the world of the text. Reading itself becomes a fragmented activity whereby readers must paradoxically stop reading in order to crack and then read the code. At times, as is the case with Foer's *Extremely Loud & Incredibly Close*, the text is ultimately illegible: the code is uncrackable and the point is precisely the fragmented experience of failed communication.

❖ Fragmentary writing and fragmentary fictions are – in many ways, and through varying formal or, even, avant-garde strategies – an example of what Brian Richardson, amongst others, has called "unnatural narratives," texts that "contain significant antimimetic events, characters, settings, or frames" and thus "violate mimetic expectations and practices of realism, and defy the conventions of existing, established genres" (3). However, many of the contributors in the present volume argue the inverse: that fragmentation and fragmentary writing function – particularly in late twentieth and early twenty-first century prose – as a mimetic or realist mode: Tereszewski, for instance, sees the fragmentariness of Ballard's fiction as "more real, more immediate than that manufactured state of wholeness"; Hetman similarly reads Wallace's formal innovations as "lower case realism" (vs. Realism as a more popular mode of writing), that is "an essentially recognizable way of depicting a chaotic, fragmented world"; and Maria Antonietta Struzziero suggests that the aim of fragmentation is "to evoke the polymorphous and chaotic essence of modern life, which, in its complexity, resists full comprehension and does not yield to a conventional narrative." The chapters in *The Poetics of Fragmentation in Contemporary British and American Fiction* might collectively, therefore, enable a critical appraisal of formal strategies in contemporary prose as (what we might call) *fragmentary realism*. Furthermore, fragmentary realism sits within the bounds of what Ulka Anjaria has called "the return to realism" in the twenty-first century, which functions "not simply as a resistance to today's new culture of heterogeneity and digitization but as a new way of imagining literary and political futures."

❖ Shields' *Reality Hunger* is both critical polemic and "uncreative writing," the latter term coined by Kenneth Goldsmith to symbolize a practice of borrowing and reassembling (see also Epstein for a critical overview of the form). Bray, Gibbons, and McHale view uncreative writing as "*all* process": "Originating nothing, it appropriates and recycles readymade verbal material, whether read, spoken or culled from the internet" (13; original emphasis). Each numbered part of *Reality Hunger* contributes to the whole and resonates with the concept of the fragment in two ways; firstly, each is a separate unit; secondly, each has been fragmented from a larger whole, extracted from another text and re-presented in *Reality Hunger*. Indeed, in the appendix, Shields explains, "This book contains hundreds of quotations that go unacknowledged in the body of the text" (p. 209). This statement from Shields is more like a confession under duress. The publishers of *Reality Hunger*, however, took a different view: "Random House lawyers determined that it was necessary for me to provide a complete list of citations" (p. 209). Yet for Shields, his text cannot, and he implies – should not – be interpreted as plagiarism. Rather, the act of fragmenting is both creative and productive: "Replication isn't reproduction. The copy transcends the original," he writes in fragment 289.

❖ Mariano D'Ambrosio, in his chapter in this book, suggests that polyphonic narratives are fragmented precisely through their employment of a variety of voices, as well as the way in which this often leads to a disparity of textual material. Dialogue and dialogic style are also discussed as fragmentary by Teresa Bruś and Maria Antonietta Struzziero. Bakhtin argued that all novels were heteroglossic, dialogic, composite. Crudely, this would raise the question: are, then, all works of fiction fragmentary? Even pursuing D'Ambrosio's more bordered linkage between polyphony and fragmentation, might it be tempting to interpret stylistic forms such as irony or free indirect discourse – recognized for their duality of meaning and voice respectively – as fundamentally fragmentary?

❖ *Un*fragmentary writing, the "seamless whole," is itself an illusory concept as Moseley makes clear in his chapter when he resigns, "If we try to imagine such an achieved work, we will find there is none."

❖ In *Intertextuality in Practice*, Jessica Mason offers a cognitive approach to intertextuality using Schema Theory. Schemas are packages of knowledge that people construct and utilize in everyday life; for instance, we all have a "restaurant schema" that helps to guide our interactions according to familiar patterns and expectations about the process of being in a restaurant. Mason argues that readers also develop "narrative schemas," in which they store working information about a particular narrative. Encountering an intertextual reference will (so long as the reference is recognized) activate the relevant narrative schema. This means that readers can incorporate new information into – and assess the coherence of that new information – in relation to the narrative schema they have constructed in their mental archive. Such is, therefore, the cognitive process underwriting the experience of reading Jeanette Winterson's *The Gap of Time* which Struzziero, in her chapter in this volume, analyzes as an intertext of William Shakespeare's *The Winter's Tale*. The same is true at a transtextual level. In his astute transtextual account of David Mitchell's writing, Gerd Bayer explicates the "various features that establish patterns beyond individual books, be it characters that appear in more than one text or narrative ideas that are being recycled." In doing so, Bayer creates a narrative schema centered on the author that enables a tracking of characters and themes across and beyond individual books. Consequently, narrative schemas are the means by which readers make sense of, and build connections between, literary fragments.

❖ Adam Thirlwell's novella *Kapow!* (2012) is both visually and narratively fragmented (see Gibbons, "'Take that you intellectuals'"). Though short, the text continually extends and expands beyond its boundaries, with fold-out pages and bifurcating footnotes that disrupt the conventionally formatted central block layout of text and traverse the page in alternate directions. The narrator even comments,

> I was imagining a story that was made up of so many digressions and evasions that in order to make it readable it would need to be divided in every direction. So that if you wrote it out as a continuous block it would be the same but also different. (18)

Indeed, Nigel Krauth has described the book precisely in terms of fragments: "Sometimes the fragment creates a pertinent shape in contrast to the rest of the page's text, or literally takes off in another direction, like a distracted thought" (97).

❖ Contemporary fragmentary writing often uses formal devices to imitate the effects of other media. Moseley claims that a form of fragmentary prose that "probably does not register with most readers as being fragmented … is the fiction operating under many of the conventions of film," and the filmic property of fragmentary writing is noted by Struzziero, who interprets a scene of "filmic montage" in Winterson's *The Gap of Time*. Filmic effects of fragmentation can therefore be seen as a form of "intermedial evocation" – a term used by Werner Wolf to describe the way in which one medium "imitates the effects of another medium" (255).

❖ It is not only the composition of grammar or text on the page that results in the poetics of fragmentation. At a more abstract level, subjectivity is also often viewed as fragmentary. In this volume, Malcom argues, "Characters, too, are fragmented isolates"; Bruś declares "selves are accessed through fragments"; and Magnin connects trauma to fragmentation by arguing that "each character is fragmented into two separate entities so as to alleviate their pain." Catherine Emmott has shown that the split self, often achieved through pronoun choice and co-referentiality (e.g. '*I'm* not *myself* today'; my emphasis; see Lakoff) is a conceptual metaphor found in "a wide range of fictional and non-fictional narratives, since it commonly occurs at times of personal crisis" (153). In this volume, D'Ambrosio suggests that there can be an iconic relationship between the form and content: "The fragmentation of the text, thus, corresponds to the fragmentation of the self, as well as the fragmentation of reality, whose manifold, complex, plural experience is considered impossible to render in a sequential, unitary text."

❖ As both Grzegorz Maziarczyk and Deborah Bridle show in this book, transmedia and multimedia texts are a particular form of twenty-first century fragmentary writing. Bridle, in her analysis of Thomas Ligotti and Current 93's *In a Foreign Town, in a Foreign Land* shows that "musical and literary compositions may be seen as a fragmented whole." *In a Foreign Town, in a Foreign Land* is by no means an exception: Danielewski's *House of Leaves* is accompanied by the album *Haunted* by the author's sister Poe (see discussion by Evans); more recently Woodkid's album *The Golden Age* (2013) could also be purchased in a special edition format in which it was accompanied by a short novel written by Katarzyna Jerzak and Yoann Lemoine (AKA Woodkid), which features fourteen black and white illustrations.

This postscript is, perhaps, a bricolage, constructed of nineteen fragments that – holistically – represent my critical reflections on reading *The Poetics of Fragmentation in Contemporary British and American Fiction*. I hope the themes I have identified across the volume work to braid these fragments together. There are, certainly, more themes beyond those I have raised: for instance, the ethical effects of fragmentary writing and the fragments of memory. You – dear reader – will most likely have noticed others (and, in thinking about your reading experience, I wonder how you read this postscript: whether you embraced a fragmented route or sought the safety and familiarity of a linear pathway). *The Poetics of Fragmentation in Contemporary British and American Fiction* is, ultimately, an accomplished edited collection in which, as in a beautiful mosaic, each chapter resonates with others in order to produce a new image – a new understanding – of literary fragmentation in the late twentieth and early twenty-first century.

Works Cited

Akker, Robin van den, and Timotheus Vermeulen. "Periodising the 2000s, or, the Emergence of Metamodernism." *Metamodernism: Historicity, Affect, and Depth after Postmodernism*. Eds. Robin van den Akker, Alison Gibbons and Timotheus Vermeulen. London: Rowman & Littlefield, 2017. 1–19.

Anjaria, Ulka. "Twenty-First-Century Realism." *Oxford Encyclopedia of Literature*, 2017, DOI: 10.1093/acrefore/9780190201098.013.194. Accessed 26 Oct. 2018.

Bray, Joe, Alison Gibbons and Brian McHale. Introduction. *The Routledge Companion to Experimental Literature*. Eds. Bray, Joe, Alison Gibbons and Brian McHale. Abingdon: Routledge, 2012. 1–18.

Castiglione, Davide. "Difficult Poetry Processing: Reading Time and the Narrativity Hypothesis." *Language and Literature* 26.2 (2017): 99–121.

Emmott, Catherine. "'Split Selves' in Fiction and in Medical 'Life Stories.'" *Cognitive Stylistics: Language and Cognition in Text Analysis*. Eds. Elena Semino and Jonathan Culpeper. Philadelphia: John Benjamins, 2002. 153–81.

Emmott, Catherine, and Anthony Sanford. *Mind, Brain and Narrative*. Cambridge: Cambridge UP, 2012.

Epstein, Andrew. "Found Poetry, 'Uncreative Writing,' and the Art of Appropriation." *The Routledge Companion to Experimental Literature*. Eds. Joe Bray, Alison Gibbons and Brian McHale. Abingdon: Routledge, 2012. 310–22.

Evans, Mel. "This Haunted House: Intertextuality and Interpretation in Mark Danielewski's *House of Leaves* (2000) and Poe's *Haunted* (2000)." *Mark Z. Danielewski*. Eds. Joe Bray and Alison Gibbons. Manchester: Manchester UP, 2011. 68–85.

Gibbons, Alison. "'Take that you intellectuals' and 'KaPOW!': Adam Thirwell and the Metamodernist Future of Style." *Studia Neophilologica* 87.Supp 1 (2015): 29–43, https://doi.org/10.1080/00393274.2014.981959. Accessed 26 Oct. 2018.

---. "Literature and Multimodality." *Routledge Handbook of Language and Creativity*. Ed. Rodney H. Jones. London: Routledge, 2015. 293–306.

---. "Multimodal Literature and Experimentation." *The Routledge Companion to Experimental Literature*. Eds. Joe Bray, Alison Gibbons and Brian McHale. Abingdon: Routledge, 2012. 420–34.

---. *Multimodality, Cognition, and Experimental Literature*. New York: Routledge, 2012.

Goldsmith, Kenneth. *Uncreative Writing: Managing Language in the Digital Age*. New York: Columbia UP, 2011.

Konstaninou, Lee. *Cool Characters: Irony and American Fiction*. Cambridge: Harvard UP, 2016.

Krauth, Nigel. *Creative Writing and the Radical: Teaching and Learning the Fiction of the Future*. Bristol: Monolingual Matters, 2016.

Lakoff, George. "Sorry, I'm Not Myself Today: The Metaphor System for Conceptualizing the Self." *Spaces, Worlds, and Grammar.* Eds. Gilles Fauconnier and Eve Sweetser. Chicago: U of Chicago P. 91–123.

Madera, John. "O for a Muse of Fire... An Interview with Lance Olsen." *Rain Taxi*, Summer 2010, http://www.raintaxi.com/o-for-a-muse-of-fire-an-interview-with-lance-olsen/. Accessed 26 Oct. 2018.

Mason, Jessica. *Intertextuality in Practice.* Amsterdam: John Benjamins, 2019.

Olsen, Lance. *[[there.]].* Fort Wayne: Anti-Oedipus, 2014.

Richardson, Brian. *Unnatural Narrative: Theory, History, and Practice.* Columbus: Ohio State UP, 2015.

Shields, David. *Reality Hunger.* London: Penguin, 2010.

Smithson, Robert. "The Shape of the Future and Memory (1966)." *Robert Smithson: The Collected Writings.* Ed. Jack Flam. Berkeley: U of California P, 1996. 332–33.

Timmer, Nicoline. *Do You Feel It Too? The Post-Postmodern Syndrome in American Fiction at the Turn of the Millennium.* Amsterdam: Rodopi, 2010.

Updike, John. "Mixed Messages: *Extremely Loud and Incredible Close.*" *The New Yorker*, 14 Mar. 2005, https://www.newyorker.com/magazine/2005/03/14/mixed-messages. Accessed 1 Jan. 2007.

Vermeulen, Timotheus, and Robin van den Akker. "Notes on Metamodernism." *Journal of Aesthetics and Culture* 2.1 (2010): 1–14, https://doi.org/10.3402/jac.v2i0.5677. Accessed 26 Oct. 2018.

Wolf, Werner. "Intermediality." *Routledge Encyclopedia of Narrative Theory.* Eds. David Herman, Manfred Jahn and Marie-Laure Ryan. London: Routledge, 2005. 252–56.

Contributors

Mariano D'Ambrosio holds an MA in journalism from the University of Parma and a PhD in comparative literature from University Paris 3 – Sorbonne Nouvelle. The title of his doctoral thesis is "The novel of nonlinearity: A comparative study of *Tristram Shandy*, *Pale Fire*, *Life: a User's Manual* and *House of Leaves*."

Gerd Bayer is Professor and Akademischer Direktor in the English department at the University of Erlangen-Nürnberg, having previously taught at the University of Toronto, Case Western Reserve University and the University of Wisconsin-Whitewater. He is the author of a book on John Fowles and of *Novel Horizons: The Genre Making of Restoration Fiction*, as well as the (co-)editor of seven essay collections, most recently of *Early Modern Constructions of Europe* and *Holocaust Cinema in the Twenty-First Century*. He has published essays on postmodern and postcolonial literature and film, early modern narrative fiction, Holocaust Studies and heavy metal.

Deborah Bridle teaches at the Science Faculty at the University of Côte d'Azur and is a member of the CTEL research team. Her doctoral dissertation was devoted to the image of the mirror in a selection of Victorian fairy tales. Her research focuses on fiction dealing with the fantastic. She is particularly interested in occultism and mysticism in the works of authors from the end of the nineteenth century, as well as in the nihilistic philosophical approaches in the works of twentieth-century writers of horror.

Teresa Bruś is Associate Professor at the University of Wrocław. Her major fields of research include visual culture, photography and literature, and life writing. She teaches M.A. seminars on autobiography, electives on the poetry of the 1930s, English modernism and portraiture. Her doctoral dissertation focused on aspects of "profound frivolity" in W.H. Auden's poetry. She is also a graduate of the International Forum of Photography in Poland. She has published on various aspects of life writing and photography in journals, including *Biography: An Interdisciplinary Quarterly*, *Prose Studies*, *Connotations*, and *Thepes*. She is the author of *Life Writing as Self-Collecting in the 1930s: Cecil Day Lewis and Louis MacNeice* (2012).

Wojciech Drąg is Assistant Professor at the Institute of English Studies, University of Wrocław. He is the author of _Revisiting Loss: Memory, Trauma and Nostalgia in the Novels of Kazuo Ishiguro_ (2014) and co-editor of _War and Words: Representations of Military Conflict in Literature and the Media_ (2015) and _Spectrum of Emotions: From Love to Grief_ (2016). In 2018, he received The Kosciuszko Foundation fellowship at the University of Utah.

Alison Gibbons is Reader in Contemporary Stylistics at Sheffield Hallam University. She is author of _Multimodality, Cognition, and Experimental Literature_ (Routledge, 2012) and co-editor of _Mark Z. Danielewski_ (Manchester University Press, 2011), _The Routledge Companion to Experimental Literature_ (Routledge, 2012), _Metamodernism: Historicity, Affect, and Depth after Postmodernism_ (Rowman & Littlefield, 2017) and _Pronouns in Literature: Positions and Perspectives in Language_ (Palgrave Macmillan, 2018).

Vanessa Guignery is Professor of contemporary English and Postcolonial Literature at the École Normale Supérieure in Lyon. She published _The Fiction of Julian Barnes_ (2006) and _Conversations with Julian Barnes_ (co-edited with Ryan Roberts, 2009). She is the author of _Seeing and Being: Ben Okri's_ The Famished Road (2012) as well as a monograph on B.S. Johnson (2009) and another on Jonathan Coe (2015). She is the editor of several books on contemporary literature in English, including a collection of interviews with eight contemporary writers, _Novelists in the New Millennium_ (2012) and _The B.S. Johnson – Zulfikar Ghose Correspondence_ (2015).

Jarosław Hetman is Assistant Professor at the Department of English, Nicolaus Copernicus University in Toruń. His academic interests include contemporary American fiction, relationships between literature and art and selected problems of literary theory. He is also the supervisor of The Spinning Globe, a Shakespearian theatrical group operating under the auspices of the Department of English.

Zofia Kolbuszewska is Associate Professor at the Institute of English Studies, University of Wrocław. She is the author of _The Poetics of Chronotope in the Novels of Thomas Pynchon_ (2000) and _The Purloined Child: American Identity and Representations of Childhood in American Literature 1851-2000_ (2007) and several articles on Pynchon, American postmodernism, American Gothic, ekphrasis, neobaroque and forensic imagination. She edited _Thomas Pynchon and the (De)vices of Global (Post)modernity_ (2012) and co-edited _Echoes of Utopia: Notions, Rhetoric, Poetics_ (2012) and _(Im)perfection Subverted, Reloaded and Networked: Utopian Discourse across Media_ (2015).

Caroline Magnin is writing a doctoral thesis on American literature at Sorbonne University under the supervision of Professor Marc Amfreville. Her research focuses on the writing of trauma in post-9/11 American fiction. She is also a lecturer at Versailles Saint-Quentin-en-Yvelines University, where she teaches American literature and translation.

David Malcolm is Professor of English literature at the SWPS University of Social Sciences and Humanities in Warsaw. He holds a PhD from University College London. He has written, edited, and co-edited books on Jean Rhys, John McGahern, Seamus Heaney, Graham Swift, Ian McEwan and others. His research interests concentrate on poetry, short fiction and fiction in Britain and Ireland.

Côme Martin holds a PhD in contemporary American literature. His research focuses on the relations between text and image and on books with unusual shapes, in comics as well as novels. He is an associate member of the TIES research group at Paris Est – Créteil University and an associate member of the GRENA laboratory in Paris IV – Sorbonne.

Grzegorz Maziarczyk is Head of the Institute of English Studies at John Paul II Catholic University of Lublin, Poland. His main research interests include textual materiality, multimodal storytelling, transmediality and dystopia. He is the author of two monographs – *The Narratee in Contemporary British Fiction* (2005) and *The Novel as Book: Textual Materiality in Contemporary Fiction in English* (2013), as well as co-editor of five collections of essays, including *(Im)perfection Subverted, Reloaded and Networked: Utopian Discourse across Media* (2015) and *Explorations of Consciousness in Contemporary Fiction* (2017).

Merritt Moseley is the editor of four volumes on British and Irish Novelists Since 1960, one on Booker Prize-Winners and one on the academic novel, and the author of monographs on David Lodge, Kingsley Amis, Julian Barnes, Michael Frayn, Pat Barker and Jonathan Coe. He was a Professor of Literature at the University of North Carolina at Asheville.

Alicia J. Rouverol, PhD, is Visiting Lecturer in Creative Writing, Fiction, at the University of Sheffield and has taught Creative Writing/Literature previously at the University of Manchester and at Sheffield Hallam University. She is the co-author of *"I Was Content and Not Content": The Story of Linda Lord and the Closing of Penobscot Poultry* (2000) and other articles in oral history. Her research focuses on contemporary British and American fiction, women's experimental writing and globalization.

Maria Antonietta Struzziero is an independent scholar. She completed a PhD in Linguistic and Literary Studies at the University of Salerno. Her doctoral dissertation concentrated on Jeanette Winterson and the love discourses in some of her novels. She has published articles on Thomas Hardy, Italo Calvino, Julian Barnes and Jeanette Winterson, and given papers at international conferences. She has co-edited "Voci ed echi: Quaderni di letteratura comparata" and translated two novels. She is currently working on mythology in contemporary novels, particularly Colm Tóibín's *House of Names* and Madeline Miller's *Circe*.

Marcin Tereszewski is Assistant Professor at the University of Wrocław, where he specializes in modern British fiction and literary theory. He is the author of *The Aesthetics of Failure: Inexpressibility in Samuel Beckett's Fiction* (2013) and co-editor of *Production of Emotions: Perspectives and Functions* (2016). His current research interests include an examination of psychogeographical aspects of dystopian fiction, particularly in relation to J.G. Ballard's fiction and architecture.

Index

Printed in April 2021
by Rotomail Italia S.p.A., Vignate (MI) - Italy